# Negotiating Trade Liberalization in Argentina and Chile



"This volume examines the interaction between domestic and international negotiations in trade politics. With its focus on Argentina and Chile it provides an important empirical contribution to the debate."

**Eugénia da Conceição-Heldt**, *Technical University of Munich*

"This book offers a major contribution to our understanding of how international trade negotiations – South-South, North-South, and multilateral – affect domestic trade politics. Andrea Bianculli delivers a clear and engaging account of Argentina and Chile at a historic turning point in Latin America's trade relations."

**Soo Yeon Kim**, *National University of Singapore*

How do international negotiations affect domestic politics? Starting in the 1990s, countries throughout Latin America embarked on many and simultaneous negotiations. On the shifting ground of widening and deepening trade agendas and diverse arenas, what factors determined trade politics?

This book examines the domestic political dynamics triggered by South-South, North-South and multilateral agendas in Argentina and Chile between 1990 and 2005. Using a much-needed cross-negotiation and cross-country comparative perspectives, and through detailed empirical analyses of several key negotiations, it proposes an explanation that emphasizes the interplay between international negotiations and domestic trade politics, taken as the result of the complex and dynamic interdependencies and interrelations between state and society.

Informed by interviews with public officials, businesses and civil society, the analysis reveals that variation in the depth of agendas, the distributional effects and the uncertainty of political outcomes all have important consequences for domestic preference formation, collective action strategies and types of relationships. Given this, the variety of negotiations, when considered separately and comparatively, show that South-South, North-South and multilateral processes promote different patterns of trade politics. In sum, although national specificities and historical legacies are important, the book argues that trade policy comes first in creating domestic politics in Latin America.

**Andrea C. Bianculli** is Juan de la Cierva-Incorporación Fellow at Institut Barcelona d'Estudis Internacionals (IBEI). Her research crosses international and comparative political economy, and lies in the areas of global and regional governance, trade, regulation and development, with a particular focus on Latin America.

## Routledge Studies in Latin American Politics

For a full list of titles in this series, please visit www.routledge.com

10 **Transforming Brazil**
A History of National Development in the Postwar Era
*Rafael R. Ioris*

11 **Pharmaceutical Autonomy and Public Health in Latin America**
State, Society, and Industry in Brazil's AIDS Program
*Matthew Flynn*

12 **Civil-Military Relations in Post-Conflict Societies**
Transforming the Role of the Military in Central America
*Orlando J. Pérez*

13 **Re-Imagining Community and Civil Society**
In Latin America and the Caribbean
*Edited by Gordana Yovanovich and Roberta Rice*

14 **Revolutionary Violence and the New Left**
Transnational Perspectives
*Edited by Alberto Martín Álvarez and Eduardo Rey Tristán*

15 **Business-State Relations in Brazil**
Challenges of the Port Reform Lobby
*Mahrukh Doctor*

16 **The Politics of Capitalist Transformation**
Brazilian Informatics Policy, Regime Change, and State Autonomy
*Jeffrey G. Seward*

17 **Negotiating Trade Liberalization in Argentina and Chile**
When Policy Creates Politics
*Andrea C. Bianculli*

# Negotiating Trade Liberalization in Argentina and Chile

## When Policy Creates Politics

**Andrea C. Bianculli**

Routledge
Taylor & Francis Group
LONDON AND NEW YORK

First published 2017 by Routledge

2 Park Square, Milton Park, Abingdon, Oxfordshire OX14 4RN
711 Third Avenue, New York, NY 10017

*Routledge is an imprint of the Taylor & Francis Group, an informa business*

First issued in paperback 2018



*Library of Congress Cataloging in Publication Data*
A catalog record for this book has been requested

ISBN: 978-1-138-94926-3 (hbk)
ISBN: 978-1-138-36818-7 (pbk)

Typeset in Times New Roman
by Apex CoVantage, LLC

**To the memory of my Mum**

# Contents

# Illustrations

## Figure



## Tables

# Abbreviations

| | |
|---|---|
| ABAC | APEC Business Advisory Council |
| ABF | Americas Business Forum |
| ABIF | Chilean Association of Banks and Financial Institutions |
| ACIEL | Coordinating Association for Free Businessmen's Institutions |
| ACJR | Chilean Alliance for Fair and Responsible Trade |
| AD | Democratic Alliance |
| ADIMRA | Argentine Association of Metallurgical Industry |
| AEA | Argentine Business Association |
| AFL-CIO | American Federation of Labour-Congress of Industrial Organizations |
| ALBA | Bolivarian Alliance of the Americas |
| AmCham | American Chamber of Commerce |
| APA | Chilean Association of Poultry Producers |
| APEC | Asia Pacific Economic Cooperation |
| APLA | Latin American Petrochemical and Chemical Association |
| APYME | Assembly of Small and Medium Entrepreneurs |
| ASEXMA | Association of Manufacture and Services Exporters |
| ASOEX | Chilean Association of Fruit Exporters |
| BNHI | Business Network for Hemispheric Integration |
| CAC | Argentine Chamber of Commerce |
| CACE | Advisory Council on Foreign Trade |
| CAFTA-DR | Dominican Republic-Central America FTA |
| CAMARCO | Argentine Chamber of Construction |
| Camport | Chamber of Maritime Transport and Ports |
| CAN | Andean Community |
| CAP | Common Agricultural Policy |
| CARBAP | Confederation of Rural Associations of Buenos Aires and La Pampa |
| CChC | Chilean Construction Chamber |
| CCFTA | Canada-Chile Free Trade Agreement |
| CCS | Santiago Chamber of Commerce |
| CCSC | Civil Society Consultative Council |
| CCSCS | Southern Cone Coordinator of Central Trade Unions |

| | |
|---|---|
| CEA | Argentine Entrepreneurial Council |
| CEDHA | Centre for Human Rights and Environment |
| CEI | Centre for International Economy |
| CEP | Centre for Production Studies |
| CERA | Argentine Chamber of Exporters |
| CES | Coalition of Service Exporters |
| CES | Social and Economic Conference (Argentina) |
| CES | Social and Economic Council (Chile) |
| CET | Common External Tariff |
| CGE | General Economic Confederation |
| CGT | General Confederation of Labour |
| CIARA | Argentine Oil Industry Chamber |
| CICI | Inter-Ministerial Commission of International Trade |
| CIEPLAN | Corporation of Studies for Latin America |
| CILFA | Industrial Chamber of Argentine Pharmaceutical Laboratories |
| CIOSL | International Confederation of Free Trade Unions |
| CIPA | Chamber of Industrial Food Products Manufacturers |
| CIQyP | Chamber of the Chemical and Petrochemical Industries |
| CIS | Centre of Iron and Steel Industrialists |
| CNC | National Chamber of Commerce |
| CNCE | National Commission of Foreign Trade |
| CNCI | National Council on International Trade |
| CNE | National Corporation for Exporters |
| CNM | MERCOSUR Committee of Normalization |
| CNS | National Trade Union Coordinating Body |
| CONUPIA | National Confederation for Medium Sized, Small and Micro Industry, Service and Craftsmen of Chile |
| COPAL | Coordinator for Food and Beverage Industries |
| CORA | Corporation of Agrarian Reform |
| CORFO | Chilean Economic Development Agency |
| CPC | Confederation for Production and Commerce |
| CPPDE | Public-Private Council for Export Development |
| CSO | Civil Society Organization |
| CTA | Argentine Workers' Central Union |
| CUT | Unitary Workers Confederation |
| DIRECON | General Directorate for International Economic Relations |
| ECA | Economic Complementation Agreement |
| ECLAC | Economic Commission for Latin America and the Caribbean |
| ETUC | European Trade Union Confederation |
| EU | European Union |
| EU-CELAC Summit | EU-Community of Latin American and Caribbean States Summit |

| | |
|---|---|
| EU-LAC Summit | EU-Latin America and the Caribbean Summit |
| FAA | Argentine Agrarian Federation |
| FDI | Foreign Direct Investment |
| Fedefrutas | Federation of Chilean Fruit Growers |
| FOCO | Citizens' Justice and Human Rights Forum |
| FTA | Free Trade Agreement |
| FTAA | Free Trade Area of the Americas |
| FTC | Copper Workers Confederation (now Copper Workers Federation) |
| FUT | Workers' United Front |
| GATT | General Agreement on Tariffs and Trade |
| GDP | Gross Domestic Product |
| HSA | Hemispheric Social Alliance |
| IADB | Inter-American Development Bank |
| IAPI | Argentine Institute for Trade Promotion |
| IMF | International Monetary Fund |
| INAI | International Negotiation on Agriculture Institute |
| INTAGRO | Institute of Agrarian Studies |
| IPE | International Political Economy |
| IPR | Intellectual Property Rights |
| IRAM | Argentine Institute of Standardization and Certification |
| ISEN | National Foreign Service Institute |
| ISI | Import-substituting industrialization |
| ITUC | International Trade Union Confederation |
| LAFTA | Latin American Free Trade Association |
| LAIA | Latin American Integration Association |
| MEBF | MERCOSUR-EU Business Forum |
| MERCOSUR | Common Market of the South |
| MIDEPLAN | Ministry of Planning and Cooperation |
| NAMA 11 | Non-Agricultural Market Access 11 |
| NAFTA | North American Free Trade Agreement |
| NGO | Non-governmental organization |
| NTB | Non-Tariff Barriers |
| OAS | Organization of American States |
| ODECU | Organization of Consumers and Users of Chile |
| ODEPA | Agrarian Research and Policy Office |
| ODEPLAN | Office of National Planning |
| ORIT | Inter-American Regional Workers' Organization |
| PICE | Programme for Economic Integration and Cooperation |
| ProChile | Direction for the Promotion of Exports |
| PS ECA | Partial Scope Economic Complementation Agreement |
| PTA | Preferential Trade Agreement |
| RTA | Regional Trade Agreement |
| SECOFI | Mexican Secretariat of Commerce and Industrial Promotion |
| SEGPRES | Ministry General Secretariat of the Presidency |

| | |
|---|---|
| SERPAJ | Peace and Justice Service of Argentina |
| SME | Small and medium-sized enterprise |
| SNA | National Agriculture Society |
| SOFOFA | Society for Promoting Manufacturing |
| SONAMI | National Mining Society |
| SONAPESCA | National Fishing Society |
| SRA | Argentine Rural Society |
| TFA | Trade Facilitation Agreement |
| TPA | Trade Promotion Authority |
| TRIMs | Trade-Related Investment Measures |
| TRIPs | Trade Related Aspects of Intellectual Property Rights |
| UIA | Argentine Industrial Union |
| UNASUR | Union of South American Nations |
| UNDP | United Nations Development Programme |
| UNT | National Union of Workers |
| UP | Popular Unity |
| UR | Uruguay Round |
| USTR | United States Trade Representative |
| WB | World Bank |
| WTO | World Trade Organization |

# Acknowledgments

This book is the result of almost ten years of research, which started as a doctoral project at the Universitat Pompeu Fabra. During these years, I have incurred significant debts of gratitude to colleagues, friends and family, who have provided constant support on both sides of the Atlantic.

A special thank you belongs to Jacint Jordana, my PhD supervisor, and to Mercedes Botto for their guidance and support. Gratitude and warm thanks for encouragement and intellectual inspiration go to Diana Tussie and Jean Grugel. I would also like to thank Diego Muro and Sebastian Hellmeier, as well as all the colleagues and friends whom I have encountered over the years at FLACSO-Argentina, the Universitat Pompeu Fabra, the Institut Barcelona d'Estudis Internacionals (IBEI) and the KFG 'The Transformative Power of Europe' at the Free University of Berlin. In addition, the research would not have been possible without the help of the many interviewees in Argentina and Chile.

I thank Natalja Mortensen and Lillian Rand at Routledge for their professionalism and their patience, as well as two anonymous reviewers, whose comments helped to improve this study. I am also grateful to Sylvia Jones, who helped bring clarity to my prose and make this a better book by doing an excellent job of editing my manuscript.

Finally, I would like to thank my father and sister for their love and constant support. Deep appreciation and gratitude go to Fernando, my life partner, whose love and encouragement made each step in this long journey a brighter one. Last, but far from least, I thank Chiara, my daughter, for all the wonderful joy she brings and for helping me keep things in perspective as I faced the challenges and rewards of being a mother and a scholar. To both of you, all my love.

Barcelona, July 2016

# Part I

# Making Sense of Trade

## Arguments and Politics

# 1 The Contours of Trade Politics

In 2005, in Mar del Plata, Argentina, under the attentive eyes of the leaders of all the countries of the American continent—except for Cuba—five presidents who had recently come to power said 'no' to the continuation of the negotiation for the Free Trade Area of the Americas (FTAA). Thus, Néstor Kirchner (Argentina), Lula da Silva (Brazil), Tabaré Vázquez (Uruguay) and Duarte Frutos (Paraguay), standing for the Common Market of the South (MERCOSUR), together with Hugo Chávez (Venezuela), put a definitive end to what had become the dominant agenda within the Summit of the Americas Process since the first meeting in Miami in 1994. What until then seemed to be a strong consensus on free trade was thus broken. Still, something else broke for several countries in Latin America: the idea that free trade was a unique recipe, the only way for them to integrate regionally and internationally. Discrepancies among countries, until then rather obscure, became increasingly apparent. Hence, the year 2005 marked a crucial turning point for Latin American countries' international strategies.

To understand fully this veto of the FTAA and later developments as well, we need to look back in time and scrutinize trade strategies that started in the late 1980s and early 1990s. After more than half a century of protectionism, by the mid-1980s, Latin American countries undertook structural adjustment programs aimed at promoting trade liberalization, including tariff reduction and the elimination of subsidies, together with (de)regulation and privatization. Even if countries moved forward at different speeds, major transformations were required. Thus, Latin America embarked on a significantly new course towards international integration.

This book takes the reader through those years. They were years of immense change in the Latin American countries with the implementation of trade liberalization being one of the most advanced aspects of reform. Once its benefits were exhausted, general and unilateral liberalization of trade and investments were followed by the articulation of a complex network of regional agreements. This involved the revival of old initiatives and the launch of new schemes, while at the same time endorsing multilateral trade rules through the World Trade Organization (WTO). Consequently, the region became immersed in multiple and simultaneous trade negotiations, including both South-South and

North-South initiatives and multilateral negotiations, which involved important challenges and novelties for countries in the region.

From a global perspective, the completion of the Uruguay Round (UR) and the creation of the WTO through the 1994 Marrakesh Agreement marked a move towards the promotion of deep integration through the negotiation of rules and regulations in new issues, more technically complex and falling within areas of the exclusive competence of states. These transformations at the multilateral level ran parallel to the expansion of the forces of regional cooperation and regionalism, and found their correlate in North-South agreements, i.e. negotiations and agreements pulling together developed and developing countries. As a result of these advances, the trade arena became far more multifaceted and politically and socially more challenging, especially in the case of countries that—as with those in Latin America—had remained closed for more than 50 years. On the shifting ground of widening and deepening trade agendas and diversifying arenas, what factors determined domestic trade politics?

At the core of this book is the unfolding political dynamics triggered by trade negotiations in Latin America from the 1990s until 2005. Equally, the book is concerned with the challenges and dilemmas these countries faced as they became enmeshed in simultaneous and nested games at the regional and multilateral levels. This study suggests, first, that given the increasing complexity and variation of the negotiation agendas at stake, together with their simultaneity, trade negotiations impacted on domestic trade politics in ways not experienced during the previous model of development and integration into the regional and international economic systems. Second, it argues that grasping domestic political dynamics calls for an ample understanding of trade politics, which is herewith defined as the result of the complex and dynamic interdependencies and interrelations between state and society. Which state and non-state actors become activated after the launch of trade negotiations? How do they form their preferences? Which collective strategies emerge? Why do governments and societal actors resort to such strategies? Furthermore, a key premise of the book is that domestic patterns of trade politics, that is to say, state-society relations, vary according to the type of negotiation.

By looking into this question, the book makes three relevant theoretical and empirical contributions. First, it shows that the variation in the scope of the agenda and the uncertainty of political outcomes has important consequences for the ways in which domestic state and non-state actors define their preferences and collective strategies after the launch of different trade negotiations. Thus, South-South, North-South and multilateral trade negotiations elicit different trade politics dynamics. In other words, 'policy creates politics' (Lowi 1964). Second, through detailed empirical investigation of several key negotiations, the book provides a systematic and contextualized comparative analysis of the complex constellations of governmental and societal actors, their preferences, relations and collective action strategies across North-South, South-South and multilateral trade negotiations in two countries in Latin America: Argentina and Chile between 1990 and 2005. Finally, this cross-negotiation and cross-country assessment is intended to advance a new understanding of the domestic political dynamics of international trade in Latin America, which has been a rather neglected region in studies of international political economy (IPE) until very recently. Models inspired by and designed to account for trade politics in the United States and to a lesser extent on the European Union (EU) have dominated this academic field. The book covers 15 years of trade negotiations and adopts a theoretical and methodological approach that is especially designed to capture and analyse mutations through time and variation across countries and types of negotiations.

## What Is Trade Politics? Why Trade Politics?

Trade is a contentious issue. The long-standing presumption that international trade—by means of comparative advantage—generates mutual gains has been increasingly refuted by the unequal distribution of these gains within and across countries. Promoting free trade over protectionist measures or assuming a protectionist stance over trade liberalization is likely to have a differential impact on social groups within and across national borders. Trade generates winners and losers. The shaping of trade policies is thus one of the most politically contentious exercises.

It is not surprising, then, that trade politics has been a matter of interest for scholars and an issue looming in the minds of policymakers, and in recent decades has raised the stakes and elicited responses from a wider set of societal actors.

Trade politics brings us back to the nature of markets, politics and society; the role they play; and how they interact to shape the policy process and outcomes. There is however significant debate concerning these interactions, and examining these roles and relationships with respect to the international system entails a complex undertaking. When analysing the determinants of trade policy, but also its social and political consequences, the central problem has been disentangling the relation between international trade and domestic political dynamics. This implies not only the interaction between markets, politics and society, but also between the domestic and international levels.

I propose to define 'trade politics' as the result of the complex and dynamic interdependencies and interrelations between state and society as they attempt to respond to the pressures and challenges posed by regional and international negotiations. My definition thus moves beyond traditional explanations of trade politics, which broadly speaking, and despite wide theoretical variations, assume either a society- or a state-centred perspective.

Society-centred approaches define the state as an arena of competing social forces and conceptualize it as a transmission belt for the demands of domestic actors who attempt to maximize their material welfare (Frieden 1991, Milner 1988, Rogowski 1989). In contrast, state-centred approaches treat the state as an actor relying on specific administrative and political resources in pursuit of its own interests, irrespective of where domestic actors' preferences lie (Ikenberry 1988, Krasner 1984). My definition of trade politics, however, recognizes that, though institutionally distinct, state and society are in constant interaction.

Contrary to many of the mainstream approaches, in this book, the state is not a passive political actor and an 'impartial' referee among actors competing for either protection or free trade. Nor is it an autonomous actor impermeable to societal demands. On the contrary, nation states play a pivotal and decisive role in regional and international scenarios.

This centrality is more than pertinent to the object of this study, given that the state is the main authority in the negotiation of regional and international agreements and remains the source of democratic governance and accountability both at the domestic and international levels. However, rather than taking the state as a unitary actor, pursuing a clear and identifiable interest based on a set of powers and capabilities derived from its constitutional and legal powers, my definition disaggregates the state. It looks into its complexities as an entity where institutionalized agencies, structures and procedures coexist with informal mechanisms and practices. The aim is to assess how the state relates to and coordinates with various societal actors as it attempts to build its own capacity to respond to trade negotiations. This relational capacity is thus crucial. Capacities are created and recreated through the coordination and interaction between state and society in the process of trade negotiations.[1] Accordingly, my approach attempts to unravel how particular changing contexts affect governments' incentives to coordinate with societal actors and thus shape collective action, this being a neglected aspect of statist debates (Schneider 2004).

This definition of trade politics purposely implies a larger and necessarily diverse universe of societal actors relying on quite varied modes of organization and goals. It sheds light on their identities, their roles and preferences, and the different ways through which they interact and interrelate, but especially with the state as the ultimate locus of decision-making power. 'Non-state actors' refers here to business organizations and civil society entities understood in wide terms, including trade unions, academia and the more formally constituted-non-governmental organizations (NGOs), along with social movements, interest groups and other non-state groups composed under the term of civil society organizations (CSOs) (Friedman and Hochstetler 2002). Thus, it captures the role of societal representatives, largely ignored in the literature, whose preferences and strategies seem difficult to comprehend just by resorting to traditional interest-based approaches. Given the almost exclusive focus on comparative benefits and costs that classical economic theory attributes to protectionism and free trade, these analytical schemes seem insufficient today. Apart from downplaying the role of the state, their treatment of societal actors is highly oversimplified as they focus almost exclusively on the demands of business, whereas the preferences and strategies of labour, academia and the vast array of NGOs remain largely unexplained by these analytical approaches (Walter and Sen 2009). However, the changes in the nature of the trade agenda and its impact on sensitive domestic issues impinge on the interests of wider constituencies, whose demands are underpinned by different conceptions of the appropriate relationship between the state and the market.

In sum, rather than taking state and society as mutually exclusive categories, my definition of trade politics delves into the complex constellation of state and non-state actors, their preferences and strategies. Furthermore, it focuses on the interactions and interrelations between state and society. These interrelations are not necessarily continuous through time and may not be based on institutionalized and formal mechanisms. On the contrary, cross-time variation may be observed, and hybrid and mixed institutional forms may emerge. Moreover, these relations and connections will be largely determined by the resource interdependency between state and non-state actors as countries become involved in different trade negotiations. Trade politics is thus a dynamic process of configuration and reconfiguration of state-society interactions.

## The New Trade Agenda

Trade has been a central issue in national, regional and international politics throughout the history of the modern international system. Even in the late nineteenth and early twentieth centuries, international trade and investments were relatively free, under the umbrella of the British, French and Germans. After the interruptions of two world wars and the Great Depression, the post-Second World War period witnessed the emergence of multilateralism and the liberalization of world trade with the signing of the General Agreement on Tariffs and Trade (GATT) by 23 countries in Geneva in 1947.

As an exclusively negative integration project, the GATT relied on a basic and common framework for reducing tariffs. Years later, however, the establishment of the WTO signalled the evolution of the multilateral trade agenda into wider and more thorough rules for world trade, while the number of member countries has been increasing ever since.[2]

Even if demands for further liberalization have not been exhausted—as shown by current negotiations in agriculture, textiles, automobiles and the banking and insurance sectors—the completion of the WTO increased the pressures for negotiating international regulatory agreements over issues falling within the domestic arena and reaching deep into domestic governance mechanisms (Dymond and Hart 2001). These refer to intellectual property rights (IPRs), competition policy, non-trade barriers, investments and services, including sensitive issues, as in the cases of education and health. As a positive integration project, the multilateral trade agenda thus aims at 'the reconstruction of a system of economic regulation' (Scharpf 1999:45) to guide trade across national boundaries through rules specifying how exchanges will be governed (Fligstein 2005).

Multilateral trade liberalization has run parallel to the expansion of the forces of regionalism. Regional cooperation initiatives of varying scope, size and commitment have emerged, re-emerged and consolidated since the end of the 1980s in Europe, but also in the Americas, Africa and Asia, while trade agreements have also multiplied.[3] The new trade agenda[4] thus found a correlate in bilateral and regional trade negotiations. Apart from the more traditional issues relating to trade liberalization and market opening, these initiatives aimed at extending regulatory standards and disciplines to new areas, namely, IPRs, investment, services and government procurement (Dent 2006, Phillips 2007, Roffe and Santa Cruz 2006). This was most marked in North-South agreements, which pulled together developed and developing countries. Starting with the establishment of the North American Free Trade Agreement (NAFTA) between Canada, Mexico and the United States in 1994, the number of North-South trade agreements has also been on the rise and was later reinforced by the failure of the Cancun Ministerial Conference in 2003 and the subsequent deadlock of the Doha Round. The trade agenda has thus become far more multifaceted and policy challenging, while negotiation scenarios have multiplied. This certainly affected trade politics.

Furthermore, these developments have had major implications for both governments and society. First, these transformations have created a far more testing environment for governments in terms of both their trade capabilities and expertise and their legitimacy. On the one hand, this new trade agenda, together with the sophistication of trade policy instruments, requires enhanced expertise and specialized information in trade issues; all of which was less relevant under the old GATT system (Hocking and McGuire 2004, Kelly and Grant 2005, Ostry 1997, 2002). It also calls for greater coordination among different public agencies (Goldstein and Martin 2000, Shaffer 2006). On the other hand, governments confront more and more heterogeneous demands both at the domestic and international levels. Second, from a societal perspective, the new trade agenda and its more intrusive issues affect the political incentive structure of a wider array of actors, whose interests do not fall within the traditional distinction between free traders and protectionists. In fact, this division is now interwoven with new issues sponsored by a wide range of societal representatives, including not only business, but also labour and an ever-expanding catalogue of CSOs whose interests and concerns impinge on the trade politics agenda, cutting across the preferences and objectives of governments and firms. This new trade agenda has raised concerns among a myriad of societal actors about the social and environmental implications of free trade policies, their impact on IPRs and on the provision of public services provision, among others. Trade turned into a critically and increasingly contentious issue, as attested by the massive mobilizations taking place in cities like Quebec in 2001, where over 50,000 people voiced their concerns about the FTAA, or during the Fifth Ministerial Meeting under the banner of the WTO, in Cancun, Mexico, in 2003.

Hence, there is little disagreement that the trade agenda has undergone important transformations during the last 25 years. In the context of globalization, the landscape and nature of trade politics were deeply transformed, not only because of changes in the agenda but also because of the multiplication of negotiation arenas and the emergence of new actors. Consequently, contemporary trade politics involves interactions between a wider diversity of actors—states, business, labour and civil society—over the old and the new issues on the trade agenda, and simultaneously interrelates and interacts in different negotiation arenas.

## Why Latin America? Why the 1990s?

Free trade is certainly not a new phenomenon in Latin America. However, for decades the region had remained closed to international trade flows, and for many years after the Second World War, the countries in the region followed an inward-looking development model centred on an import-substituting industrialization (ISI) strategy through the direct intervention of the state in the economy. Regional and international trade strategies were thus intended to promote industrial development in order to achieve some degree of autonomy vis-à-vis the developed world. More specifically, whereas trade negotiations were directed at reducing or eliminating trade barriers, and trade remained confined to the interchange of primary—except agricultural—and manufactured products, at the multilateral level, negotiations within the GATT revolved around the ideal of reciprocity, namely mutual changes to bring about equal modifications in traded volumes across partners. Trade policy decisions remained in the hands of a small number of public officials and policymakers and with those actors most directly affected by such negotiations: labour and business organizations, which would push either for protection or trade liberalization (Botto 2003, Bouzas 2004). Under the ISI model, trade policymaking remained thus a rather secretive and hardly accessible process.

This close-economy strategy endured until 1970 when, beginning with Chile and then increasingly throughout the region during the late 1980s, different national governments initiated commercial and trade liberalization. By the mid-1990s, Latin American countries had already experienced extensive market reforms to achieve deregulation, privatization and trade liberalization, including tariff reduction and the elimination of subsidies.

After almost 50 years of sealed domestic markets based on high levels of protectionism and state intervention, the conversion to trade liberalization was especially drastic and abrupt. Except for Chile, countries carried out sweeping liberalization reforms over a period of just two to three years; Argentina, as an extreme case, implemented the country's liberalization program in practically one month (Agosin and Ffrench-Davis 1995). Unilateral bids to open up the economies were soon complemented by free trade agreements of various kinds, including bilateral, regional and multilateral commitments. In the process, countries promoted a complex network of regional agreements, both through the revival of old initiatives and under the format of the so-called 'new' or 'open' regionalism.

Two different visions imbued these new regional strategies. While the notion of new regionalism fuelled the policy recommendations of the World Bank and the International Monetary Fund, acting as the champions of the Washington

Consensus, the Economic Commission for Latin America and the Caribbean (ECLAC) encouraged 'open regionalism' (ECLAC 1994).[5] The latter implied a comprehensive strategy aimed at encouraging technological innovation and production integration and social equity, through more active social policy, to promote thus high quality insertion of these countries in the global economy.[6] In practice, however, these recommendations remained rather irrelevant and new regionalism initiatives would more strongly pursue free trade to enhance the region's participation in the global economy (Bianculli 2016). In all, the objective was to achieve political and economic objectives by exploiting a wide range of external linkages (Mittelman 2000), including the regional, the interregional and the multilateral arenas.

Consequently, as countries abandoned all traces of the ISI, they became confronted with different and simultaneous trade negotiations, dealing with wider and deeper agendas and raising domestic sensitivities, thus, activating the demands of wider constituencies and sowing the seeds of contestation. Trade increasingly became a complex, multi-layered arena, having an impact on larger and more diverse constellations of actors and leading to a variety of collective action strategies and state-society relations.

The old-style trade politics of the ISI model was disrupted as the environment of regional and world trade changed considerably, all of which involved important challenges and novelties for Latin American countries. Whereas the lack of transparency and accountability was increasingly challenged and contested by new actors, high requirements for technical expertise increased the challenge for both governments and societal representatives. Furthermore, these new actors would not only demand to be heard at the domestic level but would also promote coalitions across countries and at other levels. In a context marked by a concerted move towards political liberalization and democratization as countries shed military rule and moved to establish democratic practices, this dramatic reversal of economic policy and international trade strategies definitely affected domestic trade politics.

## Why Argentina and Chile?

The countries of Latin America are certainly diverse in terms of their economic size, level of development and more importantly, their national political economies and their place in the world economy. Disparity is also evident regarding the particular shape and pace structural reforms assumed across North, Central and South America. Therefore, providing a detailed account of the political dynamics of trade negotiations requires further focus. The book analyses trade politics in two countries in the Southern Cone: Argentina and Chile.

Argentina and Chile may show important areas of divergence and diversity and undeniable structural differences—namely, their economic size, the intensity of integration into the world trading system and the commodity and regional composition of foreign trade flows.[7] Nevertheless they share common features due to their political history, political systems, dominant models of development and modes of economic organization. As put by Phillips (2004b), these two countries, together with Brazil, Paraguay and Uruguay, are part of the Southern Cone model of capitalist development. This model rests at the intersection of traits that these countries share and their insertion into an emerging regional political economy, being this embedded within and forged by the structures and processes of the global political economy.

Clearly, both countries operated hence within a similar regional and international context. Furthermore, whereas they diverge in terms of the particular moment when they embarked on market reforms and trade liberalization, Argentina and Chile became active players in regional and international trade negotiations starting in the 1990s. They were then engaged in South-South, North-South and multilateral negotiations. The question that comes next is to what extent this variation in the liberalization process led to differences when it came to the constellation of domestic actors, preferences and collective action strategies across trade negotiations.

## Comprehending Trade Politics Today

This book explores trade politics in Latin America during the roaring years of market opening and drastic trade liberalization, just when trade attained an unparalleled salience in domestic politics. Whereas conventional political economy approaches do not travel well from one setting to another (Alt et al. 1996), studies dealing with Latin American trade politics have largely neglected a relevant question: to what extent do various trade negotiations impact differently on domestic trade politics?

Trade politics is certainly not a static process. It occurs at the intersection between economics and politics, the domestic and the regional and international levels, and results from the intricate interplay between continuing national specificities and the reconfiguring pressures and challenges posed by regional and international negotiations.

Without succumbing to the idea that developing areas require separate studies, unique theoretical constructs and distinct analytical strategies given their '*exceptionalism*', it is my argument that studying and analysing how international negotiations affect domestic political dynamics call for a comparative and empirically grounded approach.[8] Such an approach relies on a more precise acknowledgement of these countries' positions in the regional and wider global political economy, together with their historical context (Fawcett and Hurrell 1995a, Gamble and Payne 1996b, O'Brien 2005, Phillips 2005) and the recoupling of political and economic spheres at the domestic and the international levels.

Furthermore, given that globalization and national governance are interdependent and not opposites (Weiss 1997, 1999), fully accounting for trade politics requires a constructive (re)engagement between comparative and international political economy (Caporaso 1997, Phillips 2004a, Da Conceição-Heldt 2011) to assess the weight of domestic institutional factors vis-à-vis the challenges posed by the negotiation of particular trade agreements. Do preferences, strategies and state-society relations vary across trade negotiations? Do these relate to already institutionalized and established patterns? Alternatively, do they imply new institutional arrangements to cope with the specific challenges trade negotiations bring about, thus producing similar patterns of trade politics among countries? This reengagement between comparative and international political economy is crucial to showing how and to what extent domestic actors' preferences, strategies and responses to different regional and international challenges are conditioned by a country's historical, institutional and social configurations, and by politics. Nevertheless, whereas the domestic configuration of actors and strategies depends heavily on national institutional structures and established traditions, and particular sets of political and policy choices on the part of governments, and a myriad of social actors, they can also be transformed as domestic actors attempt to participate effectively on the global scene. In all, the preferences and strategies implemented by state and non-state actors—even though they are path-dependent or path-conditioned—are transformed and redefined as they interpret and weigh the specific challenges and opportunities posed by South-South, North-South and WTO trade agendas

Research for this book involved 49 in-depth and semi-structured interviews with key actors in the state and societal arenas, including public officials, business, labour and civil society representatives, who possessed first-hand knowledge and expertise on trade negotiations and who were selected partly for convenience but also through snowball sampling. The interviews were carried out in Argentina and Chile in November 2007, July-August 2008 and July 2009 to provide depth and empirical strength to the analytical narrative. In addition, the material allowed for a structured and focused comparison of the emerging patterns of domestic trade politics. In other words, the case-based analysis served to explore the dynamic process of preference formation and articulation in particular contexts marked by the institutional setting of each country, on the one hand, and the specific challenges different trade negotiations pose to domestic actors, on the other. The emphasis is on the contextual understanding of the processes following the launch of South-South, North-South and multilateral trade negotiations, rather than on causal theory or statistical testing of elaborate models. Along with context, the focus is also on how events and patterns evolve in a particular trade negotiation and both across countries and across negotiations. Finally, this extensive interview material, together with informal conversations, was combined with a range of written resources, both primary and secondary, to corroborate, deepen and complement the former and to assure data richness. Appendix 1 provides a descriptive breakdown of the interviews for each country.

Based on these insights and methodology, the book provides a cross-negotiation and cross-country comparative assessment of the domestic political dynamics generated by the launch of different trade negotiations in Argentina and Chile between 1990 and 2005. In all, this study contributes to understanding the impact of trade negotiations on state and society preferences, strategies and relations, thus deepening our knowledge of trade politics in Latin America.

## The Plan of the Book

The remainder of the book offers a detailed empirical and theoretical discussion on how trade policy creates politics in Latin America. It is divided thematically and functionally into three parts and seven chapters.

Part I sets out the context and the theoretical framework and methodological approach framing the research. Chapter 2 opens with a discussion of trade politics, organized around a number of key debates in the fields of economics, politics and IPE, and discusses the various sets of interrelated and mutually complementary issues in the domestic and international levels that affect trade politics. Thus, the analytical model relies on two fundamental notions. First, based on the idea that regionalization, globalization and national governance are interdependent, the model builds on a more constructive dialogue between comparative and international political economy approaches, as little other research has done. Second, to the extent that preferences and collective action strategies are far from unproblematic and ever-ready explanations, this model promotes a contextual and grounded understanding of trade policy preferences and strategies in Latin America. The analytical framework attempts to account for the constellation of state and non-state actors, their preferences and collective action strategies in the context of different trade negotiations. It thus integrates two fundamental dimensions: state-society relations and the logic driving actors' preferences and strategies. Based on these, it proposes four different types of trade politics: cooperative, pressured, subordinated and resistant.

Part II takes us into the contextual boundaries of trade politics in Latin America. Chapter 3 examines the historical, political and institutional dimensions of state-society interactions in the area of trade policy in Argentina and Chile over the second half of the twentieth century and the early years of the following one. This is particularly relevant to understanding the political dynamics and state-society relations triggered by the launch of different trade negotiations as these two countries became immersed in their complex web from the 1990s until 2005. Chapters 4 and 5 present a dense and analytical narrative of the domestic trade politics dynamics triggered by the launch of South-South, North-South and multilateral trade negotiations in Argentina and Chile. These chapters unravel the constellation of state and societal actors, their preferences and collective action strategies as trade agendas gained in depth and breadth, leading to more complex and technical issues, while also involving a larger number of partners and (simultaneously) taking place at different levels, all of which impact on the (un)certainty of policy outcomes.

In order to move beyond the lessons of the individual cases, Part III draws together the analyses and comparatively evaluates trade politics dynamics. Chapter 6 proceeds with the comparative analysis across trade negotiations and across countries, and thus assesses how different negotiations—South-South, North-South and multilateral—promoted different patterns of trade politics in Argentina and Chile. This analysis is done by controlling the national variable and according to the general assumption guiding this research: different trade negotiations promote diverse patterns of trade politics at the domestic level. In addition, the chapter assesses the value of the particular elements that account for these variations. While the comparison across countries acknowledges the weight of political legacies and path conditioning, the chapter considers the constellation of state and non-state actors, their preferences, collective action strategies and articulations to account for their orientation and reorientation in terms of the different trade agendas at play.

The concluding chapter lays out a synthesis and re-examination of the main arguments and broader concerns raised in this first chapter. The book ends with a reflection on what still needs to be done to understand trade politics in Latin America better and to assess its implications within the current shift in the region towards a re-evaluation of its trade and integration model, and the role of state and societal actors in such developments.

## Notes

1 This definition builds largely on the literature on governance, which yields a wider approach to the process of government. The argument is that governing operates in a new context (Chhotray and Stoker 2009) as shown by the emergence of new methods of control and regulation where neither the state nor the public sector retains an exclusive monopoly (Hirst 2000, Maier 1989). In turn, this entails the establishment of different forms of coordination and political cooperation (Pierre 2000, Pierre and Peters 2000).

2 Members include the 128 GATT signatories at the end of 1994 and the 36 countries that have joined the organization up to July 2016, making thus 164 members in all.

3 I use the term 'trade agreement' to refer to any international agreement where two or more countries reciprocally liberalize trade and promote economic integration. According to data by the WTO, which defines these as regional trade agreements (RTA), the number of trade agreements has increased notably since its creation in 1994. Hence, 460 agreements have been signed, covering more than half of world trade, of which 267 are currently in force. For further details, see the WTO: www.wto.org/english/tratop_e/region_e/region_e.htm, last accessed 10 July 2016.

4 These changes have also led to notions like the 'new deep trade agenda' (Young and Peterson 2006), 'postmodern agenda' (Dymond and Hart 2001) or 'regulatory trade agenda'(De Bièvre 2006, Woll and Artigas 2007).

5 In the 1950s, this organization, one of the five regional commissions of the United Nations, advocated economic regional cooperation and the creation of regional markets. Thus, under the decisive thrust of the ECLAC and the inspired lead of Raul Prebisch, different regional cooperation initiatives flourished in Latin America during the 1950s. These were considered to be instrumental for enhancing industrial production and promoting development and autonomy, and thus, surpassing the region's economic and political dependence on advanced industrial economies (ECLA 1950).

6 Already in 1990, and inspired in the seminal contribution of Fernando Fajnzylber (1990), this 'new cepalism' entailed a relevant transformation as the ECLAC

moved its traditional focus on economic policy to promote a rights approach in its analyses and policy recommendations (Bodemer 1988, Ocampo 1998).

7 Moreover, given that these structural elements can be affected by policy decisions only in the long-term, they can be taken as relatively constant in the short term (Bouzas 2006).

8 This also builds on previous debates regarding the need for more grounded theory when analysing developing areas (Fawcett and Hurrell 1995b, Gamble and Payne 1996a, Phillips 2005). Luna et al.'s call for 'empirically grounded studies that can help understand, let alone respond to, Latin America's transformations' (Smith et al. 2014:4) has recently reignited this debate.

## References

Agosin, M. R. and R. Ffrench-Davis (1995). Trade Liberalization and Growth: Recent Experiences in Latin America, *Journal of Interamerican Studies and World Affairs* 37(3): 9–58.

Alt, J. E., J. Frieden, M. J. Gilligan, D. Rodrik and R. Rogowski (1996). The Political Economy of International Trade: Enduring Puzzles and an Agenda for Inquiry, *Comparative Political Studies* 29: 689–717.

Bianculli, A. C. (2016). Latin America, in T. A. Börzel and T. Risse (Ed.) *The Oxford Handbook of Comparative Regionalism*. Oxford, Oxford University Press: 154–177.

Bodemer, K. (1988). Del "viejo" Cepalismo a la crítica de la globalización. Cambio y continuidad en el debate sobre las estrategias de desarrollo en América Latina, *Coherencia* 5(8): 9–34.

Botto, M. (2003). The FTAA and the Participation of Civil Society: Scope and Challenges of a New Regional Agenda, *Integration & Trade* 7(19): 73–91.

Bouzas, R. (2004). *Mercosur's Experience of Preparing Trade Negotiations with the EU: A Memorandum*. Maastricht, European Centre for Development Policy Management (ECDPM)/ODI.

Bouzas, R., Ed. (2006). Domestic Determinants of National Trade Strategies: A Comparative Analysis of MERCOSUR Countries, Mexico and Chile. Paris, MERCOSUR Chair -Science Po.

Caporaso, J. A. (1997). Across the Great Divide: Integrating Comparative and International Politics, *International Studies Quarterly* 41(4): 563–591.

Chhotray, V. and G. Stoker, Eds. (2009). *Governance Theory and Practice: A Cross-Disciplinary Approach*. Basingstoke & New York, Palgrave Macmillan.

Da Conceição-Heldt, E. (2011). *Negotiating Trade Liberalization at the WTO: Domestic Politics and Bargaining Dynamics*. Basingstoke, Palgrave Macmillan.

De Bièvre, D. (2006). The EU Regulatory Trade Agenda and the Quest for WTO Enforcement, *Journal of European Public Policy* 13(6): 851–866.

Dent, C. M. (2006). The New Economic Bilateralism in Southeast Asia: Region-Convergent or Region-Divergent? *International Relations of the Asia Pacific* 6(1): 81–111.

Dymond, W. A. and M. Hart (2001). Post-Modern Trade Policy: Reflections on the Challenges to Multilateral Trade Negotiation after Seattle, *Journal of World Trade* 34(3): 21–38.

ECLA (1950). *The Economic Development of Latin America and Its Principal Problems*. New York, United Nations.

ECLAC (1994). *Open Regionalism in Latin America and the Caribbean: Economic Integration as a Contribution to Changing Production Patterns with Social Equity*. Santiago de Chile, United Nations-Economic Commission for Latin America and the Caribbean.

Fajnzylber, F. (1990). *Industrialization in Latin America: From the 'Black Box' to the 'Empty Box': A Comparison of Contemporary Industrialization Patterns*. Santiago de Chile, Comisión Económica para América Latina y el Caribe (CEPAL).

Fawcett, L. and A. Hurrell (1995a). Introduction, in L. Fawcett and A. Hurrell (Ed.) *Regionalism in World Politics: Regional Organization and International Order*. Oxford, Oxford University Press: 1–6.

Fawcett, L. and A. Hurrell, Eds. (1995b). *Regionalism in World Politics: Regional Organization and International Order*. Oxford, Oxford University Press.

Fligstein, N. (2005). The Political and Economic Sociology of International Economic Arrangements, in N. J. Smelser and R. Swedberg (Ed.) *The Handbook of Economic Sociology*. Princeton, NJ, Princeton University Press: 183–204.

Frieden, J. A. (1991). Invested Interests: The Politics of National Economic Policies in a World of Global Finance, *International Organization* 45(4): 425–451.

Friedman, E. J. and K. Hochstetler (2002). Assessing the Third Transition in Latin American Democratization: Representational Regimes and Civil Society in Argentina and Brazil, *Comparative Politics* 35(1): 21–42.

Gamble, A. and A. Payne (1996a). Conclusion: The New Regionalism, in A. Gamble and A. Payne (Ed.) *Regionalism and World Order*. London, Macmillan Press: 247–264.

Gamble, A. and A. Payne, Eds. (1996b). *Regionalism and World Order*. London, Macmillan Press.

Goldstein, J. and L. L. Martin (2000). Legalization, Trade Liberalization, and Domestic Politics: A Cautionary Note, *International Organization* 54(3): 603–632.

Hirst, P. (2000). Democracy and Governance, in J. Pierre (Ed.) *Debating Governance: Authenticity, Steering, and Democracy*. Oxford, Oxford University Press: 13–35.

Hocking, B. and S. McGuire, Eds. (2004). *Trade Politics*. London, Routledge.

Ikenberry, G. J. (1988). Conclusion: An Institutional Approach to American Foreign Economic Policy, *International Organization* 42(1): 219–243.

Kelly, D. and W. Grant, Eds. (2005). *The Politics of International Trade in the Twenty-First Century: Actors, Issues and Regional Dynamics*. Basingstoke & New York, Palgrave Macmillan.

Krasner, S. D. (1984). Approaches to the State: Alternative Conceptions and Historical Dynamics, *Comparative Politics* 16: 223–252.

Lowi, T. J. (1964). American Business, Public Policy, Case Studies and Political Theory, *World Politics* 16(4): 667–715.

Maier, C. S. (1989). Introduction, in C. S. Maier (Ed.) *Changing Boundaries of the Political*. Cambridge, Cambridge University Press: 1–24.

Milner, H. V. (1988). *Resisting Protectionism: Global Industries and the Politics of International Trade*. Princeton, NJ, Princeton University Press.

Mittelman, J. H. (2000). *The Globalization Syndrome: Transformation and Resistance*. Princeton, NJ, Princeton University Press.

O'Brien, R. (2005). The Transnational Relations Debate, in N. Phillips (Ed.) *Globalizing International Political Economy*. Basingstoke & New York, Palgrave Macmillan: 165–192.

Ocampo, J. A. (1998). Más allá del Consenso de Washington: una visión desde la CEPAL, *Revista de la CEPAL* 66: 7–28.

Ostry, S. (1997). *The Post-Cold War Trading System: Who's on First?* Chicago & London, The University Chicago Press.
Ostry, S. (2002). Preface, in IDB, and Munck Centre for International Studies (Ed.) *The Trade Policy-Making Process. Level One of the Two-Level Game: Country Studies in the Western Hemisphere*. Buenos Aires, Banco Interamericano de Desarrollo—Instituto para la Integración de América Latina y el Caribe. Ocassional Paper 13: i–iv.
Phillips, N. (2004a). "International Political Economy, Comparative Political Economy and the Study of Contemporary Development." IPEG Papers in Global Political Economy N° 8. International Political Economy Group.
Phillips, N. (2004b). *The Southern Cone Model: The Political Economy Development of Regional Capitalist Development in Latin America*. London, Routledge.
Phillips, N. (2005). "Globalizing" the Study of International Political Economy, in N. Phillips (Ed.) *Globalizing International Political Economy*. Basingstoke, Palgrave Macmillan: 1–19.
Phillips, N. (2007). The Limits of 'Securitization': Power Politics and the Process in US Foreign Economic Policy, *Government and Opposition* 42(2): 158–189.
Pierre, J., Ed. (2000). *Debating Governance: Authenticity, Steering, and Democracy*. Oxford, Oxford University Press.
Pierre, J. and B. G. Peters, Eds. (2000). *Governance, Politics, and the State: Political Analysis*. London, Macmillan Press Limited.
Roffe, P. and M. Santa Cruz (2006). *Los derechos de propiedad intelectual en los acuerdos de libre comercio celebrados por países de América Latina con países desarollados: Comercio Internacional*. Santiago de Chile, ECLAC: 82.
Rogowski, R. (1989). *Commerce and Coalitions: How Trade Affects Domestic Political Alignments*. Princeton, NJ, Princeton University Press.
Scharpf, F. W. (1999). *Governing in Europe: Effective and Democratic?* Oxford, Oxford University Press.
Schneider, B. R. (2004). *Business Politics and the State in Twentieth-Century Latin America*. Cambridge, Cambridge University Press.
Shaffer, G. (2006). What's New in EU Trade Dispute Settlement? Judicialization, Public–Private Networks and the WTO Legal Order, *Journal of European Public Policy* 13(6): 832–850.
Smith, W. C., J. P. Luna, M. V. Murillo, A. Schrank, E. Huber, J. D. Stephens, F. Limongi, K. M. Roberts, B. R. Schneider, T. G. Falleti and A. P. Montero (2014). Special Section: Political Economy and the Future of Latin American Politics, *Latin American Politics and Society* 56(1): 1–33.
Walter, A. and G. Sen (2009). The Political Economy of Trade Policy: Interests and Institutions, in A. Walter and G. Sen (Ed.) *Analyzing the Global Political Economy*. Princeton, NJ, Princeton University Press: 60–84.
Weiss, L. (1997). Globalization and the Myth of the Powerless State, *New Left Review* I/225(September–October): 3–27.
Weiss, L. (1999). Globalization and National Governance: Antinomy or Interdependence? *Review of International Studies* 25(5): 59–88.
Woll, C. and A. Artigas (2007). When Trade Liberalization Turns into Regulatory Reform: The Impact on Business-Government Relations in International Trade Politics, *Regulation and Governance* 1(2): 121–138.
Young, A. and J. Peterson (2006). The EU and the New Trade Politics, *Journal of European Public Policy* 13(6): 795–814.

# 2 Unravelling Trade Politics

## A Cross-Negotiation Perspective

The late 1980s and early 1990s witnessed a vigorous revival of regional and international economic cooperation in world politics. Explaining the 'rush to free trade' (Rodrik 1994) was a critical challenge for scholars, both empirically and theoretically. This activism triggered an extensive body of research in trade politics, an area traditionally subject to intense debate as well as being the focus of different disciplines with alternative perspectives on the domestic dynamics surrounding international trade and what policy is or should be.

Since Adam Smith's pioneering inquiry into the nature and causes of the wealth of nations in the eighteenth century, economists have developed increasingly sophisticated and complex models to assess the welfare implications of international trade. However, as they pushed for free trade as the best policy option for most countries, they remained puzzled over why policymakers regularly make use of protectionist measures: 'Perhaps no other area of economics displays such a gap between what policymakers practice and what economists preach as does international trade' (Rodrik 1995:1458). Political scientists have opened up the analysis of states, institutions and powers to solve this puzzle. They have thus explored the political determinants of trade. Contrary to economists who, starting from the idea that the sole interest of a state is to maximize economic welfare, have disregarded all non-economic motivations as irrational, political scientists have found it less difficult to account for this apparently illogical behaviour and its outcomes and have thus attempted to explain (free) trade policies and changes over time.

Though showing significant theoretical variations, explanations have typically involved two main lines of argument: respectively society-centred and state-centred approaches, emphasizing the actions taken by individuals and interest groups in shaping policymakers' preferences and the role of policymakers over the distributional outcomes of trade.

On the one hand, society-centred explanations primarily focus on the demands of societal actors, who, according to the comparative benefits and costs, which classical economic theory attributes to protectionism and free trade, are portrayed as having fixed policy preferences. Scholars have thus provided elegant explanations and predictions, often in dichotomous terms, regarding where the winners and losers from trade will stand. Considered as distributional coalitions (Mansfield and Busch 1995, Schamis 1999), economic sectors (Frieden and Rogowski 1996), firms (Gourevitch 1986, McKeown 1984, Milner 1988) or social groups and classes (Rogowski 1989), these players would then turn to the state to defend and advance their preferences. Based on these assumptions, trade policy is the result of a distributive battle between groups displaying maximizing behaviour and resorting to simple pressure lobbying strategies, either for protection or for liberalization (Magee et al. 1989, Schamis 1999), while the state remains an 'impartial' referee among these competing preferences and is 'essentially a reactor to private demands' (Frieden 1991:39).

On the other hand, while holding societal pressures constant (Mansfield and Busch 1995:727), state-centred approaches acknowledge the presence and central role of the state in shaping trade policy. Furthermore, these approaches argue that states and public actors intervene in trade policy in pursuit of their own objectives irrespective of where the preferences of domestic interest groups lie. In so doing, they examine the state, its role and strategies through two different lenses. First, they focus on the institutional structures of trade policy (Bayne and Woolcock 2003) and thus primarily conceive the state as a set of organizational structures and legal and institutional arrangements that tend to endure, emphasizing its autonomy and influence in the definition of trade policy (Goldstein 1993, Keohane and Milner 1996). A second strand underscores the abilities and resources of politicians and public officials in the Executive as of decisive relevance in shaping trade politics. In all, from this perspective, states act independently of societal demands in the policy process as their preferences respond to particular notions or 'conceptions of the "national interest" or the maximization of some social welfare function' (Ikenberry et al. 1988:12, Krasner 1983). State-centred approaches explain trade politics as the result of domestic institutional relationships, on the one hand, and the capacities of public actors to carry out their policy objectives in a context marked by particular domestic and international constraints, on the other (Ikenberry et al. 1988). By looking into the state's organizational structure and capacities, and the actions and strategies of state actors, state-centred explanations have opened up the 'black box' of policymaking.

Nevertheless, by overestimating the role either of societal actors or of the state, these approaches have characterized state and society as opposing and mutually exclusive categories, promoting in turn a dichotomous reading of trade politics. Furthermore, both state- and society-centred perspectives have remained comparative in nature. They have analysed trade politics as happening at the national level, whereas the regional or international levels have remained relatively sealed off. This 'tenacious nation-state centrism' (Robinson 2001:556) has somehow prevented full acknowledgement of the impact of and interactions with regional and international factors.

In this book, I argue that a fuller and deeper understanding of the nuances and complexities of trade politics today requires considering state and society interactions. Moreover, the international level is also to be brought in to explain variations in the ways in which state and non-state actors respond to specific international challenges.

## An Analytical Framework: Bringing Together the State and Society in Trade Politics

My definition of trade politics assumes a state-society approach. I take trade politics as a relational concept and delve deeply into the political dynamics between the state and society and vice versa.

Trade politics thus refers to a continuous and dynamic process involving the interaction of state and various societal actors through different channels, mechanisms and procedures. This multifaceted set of interdependencies and intersections between state and society gives way to new institutional forms, both formal and informal. Trade politics is the result of a series of more or less institutionalized processes and mechanisms and is also an outcome of the particular political dynamics promoted at the domestic level by international trade negotiations. However, these dynamics vary not only across time but also across different trade negotiations. Therefore, the examination of established institutional processes should be complemented with the scrutiny of the domestic process of preference formation and interaction among state and society, whose preferences and collective action strategies as well as their inclusion and influence can vary according to the trade agenda at stake. Based on this premise, the concept of trade politics goes beyond the institutional dimension and captures the complex and variegated patterns of state-society relations in the context of different trade negotiations. It is thus intended to unravel the specific constellations of actors, preferences and strategies deployed after the launch of particular trade negotiations.

## State Actors, Their Needs and the Resulting Institutional Architecture

Trade politics operates in a new context today. New and deeper agendas, which neither the state nor society have the technical expertise and resources to deal with properly, require that the state-society divide and the corresponding communication mechanisms must be redefined. On the one hand, lines of political and social fracture take place in many dimensions. Thus, heightened and more varied demands are placed on the state by a larger and more heterogeneous number of societal representatives, who demand a place and voice in the trade policy process and call for the creation of mechanisms and spaces to be informed and/or to have an effective influence on it. Moreover, they can provide the state with fundamental informational and legitimacy resources. Hence, this increasing plurality calls for different forms of coordination and political cooperation (Hirst 2000, Pierre 2000). However, the state lacks the necessary informational and legitimacy resources to formulate workable and effective policies in an environment that is becoming increasingly ungovernable (Pierre

2000:4–5). In other words, even if the state still plays a central role in trade policy and remains in control of some unique power bases, it also becomes more dependent on societal actors. Consequently, state capabilities rely not so much on the formal and institutional resources attached to instruments of government, but rather on the ability of the state to define and construct the set of relations that demarcate broad patterns of governance in a specific policy field (Jayasuriya 2004:489).

In contrast to state-centred approaches, where the focus is mainly on the state and its political and institutional capabilities for steering society and economy through political negotiations and the definition of objectives and priorities, I delve into the ways in which the state interacts with society in order to reach mutually acceptable decisions (Kooiman 1993, Rhodes 1997, 2007). Furthermore, contrary to the more traditional notions where state strength is taken as the set of powers and capabilities derived from its constitutional or legal assets, within my study, state capabilities constitute a relational term that results from the state's capacity to structure and relate with various resources and agents in particular policy areas (Jayasuriya 2004, Pierre and Peters 2000). Traditional, formal and legal 'powers over' are replaced by contextual 'powers to' (Gourevitch 1986). State effectiveness thus stems from its 'relational capacity'; it is an emergent quality of its coordination and interaction with societal actors, rather than the result of the imposition of control from above.

International trade policy rests largely in the hands of the Executive branch; this is particularly prominent in Latin America where presidents have historically played an overwhelming role in foreign policy arenas. Hence, my focus is on the state Executive and the two agencies most strongly involved in foreign trade decision making: the ministries of economics and foreign affairs, together with specific secretaries and agencies within them. The analysis does not look into legislative power, since the involvement of Congress is almost nil in this policy area, and the approval of international trade agreements appears to be just a formality (BID 2002, Bouzas 2006, Robin 2008).

Regarding state actors and their role in trade policy, two elements are worth analysing. First, there is the degree of formalization of coordination and leadership among the ministries and agencies involved in trade policy decision making. Second, there are the states' abilities to face international trade negotiations adequately, which in the context of multiple and changing negotiation scenarios may be stretched to include information and legitimacy. In the first case, the need for specialization in foreign trade compels the state to develop greater technical capacity through the creation of expert units or departments and the recruitment of specialists in this policy field (Jordana and Ramió 2002, 2003). Moreover, given that in trade policy the need for knowledge, information and expertise is constant, the state is expected to demand substantial input from different societal actors. In the second case, when its legitimacy is challenged, the state needs to strengthen and widen its base of support, this being especially crucial as the trade agenda includes even more sensitive and intrusive issues impinging on wider constituencies.[1]

### *The Institutional Architecture*

Different mechanisms will be deployed to overcome these informational and legitimacy deficits and enhance the government's effectiveness. The construction of the state's trade capacities that would make government more effective implies adding new actors to decision making. The state state will thus reach out to society to build its informational and legitimacy credentials. However, the concepts of opening and participation hold multiple meanings, and the state will deploy different channels and mechanisms to access non-state actors.

In the first case, faced with the need to build the government's informational credentials vis-à-vis its counterparts and thus negotiate effectively, governments promote the opening of channels for participation and consultation with those societal representatives capable of providing the required information. This can range from data on the vulnerability of specific sectors when trade negotiations involve tariffs and safeguards to highly technical knowledge and expertise as required in the new trade agenda. To this end, the state will more strongly promote the establishment of formal channels and mechanisms, which can vary in terms of the participating actors and the frequency and specific format of the consultations, among other features. Interestingly, however, this formalization does not entail the elimination of informal contacts. In fact, informal mechanisms and channels may persist and still be a key element in the relation between the state and those societal actors offering this fundamental added value, thus allowing an *extensive* institutional architecture to develop where non-state actors' access to trade decision making is both formally and informally facilitated. Capturing this informality is fundamental to avoiding the risk of missing much of what shapes and constrains trade politics in Latin America. An exclusive focus on formal rules 'can yield an incomplete—if not wholly inaccurate—picture of how politics work' in the region (Helmke and Levitsky 2006:2).

In contrast, when governments need to enhance their base of support in order to assure the procedural legitimacy and representativeness of trade policy decisions, they will appeal to a wider and greater variety of societal actors, though some of them may be invited to participate at a rather late stage in the decision-making process and to discuss and legitimize already-established agendas. Moreover, and even if this opening up entails the establishment of various institutional mechanisms, these will more generally present an ad hoc, fragmented and scarcely institutionalized character, whereas informal contacts and interaction with state actors will be almost nil. These more lax and softly formalized mechanisms of access, in the absence of informal facilitation, result in a *limited* institutional architecture.

Taken as a whole, the specific constellations of institutional arrangements and mechanisms provided for non-state actors to access the decision-making process that shape the institutional architecture stand quite close to the idea of 'political opportunity structure' (Kitschelt 1986) and 'institutional supply' (Mattli and Woods 2009a). These mechanisms certainly contribute to the promotion of formality and transparency—though to different extents and degrees—in countries where economic decision making tends to be opaque. Moreover, these mechanisms provide important 'selective incentives', namely material resources and privileged access to the decision-making process (Schneider 2004a). Whereas the state can thus be seen as the pivotal causal agent, not only of business organization but also of its growing specialization and professionalization (Schneider 2004a), from a civil society perspective, the blockage or ill-functioning of access mechanisms may lead to a boomerang pattern of influence (Keck and Sikkink 1998). In sum, by either blocking or allowing access to decision making, governments can spur the organization of societal actors, promoting or deterring collective action strategies, and affecting the investment in their institutional and technical capabilities.

Unravelling the particular characteristics of the institutional architecture and the variation across the established mechanisms and channels in terms of their formalization and institutionalization, but more importantly regarding the degree of inclusion they promote, is thus fundamental. Domestic political institutions impose constraints and opportunities, and thus strongly affect the ways in which societal actors define their collective action strategies. Whereas in some cases they may allow non-state actors to exert effective influence on the decision-making process, other institutional designs may impose limits on the actors' actions and hinder their influence. In sum, the opening of dialogue and participation spaces by the state provides incentives for collective action strategies. These will certainly depend on the available options somehow inscribed in the institutional architecture and the advantages and drawbacks attached to the possible courses of action. However, as long as this outreach to society can respond to two different institutional needs—information and legitimacy—there will be differences in the institutional architecture that is finally constructed. Accordingly, the state's requirements or needs have important consequences for the ways in which societal actors can transmit their demands and contribute to trade negotiations. Given that states' needs are different in each case, the participation and consultation mechanisms devised will also vary. The diverse kinds of selective incentives thus provided have significantly different effects on non-state actors, who interpret and evaluate their participation opportunities differently, all of which are expected to affect the design and deployment of collective action strategies to exert some influence on trade politics. Finally, the institutional architecture serves as a framework not only for their collective action strategies, but also for the modes of interaction between state and non-state actors and among non-state actors themselves.

## Societal Actors, Their Resources and Collective Action Strategies

Classical approaches to trade policy focus on the demand side of state-society relations. However, their analyses almost exclusively capture the demands of business and, to a lesser extent, of labour. Consequently, their models take trade policy as the result of the deliberate action of distributional coalitions (Schamis 1999), whereas lobbying over trade policy is equated with rent-seeking (Magee et al. 1989). Still, while these analyses may be appropriate when examining policies with unambiguous distributional costs and benefits and affecting a small number of stakeholders already familiar with one another, they may fail to capture the more complex trade politics dynamics.

Given its broader and deeper scope, the domestic impact of the new trade agenda turns out to be increasingly uncertain in distributional terms, on the one hand, and it affects the preference structure of many more domestic groups, on the other. As trade liberalization leads not only to deregulation but also to re-regulation at the national level (Ventura-Dias 2004), interests tend to be more indeterminate and fluid. When interests are uncertain, much depends on politics and the political construction of preferences and coalitions (Schneider 2004b). How are preferences and collective action strategies defined in the context of these more complex trade agendas?

Recent studies have developed wider frameworks for looking at the dynamics of business-government connections to show that these include not only pressure lobbying but also a more interactive relationship based on knowledge and expertise (Woll 2008, Woll and Artigas 2007). Moreover, studies have also acknowledged the role of the so-called 'transformational coalitions', which include civil society representatives 'less interested in the *division* of the pie than the *recipe* for making it' (Ostry 2002:ii, original emphasis). International trade negotiations are thus accompanied by a 'double movement' (Polanyi 1957, 2001). While governments advance the expansion of markets through regional and multilateral liberalization—'pressure from above'—civil society seeks to shape and transform the negotiation processes 'from below' (Korseniewicz and Smith 2001). Consequently, in addition to business demands, governments are required to meet a vastly increased range of claims stemming from civil society actors who request greater consultation on the elaboration of policy decisions and attempt to counterbalance the traditional weight of the private sector.

It is my argument, then, that the high complexity of the agendas and issues at stake hinder making a priori assumptions about which will be the voices in favour or against the negotiation of a particular trade agreement. To the extent that these often involve a host of obligations beyond the realm of trade policy, including the regulation of foreign direct investment (FDI), IPRs or the environment, the distributional implications of trade liberalization agreements may be relevant but are certainly not enough to understand the domestic political dynamics of trade negotiations. My definition of trade politics hence avoids an a priori assumption of where societal actors will stand on international negotiations and provides a single framework to account for these more complex domestic dynamics by looking into the preferences, strategies and relations established between them and the state.

My focus is on collective actors who aim to influence the policy process (Scharpf 1997). These actors include business chambers and trade unions, together with academia, the more formally constituted-NGOs, social movements and other non-state groups composed under the umbrella term of CSOs (Friedman and Hochstetler 2002). Assessing their preferences and strategies thus implies a focus on the mechanisms and practices through which these are defined and an analysis of the multiple means through which they are translated into strategies, which will depend not only on the societal actors' resources and capabilities but on the wider institutional architecture as well. Institutional, political and social contexts are also likely to affect the process of definition of societal preferences and the particular strategy they choose.

The state's informational and legitimacy requirements engender different institutional architectures, which offer an important selective incentive for non-state actors' collective action strategies and for the development of their organizational and technical capabilities. In addition, their preferences and strategies are mediated through domestic institutions, which can certainly influence outcomes. As well documented by Haggard (1988), institutional changes promoted by governments affect interest groups, especially in terms of their discourse and incentives to develop particular types of strategies.

However, an adequate institutional offer must be met by a strong social demand (Mattli and Woods 2009b). In other words, the extent to which societal actors are capable of participating and fully exploiting these channels largely depends on their own resources. Still, this social demand (offer) is not necessarily given in a timely manner, which is even more evident in policy areas that, as in the case of trade policy and international negotiations, require increasingly specialized and technically advanced knowledge. The ability of business and civil society to fulfil states' demands will determine to a large extent their participation and chances of impact and influence. Non-state actors' organizational and informational abilities are particularly relevant, but they will not all be equally skilled.

### *The Social Demand*

Two elements are worth analysing when depicting the social demand. First, the ability of non-state actors to represent their particular sector and to reconcile divergent positions must be considered. Certainly, irrespective of the existing institutional architecture, their effective participation and influence on the trade policymaking process depend on their ability to coordinate a common stance and to speak with a unique voice, thus showing their ability to overcome possible internal differences. Based on Olson's theory of collective action (1971), a substantial literature has discussed how much influence societal actors can have over policy outcomes. The main distinction is between groups with more specific interests and those whose interests are more diffuse. Collective action is portrayed as being easier for the former groups, whereas the latter find it difficult to translate their preferences into concrete strategies and actions. Still, from a trade policy perspective, while concentrated groups are expected to dominate (Gourevitch 1986) as diffuse groups remain largely powerless, there still may be important cleavages and conflicts among concentrated interests regarding trade policy (Destler and Odell 1987, Milner 1988). In this respect, non-state actors vary from those that organize their activities through stable and permanent organizational modes—as in the case of business chambers and trade unions—to others where activities rely on mobilization structures—NGOs, social movements, coalitions and networks—and which are included under the term of CSOs.

A second element for analysis is their institutional capabilities, namely, their ability to face issues that, as in the case of the new trade agenda, demand specialized knowledge and expertise either to elaborate a coherent and well-founded position or to respond to the technical requirements of governments. Groups with specific resources are hence expected to gain influence over policy outcomes (Henning 2004, Lohmann 1998). Clearly, even when an extensive institutional architecture is in place, non-state actors' effective participation and roles in the decision-making process will be determined by their own resources and strategies, which show a wide variety ranging from *interests* to *ideas and information.*

### *From Interests to Ideas and Information*

This categorization builds on Weber's definition of interests as the primary force driving human action, which can be material as well as idealistic.

While emphasizing the ideal, Weber indicates that even material interests are, to a large extent, culturally constructed, since they rely on social actors' ideas about the way the world is and their proper place in it. These ideas or images of the world work like railway switches: they determine 'the tracks along which action has been pushed by the dynamic of interest' (Weber [1915] 1946:280). In other words, interests drive individuals' actions, though the ideal (social) dimension determines the final expression actors give to their actions (Swedberg 2003:3). In a similar vein, other authors have argued that both ideas and interests have a causal weight in explanations of human action. Ideas frame how actors understand their interests (Goldstein and Keohane 1993). Equally, given that ideas are part of the institutional framework where action is developed, these do not only frame interests and goals but also offer a shared language and approach to problems (Mattli and Woods 2009a).

Weber's conceptualization of ideas brings in another relevant element for understanding human behaviour: 'they can also at certain junctures make human behaviour change direction' (Swedberg 2005:70). In other words, ideas, beliefs and cognitive factors may offer new roadmaps for social actors, especially where there is uncertainty.

Uncertainty is one of the most fundamental characteristics of the social and political world (Hall 2005). Trade reform and liberalization do not escape this rule. Uncertainty becomes even more explicit in trade negotiations involving regulatory issues whose impact cannot be properly anticipated and hence create a complex scenario. Under conditions of uncertainty taken as 'the lack of knowledge about the future' (Woll 2010:137), the past is not prologue (Blyth 2010). To the extent that actors lack clear and precise knowledge about the future and are unsure of what their interests are and how to achieve them, they regard situations as unique events. They need to resort to new ideas and information, assess different views and learn from them. Ideas, cognitive and information systems are then expected to play a relevant role in shaping non-state actors' strategies.

In all, my argument is that, in addition to the material incentives, cost-benefit calculations and strategic thinking emphasized by rationalist models, ideas and beliefs influence trade politics. This builds on a growing literature that highlights ideas, beliefs and cognitive factors as crucial determinants of actors' preferences and strategies in the face of uncertainty (Abdelal et al. 2010, Blyth 2002, Bukovansky 2010, Woll 2008). In fact, ideas and material interests are mutually constituted (Blyth 2002). Both material factors and ideas are necessary to account for domestic preferences given the increasingly contested and uncertain character of trade politics today.

Thus, I argue that when facing trade negotiations, social actors' actions and strategies are the result of different logics relying on interests, on the one hand, and on ideas and information, on the other. Integrating these requires exploring when and how interests and ideas/information explain these actors' strategies, and thus provide a more exhaustive account of trade politics dynamics. Two types of strategies can be distinguished.

First, when issue uncertainty is low and the distributional consequences and policy outcomes can be easily identified, non-state actors' actions and strategies are more strongly based on purely material and idealist interests, which in turn will define the repertoires of more or less acceptable courses of action (Scharpf 1997). Thus, whereas more institutionalized actors, whose activities are structured from rather stable and permanent organizational modes and who rely on relevant resources and means, will resort to traditional pressure strategies to promote the defence of their material interests, larger and more dispersed groups, having only limited resources, can overcome this deficit by building on particular ideal interests. The latter can work as a nexus and become a driving force for action as they offer a common ground or framework capable of drawing together networks or coalitions. Their loose and lax characterization permits non-state actors to choose from among competing sets of ideas, the one that best expresses their interests (Mattli and Woods 2009a). This imperfect fit provides space for ideal interests to serve as a shared ground on which coalitions and networks can develop an agenda based on common concerns.[2] Interestingly, each will converge on a *competitive* strategy vis-à-vis the state and non-state actors and will more strongly deploy traditional pressure strategies to promote the defence of their material and ideal interests. This reflects an underlying conflicting element that clearly differentiates and sets apart these groups from the government and from other societal actors as well.

Second, when uncertainty prevails, that is to say when actors regard situations as unique events because they are unsure of what their (material and ideal) interests are and how to achieve them, ideas and information are expected to play a relevant role in shaping their preferences and strategies. Ideas and information reduce uncertainty by allowing actors to interpret the challenges and problems they have to confront by setting a course of action (Blyth 2002). Non-state actors' strategies will thus be based on an ideational/informational logic and rely more strongly on the use of relevant ideas, information and technical knowledge. Those non-state actors capable of providing the state with the relevant and required expertise will thus develop a *collaborative* strategy. As noted in recent studies on regulatory trade and governance, information, together with technical expertise, turns out to be an important resource for those actors trying to gain access to the trade policy process (Woll and Artigas 2007). Social actors can resort to various mechanisms and processes to develop these information-gathering and technical capabilities—including creating technical departments or areas; outsourcing this task to specialists, consultants and think tanks; or interacting with other actors. However, the state and the institutional architecture devised for the participation and consultation with society works as a selective incentive for those seeking to exert some influence on the policy process, inducing them to communicate meaningful information. Furthermore, these actors face a trade-off between pursuing their own sectoral interests and contributing to decision making through the provision of valuable information (Broscheid and Coen 2003, Coen 2005). Non-state actors are thus expected to become privileged sources of new ideas and information for governments. Moreover, interactions between governments and societal actors may evolve towards rather stable working relationships (Woll and Artigas 2007).

## Four Ideal Types of Trade Politics

Trade politics is characterized by complex interdependencies and articulations between state and society. Governments offer important incentives to activate societal actors, but these vary according to the particular deficit the state faces. The various requirements will lead to a process of extensive or limited inclusion according to the type and number of points of access to the decision-making process or the institutional barriers or obstacles to inclusion. In turn, these different institutional arrangements affect the incentives of non-state actors for collective action and contribute to the definition of their preferences, the promotion of capacities and the design of strategies, which will more likely respond either to a collaborative or competitive logic. Thus, when confronted with non-state actors' strategies, the arrangements will produce four ideal types of trade politics as shown in Table 2.1. As I understand them, these are Weberian ideal types: I apply them knowing that they are a construct, a tool to explain and understand the dynamics of state-society relations and the patterns of trade politics. For the sake of simplicity, I discuss these ideal types in order, though in practice they might not be found just as they are described and characterized.

*Table 2.1* Four ideal types of trade politics

| *Societal demand* Non-State Actors' Strategy | *State Actors: Institutional architecture* | |
|---|---|---|
| | *Extensive* | *Limited* |
| *Collaborative* | Cooperative trade politics | Subordinated trade politics |
| *Competitive* | Pressured trade politics | Resistant trade politics |

Source: *Author-created*

### *Cooperative Trade Politics*

This ideal type refers to constellations where the government's need for information and technical expertise leads to the opening of different channels and mechanisms to allow for the participation of those societal actors capable of contributing this key informational resource. This will lead to the implementation of formal mechanisms, which will be accompanied by informal encounters and procedures, thus providing an *extensive institutional architecture* through which social actors can rely on a wide range of points of access to the trade policy decision-making process.

A pattern of *cooperative trade politics* will only emerge when the government's strategy is met on the societal demand side with a *collaborative strategy* based on the provision of information and expertise that can thus complement the state's limited knowledge or directly supply its lack of informational resources. Essentially, this pattern of cooperative trade politics depends on the informational capabilities of societal actors. However, access to decision makers can work as a positive incentive for the latter actors to invest in their own organizations and to enhance their abilities and informational resources to participate through the channels and mechanisms formally established, but also to respond to the state's demands and requirements that could be put forward through parallel, informal arrangements. Consequently, it is expected that the stability of these mechanisms will promote a process of learning by societal actors, and as a result a working and cooperative relationship with governments based on information dependency (Coen 1998) and credible commitment (Majone 1999, 2001, North and Weingast 1989) will be established.

### *Pressured Trade Politics*

State actors will build an *extensive institutional architecture* to overcome their informational and technical vulnerabilities. However, when the state's demands and requirements are met with a *competitive strategy* on behalf of non-state actors, a pattern of *pressured trade politics* will emerge.

Organizational and informational capabilities required to achieve meaningful participation are not evenly distributed among society, which means that broad and sustained participation by all those potentially affected by the negotiation of these trade agendas is difficult to achieve. These issues are beyond the interest of most citizens, who view them as distant processes having no impact on the domestic sphere. Many societal actors may lack the required technical information and expertise, whereas others may be deprived of the necessary resources in terms of strength and leadership and thus face collective action problems. Deprived of these key assets, non-state actors may base their strategy on either idealistic or material interests.

On the one hand, more concentrated societal actors who can also count on resources and means will resort to traditional pressure strategies to promote the defence of their material interests. In its narrower definition, these interests can oscillate between demands for protection from competing importing sectors and the request for more liberalization from export-oriented sectors. Even if inclusion is extended to them, their own inability to produce well-informed proposals may lead to a *pressured pattern of trade politics*. On the other hand, this may also be found when larger and more heterogeneous groups facing important collective action problems confront the state with their own ideals, without offering the information and technical expertise the government is demanding. Paradoxically, both concentrated interests and diffuse ideas can lead—in the absence of information—to similar competitive strategies, and ultimately to comparable pressured trade politics.

### *Subordinated Trade Politics*

Requirements for broader input legitimacy lead to consultation with a larger number of societal actors. Rather paradoxically, even if this means consulting with more and heterogeneous non-state actors, it does not entail extensive inclusion, but a *limited institutional architecture* instead. This is because the institutional arrangements implemented to bridge the gap with societal actors show a lower level of institutionalization and more fragmentation and include only formal mechanisms and channels. Thus, they offer fewer incentives for non-state actors when compared with those who can also count on informal access to the decision-making process.

However, the fact that there are no participation channels or that the existing mechanisms are obstructed has a varying impact on the different non-state actors according to their own abilities and the resources they can offer to the state. When state actors' need for legitimacy is faced with a *collaborative strategy* on the demand side, this will result in a *subordinated pattern of trade politics*, which refers to a constellation where non-state actors' collective action is built on a rather well-informed basis. However, the state-societal relation will be based only on formal mechanisms that, given their lower degree of institutionalization and formalization, may be only occasionally activated, either when state actors consider that societal actors can make some particular contribution and provide added value to decision making or when the latter intend to bring forward a proposal or suggestion.

### *Resistant Trade Politics*

When the state's main requirement is to gain legitimacy and support for policy decisions, it will promote the establishment of formal channels and mechanisms, but informal access will not be provided, leading thus to a *limited institutional architecture*. Faced with a *competitive strategy*, based on concentrated material interests or diffuse ideal interests on the societal demand side, this political opportunity structure will lead to a pattern of *resistant trade politics*.

In this case, public access channels are limited and inadequate. Confronted with a more concentrated or radical pressure exerted by society, the political opportunity structure is not likely to promote the aggregation of demands, thus limiting the influence of social actors on the decision-making process. Hence, *resistant trade politics* is based exclusively on formal facilitation of access, where societal representatives find it difficult to obtain concessions. In some cases, and this is especially true for those deploying more radical strategies, dialogue with the government may be impossible or even avoided.

When participation and consultation channels are limited or blocked, more dispersed and heterogeneous groups are at a distinct disadvantage compared with more organized and concentrated groups since the resources at their disposal are modest and their knowledge limited. In addition, they are too large and heterogeneous to overcome collective action problems. The creation of wider alliances and coalitions is thus a useful strategy. Launching international negotiations can generate various strategies linked to the regional and international levels while exerting pressure on the domestic policy decision-making process. In their search for allies, domestic actors join regional and international networks and coalitions and thus put pressure on national governments from outside. In addition, by talking with regional and international partners, societal actors gain access to various resources in terms of *ideas and information*, and even financial means—resources that are in short supply for many of them. In this sense, trade negotiations are likely to act as catalysts for collective action. Based on a certain repertoire of common concerns and *ideas*, these networks—though mediated regionally and internationally—direct their strategy towards the nation state.

## Trade Politics in International Negotiations

Trade politics is taken to mean the result of the particular patterns of state-society relations that result from the complex interdependencies established between governments and social actors. Essentially, state-society dynamics are context dependent and must thus be understood within a particular political-institutional setting. Nevertheless, differences are expected to emerge not only across countries and time, but also across trade negotiations. Thus understood, trade politics is the result of two factors operating at two different analytical levels: domestic institutional processes, on the one hand, and international trade negotiations, on the other.

Building on these assumptions, accounting for trade politics patterns requires the challenges raised by trade negotiations occurring simultaneously at different levels to be analysed. The ways through which governments and societal actors define and adjust their policy stances and strategies at the domestic level to respond to these external challenges also need similar treatment. In all, the underlying assumption is that political economy is increasingly not only international but comparative as well (Phillips 2004). The research design allows me to apply this framework and the classification of trade politics patterns of two different countries and three types of international trade negotiations across time (see Figure 2.1).

*Figure 2.1* Fifteen years of trade negotiations in Argentina and Chile

*Source: Author-created*

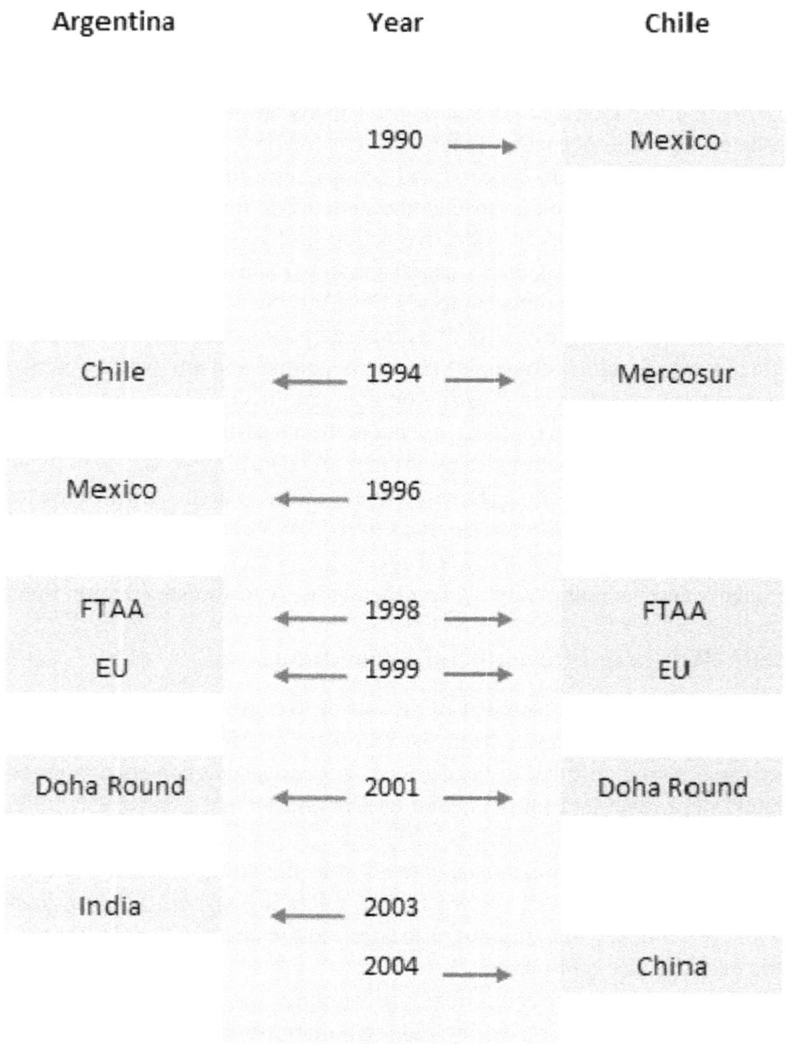

From an international perspective, the analysis compares South-South, North-South and WTO as each of them implies a particular scenario that includes the number and type of actors involved, the arena or level where they take place, and the agendas and issues involved, which range from negative to positive integration.

Though both South-South and North-South negotiations take place at the same level—the regional one—North-South brings together countries showing different levels of economic, political and institutional development. When it comes to the agendas at play, whereas South-South agreements signed in the 1990s remained limited to negative integration, that is to say, to the promotion of free trade, North-South initiatives increasingly extended regulatory standards and disciplines to new areas (Dent 2006, Roffe and Santa Cruz 2006). Thus, apart from the more traditional issues relating to negative integration, i.e. trade liberalization and market opening, in those areas where regulatory issues were relevant—namely, IPRs, investments, services and government procurement—North-South negotiations aimed at harmonizing domestic rules and regulations to promote common regulatory frameworks. In all, they introduced positive integration rules intended to shape the conditions under which markets operate. Whereas it might be relatively easy for governments to produce negative measures, thus increasing market integration by eliminating national restraints on trade and distortions of competition, agreeing on positive integration rules remains extremely difficult and in many cases almost impossible because of differences among countries in terms of normative or ideological positions, levels of economic development and institutional and policy patterns (Scharpf 1999b).

North-South negotiations also entailed deepening or extending WTO commitments, either by expanding existing WTO regulatory obligations or by regulating policy areas not covered by the organization's agenda (Horn et al. 2010). The multilateral agenda and the working of the WTO add to the complexity. They bring together a larger number of countries with important differences in terms of their levels of economic, political and institutional development, which have hence different preferences regarding positive integration regulations. Still, most of the divisive issues of the multilateral trade agenda, which aimed at promoting positive integration and which faced opposition from developing countries, became part of North-South trade negotiations. Progress towards regulatory harmonization has turned out to be more intense in the case of the latter, especially in the bilateral trade agreements signed since the early 2000s (Roffe and Santa Cruz 2006). These initiatives have placed stronger emphasis on the imposition of market disciplines than on trade liberalization itself (Dent 2006, Phillips 2007).

Moreover, as the trade agenda moves from negative to positive rule-making, it implies highly technical or interdependent policy issues, which require technical and policy analyses. It also entails higher degrees of uncertainty. When dealing with negative integration policies—as in the case of South-South agreements—aimed at dismantling trade barriers, actors are more certain about where their costs and benefits lie. On the contrary, when dealing with positive integration rules, the expected costs and benefits become blurred. The negotiation of positive commitments—as under North-South and WTO negotiations—goes beyond the removal of border barriers to trade and includes agreements on rules to allow market creation; all of which confront domestic actors with greater uncertainty. Positive policies also require the harmonization and coordination of norms and standards, or the recognition of each other's regulatory processes and standards.

In all, these negotiation agendas show variation in the extent to which they fall within the universe of national regulations and reach into domestic governance arrangements. Thus, I expect to find variation in the ways and extent to which they affect the incentives of domestic state and non-state actors. As trade agendas broaden and reach deeper into domestic governance institutions, interests and ideas/information become part of the process of definition of preferences and collective action strategies of societal actors, while governments require procedural (input) legitimacy and also costly technical and informational resources. In sum, based on these differences, South-South, North-South and multilateral negotiations are expected to give rise to particular patterns of trade politics in the Southern Cone.

To assess such variation I rely on a 'policy creates politics' (Lowi 1964, 1972) argument, thus positing that specific characteristics of the trade agenda under negotiation will lead to particular patterns of trade politics. More specifically, I contend that state-society relations—as the property that arises from the institutional architecture provided by the state and the logic guiding societal actors' strategies—depend on the degree to which the agenda under negotiation moves from negative to positive integration. In other words, variation in the breadth and depth of the agenda, its distributional effects and the uncertainty of political outcomes have important consequences for the ways in which state and non-state actors define their preferences and collective action strategies. Thus, different trade negotiations are expected to elicit particular political dynamics given their varying impact on the incentive structure and mobilization patterns of governments and social actors.

From a domestic perspective, the focus is on Argentina and Chile, two upper-middle economy countries showing important similarities and at least some rather similar background conditions stemming from their political systems, dominant models of development and modes of economic organization as part of the Southern Cone model (Phillips 2004). Both countries experienced a transition towards political liberalization and democratization during the 1980s and implemented extensive market reforms to counteract the inflationary pressures and increasing deficits in their balance of payments after the exhaustion of the ISI model. However, the pace and intensity of trade reforms followed different paths.

Instability and vicissitudes permeated trade policies in Argentina. After the first, ill-coordinated attempt at unilateral trade liberalization made under military rule in the mid-1970s, democratic governments set the basis for unilateral trade liberalization while at the same time pursuing regional and multilateral

*Table 2.2* Selected trade agreements in Argentina and Chile

| | *Argentina* | *Chile* |
|---|---|---|
| *South-South* | MERCOSUR—Chile | Chile—Mexico |
| | MERCOSUR—Mexico | Chile—MERCOSUR |
| | MERCOSUR—India | Chile—China |
| *North-South* | FTAA | FTAA |
| | MERCOSUR—EU | Chile—EU |
| *Multilateral* | WTO and the Doha Round | WTO and the Doha Round |

Source: *Author-created based on the Organization of American States' Foreign Trade Information System, www.sice.oas.org/agreements_e.asp, last accessed 15 December 2015*

initiatives. By contrast, Chile stands out for its long-standing economic liberalization strategy. In 1985, the military dictatorship implemented a flat and low import tariff rate and extensive export promotion schemes. Nevertheless, from the 1990s, both countries were actively involved in South-South, North-South and multilateral trade negotiations. In all, these countries share similar historical legacies and faced a similar policy stimulus, and provide hence a similar context. This similitude makes possible the cross-national comparative assessment.

Through the systematic comparison of negotiations and countries (see Table 2.2), the analysis sheds light on the ways in which preferences and strategies are defined and expressed across Argentina and Chile in the context of South-South, North-South and multilateral trade negotiations.[3] To what extent are the domestic patterns of state-society relations promoted after the launch of different trade agendas explained by already institutionalized and established arrangements at the national level? Alternatively, do domestic actors promote new institutional arrangements and links to meet adequately the challenges triggered by trade negotiations, leading in turn to similar trade politics patterns across countries despite particular national traditions? In all, given that globalization and domestic governance are interdependent, these transformations must be understood as the result of the complex interaction between continuing national specificities and the reconfiguring influences of globalization and regionalization. The adaptation of national political economies to these new structural contexts is mainly conditioned by their own historical, institutional and social configurations, and by politics.

## Notes

1 The issue of legitimacy has long preoccupied scholars, and both competing and complementary definitions have been provided to assess the legitimacy of processes, starting with Weber's three distinct sources of legitimacy. More recently, Scharpf (1999a) has distinguished between two forms of democratic legitimacy: one focused on the policy process and the other on policy outcomes. Given that the focus of analysis of this book is the process through which state and non-state actors define their preferences and strategies and their mutual relations, I have adapted Scharpf's distinction for the study of trade politics in Latin America in

order to assess the legitimacy of the process by which decisions are made. Trade politics is thus legitimate when citizens participate directly in the decision-making process; policy-makers are accountable to them, and the decision-making procedure is transparent.

2 Building networks and coalitions of allies is one of the four major activities that civil society performs. The other three include agenda setting by identifying a problem and producing information, developing solutions by either creating norms or making policy recommendations, and implementing solutions through tactics of persuasion and pressure to transform practices and/or promote compliance with norms (Price 2003).

3 See Appendix 2 for the list of trade agreements signed by Argentina and Chile between 1990 and 2005.

## References

Abdelal, R., M. Blyth and C. Parsons, Eds. (2010). *Constructing the International Economy*. Ithaca, NY, Cornell University Press.

Bayne, N. and S. Woolcock, Eds. (2003). *The New Economic Diplomacy: Decision-Making and Negotiation in International Economic Relations*. Aldershot, Ashgate.

BID (2002). *Más allá de las fronteras: el nuevo regionalismo en América Latina*. Washington, DC, BID.

Blyth, M. (2002). *Great Transformations: Economic Ideas and Institutional Change in the Twentieth Century*. Cambridge, Cambridge University Press.

Blyth, M. (2010). Ideas, Uncertainty and Evolution, in R. Cox and D. Béland (Ed.) *Ideas and Politics in Social Science Research*. Oxford, Oxford University Press: 83–101.

Bouzas, R., Ed. (2006). Domestic Determinants of National Trade Strategies: A Comparative Analysis of MERCOSUR Countries, Mexico and Chile. Paris, MERCOSUR Chair -Science Po.

Broscheid, A. and D. Coen (2003). Insider and Outsider Lobbying of the European Commission: An Informational Model of Forum Politics, *European Union Politics* 4(2): 165–189.

Bukovansky, M. (2010). Institutionalized Hypocrisy and the Politics of Agricultural Trade, in R. Abdelal, M. Blyth and C. Parsons (Ed.) *Constructing the International Economy*. Ithaca, NY, Cornell University Press: 68–89.

Coen, D. (1998). The European Business Interest and the Nation State: Large-Firm Lobbying in the European Union and Member States, *Journal of Public Policy* 18: 75–100.

Coen, D. (2005). Business-Regulatory Relations: Learning to Play Regulatory Games in European Utility Markets, *Governance: An International Journal of Policy, Administration and Institutions* 18: 375–398.

Dent, C. M. (2006). The New Economic Bilateralism in Southeast Asia: Region-Convergent or Region-Divergent? *International Relations of the Asia Pacific* 6(1): 81–111.

Destler, I. M. and J. S. Odell (1987). *Anti-Protection: Changing Forces in United States Trade Politics*. Washington, DC, Institute for International Economics.

Frieden, J. (1991). *Debt, Development and Democracy: Modern Political Economy and Latin America, 1965–1985*. Princeton, NJ, Princeton University Press.

Frieden, J. A. and R. Rogowski (1996). The Impact of the International Economy on National Policies: An Analytical Overview, in R. O. Keohane and H. V. Milner

(Ed.) *Internationalization and Domestic Politics*. Cambridge, Cambridge University Press: 25–47.

Friedman, E. J. and K. Hochstetler (2002). Assessing the Third Transition in Latin American Democratization: Representational Regimes and Civil Society in Argentina and Brazil, *Comparative Politics* 35(1): 21–42.

Goldstein, J. (1993). *Ideas, Interests, and American Trade Policy*. Ithaca & London, Cornell University Press.

Goldstein, J. and R. O. Keohane (1993). Ideas and Foreign Policy: An Analytical Framework, in K. Goldstein and R. O. Keohane (Ed.) *Ideas and Foreign Policy: Beliefs, Institutions, and Political Change*. Ithaca & London, Cornell University Press: 3–30.

Gourevitch, P. A. (1986). *Politics in Hard Times: Comparative Responses to International Economic Crises*. Ithaca & London, Cornell University Press.

Haggard, S. (1988). The Institutional Foundations of Hegemony: Explaining the Reciprocal Trade Agreements Act of 1934, *International Organization* 42(1): 91–119.

Hall, P. A. (2005). Preference Formation as a Political Process: The Case of the Monetary Union in Europe, in I. Katsznelson and B. R. Weingast (Ed.) *Preferences and Situations: Points of Intersection between Historical and Rational Choice Institutionalism*. New York, Russell Sage Foundation: 129–160.

Helmke, G. and S. Levitsky (2006). Introduction, in G. Helmke and S. Levistky (Ed.) *Informal Institutions and Democracy: Lessons from Latin America*. Baltimore, The Johns Hopkins University Press: 1–30.

Henning, C. H. C. A. (2004). Modelling the Political Influence of Interest Groups: Theory and Empirical Evidence from European Agricultural Policy, in A. Warntjen and A. Wonka (Ed.) *Governance in Europe: The Role of Interest Groups*. Baden-Baden, Nomos: 94–112.

Hirst, P. (2000). Democracy and Governance, in J. Pierre (Ed.) *Debating Governance: Authenticity, Steering, and Democracy*. Oxford, Oxford University Press: 13–35.

Horn, H., P. C. Mavroidis and A. Sapir (2010). Beyond the WTO: An Anatomy of the EU and US Preferential Trade Agreement, *The World Economy* 33(11): 1565–1588.

Ikenberry, G. J., D. A. Lake and M. Mastanduno (1988). Introduction: Approaches to Explaining Foreign Economic Policy, in G. J. Ikenberry, D. A. Lake and M. Mastanduno (Ed.) *The State and American Foreign Economic Policy*. Ithaca, NY, Cornell University Press: 1–14.

Jayasuriya, K. (2004). The New Regulatory State and Relational Capacity, *Policy & Politics* 32(4): 487–501.

Jordana, J. and C. Ramió (2002). *Diseños institucionales y gestión de la política comercial en América Latina*. Buenos Aires, Inter-American Development Bank—Instituto para la Integración de América Latina y el Caribe.

Jordana, J. and C. Ramió (2003). Trade Policy Institutions: A Comparative Analysis, in R. Delvin and A. Estevadeordal (Ed.) *Regional Integration and Trade in the Development Agenda*. Washington, DC, Inter-American Development Bank-Johns Hopkins University Press: 179–201.

Keck, M. E. and K. Sikkink (1998). *Activists Beyond Borders: Advocacy Networks in International Politics*. Ithaca & London, Cornell University Press.

Keohane, R. O. and H. V. Milner, Eds. (1996). *Internationalization and Domestic Politics: Cambridge Studies in Comparative Politics*. Cambridge, Cambridge University Press.

Kitschelt, H. P. (1986). Political Opportunity Structures and Political Protest: Anti-Nuclear Movements in Four Democracies, *British Journal of Political Science* 16(1): 57–85.

Kooiman, J., Ed. (1993). *Modern Governance: New Government-Society Interactions*. London, Sage.
Korseniewicz, R. P. and W. C. Smith (2001). "Protest and Collaboration: Transnational Civil Society Networks and the Politics of Summitry and Free Trade in the Americas." The North-South Agenda Papers 51. Miami, The Dante B. Fascell North-South Center, University of Miami.
Krasner, S. D., Ed. (1983). *International Regimes*. Ithaca, NY, Cornell University Press.
Lohmann, S. (1998). An Information Rationale for the Power of Special Interests, *American Political Science Review* 92(4): 809–827.
Lowi, T. J. (1964). American Business, Public Policy, Case Studies and Political Theory, *World Politics* 16(4): 667–715.
Lowi, T. J. (1972). Four Systems of Policy, Politics, and Choice, *Public Administration Review* 32(4): 298–310.
Magee, S. P., W. A. Brock and L. Young (1989). *Black Hole Tariffs and Endogenous Policy Theory: Political Economy in General Equilibrium*. Cambridge, Cambridge University Press.
Majone, G. (1999). The Regulatory State and its Legitimacy Problems, *West European Politics* 22: 1–24.
Majone, G. (2001). Non-Majoritarian Institutions and the Limits of Democratic Governance: A Political Transaction-Cost Approach, *Journal of Institutional and Theoretical Economics* 15: 57–78.
Mansfield, E. D. and M. L. Busch (1995). The Political Economy of Nontariff Barriers: A Cross-National Analysis, *International Organization* 49(4): 723–749.
Mattli, W. and N. Woods (2009a). In Whose Benefit? Explaining Regulatory Change in Global Politics, in W. Mattli and N. Woods (Ed.) *The Politics of Global Regulation*. Princeton, NJ, Princeton University Press: 1–43.
Mattli, W. and N. Woods, Eds. (2009b). *The Politics of Global Regulation*. Princeton, NJ, Princeton University Press.
McKeown, T. J. (1984). Firms and Tariff Regime Change: Explaining the Demand for Protection, *World Politics* 36(2): 215–233.
Milner, H. V. (1988). *Resisting Protectionism: Global Industries and the Politics of International Trade*. Princeton, NJ, Princeton University Press.
North, D. and B. Weingast (1989). Constitutions and Commitment: The Evolution of Institutions Governing Public Choice in Seventeenth-Century England, *Journal of Economic History* 69: 803.
Olson, M. (1971). *The Logic of Collective Action: Public Goods and the Theory of Groups*. Cambridge, MA, Harvard University Press.
Ostry, S. (2002). Preface, in IADB, and Munck Centre for International Studies (Ed.) *The Trade Policy-Making Process: Level One of the Two-Level Game: Country Studies in the Western Hemisphere*. Buenos Aires, Banco Interamericano de Desarrollo—Instituto para la Integración de América Latina y el Caribe. Occasional Paper 13: i–iv.
Phillips, N. (2004). *The Southern Cone Model: The Political Economy Development of Regional Capitalist Development in Latin America*. London, Routledge.
Phillips, N. (2007). The Limits of 'Securitization': Power Politics and the Process in US Foreign Economic Policy, *Government and Opposition* 42(2): 158–189.
Pierre, J. (2000). Introduction: Understanding Governance, in J. Pierre (Ed.) *Debating Governance: Authenticity, Steering, and Democracy*. Oxford, Oxford University Press: 1–10.

Pierre, J. and B. G. Peters, Eds. (2000). *Governance, Politics, and the State: Political Analysis*. London, Macmillan Press Limited.

Polanyi, K. (1957, 2001). *The Great Transformation*. Boston, MA, Beacon Press.

Price, R. M. (2003). Review Article: Transnational Civil Society and Advocacy in World Politics, *World Politics* 55(4): 579–606.

Rhodes, R. A. W. (1997). *Understanding Governance: Policy Networks, Governance, Reflexivity, and Accountability*. Buckingham, Open University Press.

Rhodes, R. A. W. (2007). Understanding Governance: Ten Years On, *Organization Studies* 28(8): 1243–1264.

Robin, C. (2008). *A Domestic Policy-Making Approach to World Market Integration Strategies in Developing Nations: Chile, Argentina, Peru, and Bolivia in Comparison*. Dissertation Doctor of Philosophy, University of Zurich.

Robinson, W. I. (2001). Transnational Processes, Development Studies, and Changing Social Hierarchies in the World System: A Central American Case Study, *Third World Quarterly* 22(4): 529–563.

Rodrik, D. (1994). The Rush to Free Trade in the Developing World: Why So Late? Why Now? Will It Last? in S. Haggard and S. B. Webb (Ed.) *Voting for Reform: Democracy, Political Liberalization, and Economic Adjustment*. New York, Oxford University Press: 61–88.

Rodrik, D. (1995). Political Economy of Trade Policy, in G. M. Grossman and K. Rogoff (Ed.) *Handbook of International Economics*. Amsterdam, Elsevier Science 3: 1457–1494.

Roffe, P. and M. Santa Cruz (2006). *Los derechos de propiedad intelectual en los acuerdos de libre comercio celebrados por países de América Latina con países desarollados: Comercio Internacional*. Serie Comercio Internacional, N° 70, Santiago de Chile, ECLAC.

Rogowski, R. (1989). *Commerce and Coalitions: How Trade Affects Domestic Political Alignments*. Princeton, NJ, Princeton University Press.

Schamis, H. E. (1999). Distributional Coalitions and the Politics of Economic Reform in Latin America, *World Politics* 51(2): 236–268.

Scharpf, F. W. (1997). *Games Real Actors Play: Actor-Centered Institutionalism in Policy Research*. Boulder, Westview.

Scharpf, F. W. (1999a). *Governing in Europe: Effective and Democratic?* Oxford, Oxford University Press.

Scharpf, F. W. (1999b). Negative and Positive Integration in the Political Economy of European Welfare States, in G. Marks, M. Schulz, P. C. Schmitter and W. Streeck (Ed.) *Governance in the European Union*. London, Sage: 15–39.

Schneider, B. R. (2004a). *Business Politics and the State in Twentieth-Century Latin America*. Cambridge, Cambridge University Press.

Schneider, B. R. (2004b). Organizing Interests and Coalitions in the Politics of Market Reform in Latin America, *World Politics* 56(3): 456–479.

Swedberg, R. (2003). *Principles of Economic Sociology*. Princeton, NJ, Princeton University Press.

Swedberg, R. (2005). *Interest*. Berkshire, Open University Press.

Ventura-Dias, V. (2004). Introduction: Juggling with WTO Rules in Latin America, in M. F. Lengyel and V. Ventura-Dias (Ed.) *Trade Policy Reforms in Latin America: Multilateral Rules and Domestic Institutions*. Basingstoke & New York, Palgrave Macmillan: 1–23.

Weber, M. ([1915] 1946). The Social Psychology of the World Religions, in H. Gerth and C. Mills Wright (Ed.) *From Max Weber*. New York, Oxford University Press: 267–301.

Woll, C. (2008). *Firm Interests: How Governments Shape Business Lobbying on Global Trade*. Ithaca & London, Cornell University Press.

Woll, C. (2010). Firm Interests in Uncertain Times: Business Lobbying in Multilateral Service Liberalization, in R. Abdelal, M. Blyth and C. Parsons (Ed.) *Constructing the International Economy*. Ithaca, NY, Cornell University Press: 137–154.

Woll, C. and A. Artigas (2007). When Trade Liberalization Turns into Regulatory Reform: The Impact on Business-Government Relations in International Trade Politics, *Regulation and Governance* 1(2): 121–138.

## Part II

# Latin America in a Complex Web of Trade Negotiations

# 3 Trade Politics in Latin America

## Institutional Legacies and Political Dynamics

Trade politics implies a complex and dense phenomenon where the interaction and coordination between state and non-state actors, the distribution of responsibilities between them, and the limits between state and society are fluid and changing. The nature of trade politics depends heavily on the historical and institutional legacies of domestic politics. A brief journey through the historical political economy of Argentina and Chile starting with the early years of ISI provides insight into the main institutional and political contours of state-society relations and their respective international trade paths.

Although the political systems and the nature of the state-society relations in the two countries were distinct, there remain some very broad similarities. Highly interventionist states played a leading role in the industrialization process through heavy industrial protection and by involving large state enterprises in both. Furthermore, the state remained the pivotal actor for collective action and was the focal point for all demands and pressures. In 1975, Chile underwent a sea change in the dominant development model, and Argentina, also under military rule, followed suit in 1976, but this program was not very radical. Such a plan was implemented only in the 1990s. In both countries, this entailed the dramatic reversal of the statism and the economic and social policies that had prevailed for decades; all of which had an impact on the pattern of state-society relations.

### Argentina: Fragmentation and Politicization of State-Society Relations

Throughout most of the twentieth century, a succession of political and economic swings of the 'democracy-authoritarianism pendulum' and the high volatility of public policies, most prominently in the economic realm, shaped Argentina's political economy. In all, these crises resulted from the traditional clash between export agriculture and industry, but also from class conflicts cutting across labour and capital. Because the state was the 'natural' mediator, these cleavages were exacerbated and reinforced depending on the state's inclinations.

## *Peronism, Industrialization and the Politicization of State-Society Relations (1946–1955)*

The collapse of international trade and finance after the Great Depression triggered in Argentina—as in Chile and other countries in Latin America—a process of state-led industrialization to promote import substitution. The ISI model thus started rather spontaneously. Consequently, as graphically described by Love: 'Industrialization in Latin America was a fact before it was policy, and policy before it was theory' (1994:365).

At a time of strong political unrest and the instauration of a military coup after 14 years of democracy, these initial steps towards ISI did not entail a rupture with the hegemonic agro-export model imposed by the rural elite after 1860. State incentives remained concentrated on already established nondurable goods industries (Bulmer-Thomas 2003) while also supporting beef and wheat production (Smith 1983). Hence, the landowning elite maintained its economic and political influence, and remained heavily represented among political powers and decision makers (McGuire 1997).

Nevertheless, this timid industrialization accelerated the emergence of a domestic industry and the development of an urban working class, all of which affected the distribution of political power and provided the basis for a wide populist coalition among relatively new sectors (O'Donnell 1973b). Peronism (1946–1955) reinforced this. Peronist industrial policy marked a turning point. First, this policy, mainly financed through the Industrial Bank created in 1944, encouraged a more diversified economy, less focused on external markets as the driving economic force, and aimed at a better redistribution of wealth and social stability. Second, the Argentine Institute for Trade Promotion (IAPI), established in 1946, gave the state the monopoly over the export of agricultural products. The resulting windfall was to subsidize national industries, public employment and the incipient welfare state. Resources were thus transferred from agricultural exporters to industrialists and urban workers.

The intensification of industrialization triggered a more complex matrix of state-society relations. It resulted in the creation of an important union movement and the diversification of business interests, all of which challenged the monopolistic power of representation that traditional associations had enjoyed until then.

By the time Peronism came on the scene, business associations had a long and active tradition, with the Argentine Rural Society (SRA) and the Argentine Industrial Union (UIA) being the major political representatives of the landowning and industrial elites respectively. Created in 1866, the SRA brought together the most important export producers of the Pampas and constituted a particularly homogeneous and solid organization. Until 1946, it exercised a remarkable lobbying power and enjoyed close relations with most governments.[1] Moreover, it managed to maintain both its hegemonic role and its close relations with the state, despite the increasing competition from new organizations representing the more heterogeneous interests.[2] Additionally, the SRA was closely related to the UIA, which, in fact, was partly a result of the diversification of agricultural business into industrial endeavours—i.e. food processing—to complement rural production. Hence, their performance and evolution resembled that of a club rather than a business organization, leading to the formation and consolidation of an elitist management based on economic influence and socio-political relations, irrespective of their sectoral representativeness (Schvarzer 1996).

Under Peronism, relations with the state were quarrelsome and unstable. Rural interests were neglected and even discriminated against, as they were forced to subsidize industrialization and large-scale industries tied to them (Waisman 1987). As their economic and political positions deteriorated, they engaged in constant struggles with the state against interventionist policies. On the other hand, the state provided significant economic incentives for the organization of small and medium industrial associations to counterbalance the traditional power of an increasingly opposed UIA. Even if these initiatives failed to mature into fully-fledged institutions, the industrial sector's lack of a dominant group reinforced permanent intra-industrial conflict (Acuña 1998).

As confrontation rose, the state sought the alternative backing of business and labour representatives and promoted specific mechanisms according to its perceived vulnerabilities. Thus the General Economic Confederation (CGE), created in 1952 with the direct support of the government, supplanted the UIA, which was amended and finally dissolved in 1953. The CGE, which encompassed provincial, small and new business, gathered industry support for an economic policy that was already undergoing increasing difficulties as trade deficits and inflation rose. The government also attempted to reduce its dependence on the unions as labour productivity declined while its demands increased (Brennan 1998:96). However, given the highly centralized nature of the policymaking process, these mechanisms and channels lacked proper institutions.

Institutionalization came at a later stage through the creation of the Consultative Economic Commission. It had a leading role on various committees, including foreign trade, labour relations, prices and housing (Teichman 1981:150). With the exception of this participatory mechanism, which was biased towards amicable business institutions,[3] informality in the relation between state and non-state actors prevailed during these years. State actors had privileged links with associations representing specific sectors, of which the metalworking industry was the most effective. When not ignoring opposing interests, the government pursued a direct, one-to-one dialogue with business representatives, who enjoyed personal influence with Perón and who demanded mainly promotional incentives and tariff protection (López 2006).

The absence of adequate mechanisms of dialogue and the direct interference of the government in business organizations contributed to the increasing division of business interests along political, rather than economic, lines. Additionally, the expansion of political participation and the opening to labour unions and workers did not include a strategy of stable institutional inclusion in the decision-making process. The General Confederation of Labour (CGT) led union support for Peronism and received a wide range of material, organizational and symbolic benefits. Under Peronism, no single political grouping was able to achieve sustained access to political power and decision-making processes (O'Donnell 1988:43). The growing politicization of the relationship between state and business actors and the difficulties of the institutional system in channelling these heterogeneous and conflicting societal demands escalated institutional overload to unprecedented levels. Partly, as a result, Perón was overthrown by a coup d'état in 1955, which in turn, ushered in a period of persistent institutional stability.

### *The 'Argentine Interregnum': Governance and Institutional Instability (1955–1983)*

The 1950s experienced a long cycle characterized by oscillation between limited democracy (because of the proscription of Peronism) and military coups. Democracy fell victim to the 'impossible game' (O'Donnell 1973a). On the economic side, the ISI model experienced stop-and-go cycles because of recurring trade imbalances.

Despite the marked institutional and political instability, the core aspects of economic policy were quite stable. Between 1955 and 1973, all governments—whether military or democratic—supported the ISI model. Manufacturing reached its peak in the 1960s because of the moderate developmental program implemented by Arturo Frondizi (1958–1962): it made up 28.18 per cent of GDP (Gross Domestic Product), whereas manufactured exports rose from almost zero in the 1950s to a quarter of all exports in the early 1970s (Kosacoff 2000:38–42). For the first time, heavy industry was at the core of the economy, while the country opened to regional and international economic flows. Argentina negotiated entry into the International Monetary Fund (IMF) and the World Bank (WB), and actively promoted the creation of the Latin American Free Trade Association (LAFTA), together with Brazil, Chile and Uruguay. Still, these developments were only short-lived because the government lacked political support, and the policies, which mainly stemmed from political technocrats, were not broad enough to gain new support (Manzetti 1994). Thereafter, industrial activity remained the motor of economic growth, employment creation and capital accumulation. However, as the political system swung from side to side, economic policy rocked between expansionary populism and orthodox stabilization, with occasional attempts at compromise through heterodoxy in response to shifting political coalitions (Teichman 2001). Military governments that could more easily reverse inclusive social policy mostly undertook corrections and adjustments to the model (Silva 2007). Grave and increasing political divergences made it almost impossible to design and implement public policies with long-term horizons. Furthermore, instability prevented the formation of strong and institutionalized mechanisms for developing relations between state and societal actors. Politicization was hence the norm for most of both business and labour actors.

Labour organizations more generally advocated distributional policies and an alliance between the national bourgeoisie and the working class. In so doing, they hindered the complete implementation and consolidation of stabilization programs in the late 1950s and early 1960s, but failed to reverse the important transformations the national economy had undergone since 1959, namely, the development of more capital intensive industrial sectors and more penetration by FDI (Cavarozzi 2009:25–29).

The business sector remained greatly divided over the dyad protectionism-liberalism and the role of state and business actors in the economy. The CGE was outlawed (1955–1958), whilst the UIA became an association of small, middle-sized and domestic market-oriented industrialists. Major industries withdrew from the latter and, in alliance with the (anti-Peronist) Coordinating Association for Free Businessmen's Institutions (ACIEL, 1958–1973), formed the Argentine Entrepreneurial Council (CEA) in 1967. The CEA brought together the big landed and commercial industrial interests under the SRA, UIA and the CAC, together with the large conglomerates, or '*grupos económicos*' in the Argentine political vernacular. These emerged from dynamic medium-sized companies established in the 1950s, which were expanded and diversified through state incentives and export promotion subsidies in the late 1960s (Bisang and Kosacoff 1995).[4]

Differences prevailed among the business community. Whereas the CGE called for strong involvement of the state in the economy, the participation of labour in the elaboration of socioeconomic policy and a reduced presence of multinational capital in strategic areas, ACIEL demanded only a minor role for the state and called for the investment of international capital. The CGE and ACIEL were thus trapped in a web of competing political and social alliances, whilst the resolution of their conflicts depended on the settlement of political struggles at the national level. Already by the late 1960s, industrialists recognized that these political differences reduced their influence on the decision-making process (Freels 1970). Their failure to intervene effectively in politics was also due to continuing institutional and political instability, which hindered the establishment and consolidation of access mechanisms. In turn, this prevented business associations from developing institutional strength (Schneider 2004). On the contrary, the economic and political power of conglomerates under the CEA increased as their oligopolistic control of key markets grew (Manzetti 1994).This in turn had a positive impact on their technical expertise, and in time, they came to play a major political role in economic decision making (Viguera 2000).

By then, the shortfalls of ISI were quite evident. Argentina's macroeconomic performance worsened severely, and trade deficits increased. Political polarization reached its height under the third Peronist administration (1973–1976). As the economy worsened, inflation rocketed, and the rise in oil prices negatively affected the balance of payments. The Social Pact signed in 1973 with both the CGT and the CGE lost ground. Disputes over economic policy grew in intensity. While large business groups organized lockouts, trade unions put growing pressure on the government to establish new wage agreements, and urban guerrilla activity escalated, all of which contributed to the growing climate of economic, political and social instability. The stage was set for a new military coup d'état.

Aiming for a radical restructuring of the economy and society, the military government embarked on a Process of National Reorganization (1976–1983). This included market reform through an unconventional and often contradictory mix of price and exchange controls, selective tariff reductions, privatization and state expansion. Tariff rates dropped from an average 55 per cent in 1976 to 29 per cent in 1978, and most of the existing quantitative restrictions on imports were removed (Teichman 2001). Yet, the reform was far from homogeneous. Some activities attracted new subsidies and incentives, but other core branches, under military control and enjoying strong protection, were exempted. One of the most important structural effects of these discretionary measures was the expansion and consolidation of domestically-funded economic groups, which gathered around a mother company—enjoying the protection—and became active in several activities, including industry, financing, agriculture, trade and foreign investment (Schvarzer 1986). Underlying this economic restructuring program, we find the interests of large conglomerates under the CEA, which strongly supported the military regime and demanded orthodox economic policies. Self-identified as the Captains of Industry, this new distributional coalition benefitted from state contracts. In contrast, domestic-oriented industrial interests were disregarded: the CGE was dissolved, and the UIA remained under military control during the liberalization process.

Furthermore, the military dictatorship's economic plan intended to 'discipline' the domestic-market-oriented coalition, whose demands had contributed to the distortion of the country's economy (Canitrot 1980). Deindustrialization was thus crucial as an effort to weaken the labour movement. While this led to the *extranjerización* (rapid transference to foreign hands) of the economy, deindustrialization decimated the industrial workforce: employment in this sector declined by 36 per cent between 1975 and 1981, and by more than a third between 1970 and 1990 (Smith 1989). The military government's policy of repression and violation of human rights further weakened the labour movement. This could not prevent cooperative labour leaders being granted access to decision makers and thus lobbying directly against particular aspects of the market reform process.[5]

However, this poorly structured program proved unsustainable and led to a severe financial and balance of payments crisis in 1980–1981. A period of 'chaotic adjustment' followed, including strong devaluations, price controls, intense restrictions on lending and the rescue of the extremely indebted private sector. The government's growing lack of control over the economy and its increasing political weakness (Damill and Frenkel 1996:59), combined with the defeat in the 1982 war against Great Britain, contributed to the general sense that the military was unfit to rule, thus precipitating democratic transition.

### *Democracy, Market Reform and the Rebuilding of State-Society Relations (1983–1999)*

The first democratic government under Raúl Alfonsín (1983–1989) coincided with a deep economic crisis. To begin with, the new administration resisted strict austerity and market liberalizing measures and tried to satisfy the demands of all relevant societal groups through an expansionary program. In 1985, the rapid deterioration of the economy led to a heterodox reform program to control inflation without economic contraction. After some initial success, the Austral Plan finally collapsed under the pressure of affected groups. Two years later, the country was already experiencing rising inflation and a surge in the fiscal deficit, whilst the Radical administration faced defeat in midterm elections.

The government then launched an important trade liberalization reform, which led to a significant reduction in nominal protection—the average import tax was reduced from 45 per cent in 1987 to 29 per cent at the end of 1988—and tariff positions subject to quantitative restrictions. Nevertheless, this reform could not reverse industrial decline and hyperinflation. Moreover, the government faced serious difficulties in institutionalizing economic governance effectively to resolve the distributional conflicts among unions, industrialists and agro-exporters. It thus attempted a consensual style of policymaking with the Social and Economic Conference (CES), which brought together labour, industrialists and the state to promote tripartite dialogue and replace the traditional zero-sum game. Even if economic authorities acquiesced in the creation of this new mechanism, which granted privileged representation to organized labour and industrialists, in practice they denied any real input into decision making (Smith 1990). Furthermore, the Radical administration faced strong opposition. On the one hand, the Peronist-led CGT rejected the economic plan and led 13 general strikes against the government. On the other, the private sector—mainly large economic groups and transnational companies—did not show immediate support for the reform program, whereas the agricultural, banking, commercial and construction sectors were not part of the CES (Acuña 1995). The government then resorted to bypassing business associations and having direct contact with the Captains of Industry; an initiative business men welcomed as it enabled quick coordination (Ostiguy 1990). They therefore discarded associations like the UIA, whose representativeness and democratic character was inversely proportional to their responsiveness. This initiative was also short-lived and, by the end of 1987, just after defeat in the legislative elections, the axis between the government and the Captains of Industry vanished.

New stabilization plans and new efforts at dialogue were then promoted, now with traditional actors under the UIA and the CAC. Nevertheless, these initiatives met mounting opposition from both labour unions and business actors. In 1984, opposition to wage and price controls led to an unprecedented alliance between the CGT and 10 business associations under the 'Group of 11'.

In all, attempts at promoting consensual economic governance failed to produce a stable institutional framework. Most of the overtures were short-lived and often ended up deepening sectoral divisions among associations rather than facilitating more encompassing collective action (Schneider 2004). By the end of 1988, the government faced a complex situation characterized by hyperinflation and economic collapse but also by political instability and increasing opposition. Early presidential elections were called, and Peronism came back to power.

Despite being elected on a populist Peronist platform based on large wage increases (*salariazo*), social justice and 'the productive revolution', Carlos Menem (1989–1999) undertook a programme of 'neoliberalism by surprise' (Stokes 2001). This rapid and thorough market reform programme included the privatization of the most important and politically sensitive state-owned companies and trade liberalization. The average tariff was reduced from 45 per cent in 1987 to about 13 per cent in 1994 (Viguera 2000). State employment was slashed, and public expenditures in education, housing and health underwent drastic cutbacks. By 1994, the reform process was almost complete.

The centrepiece of the reform program was the Convertibility Plan introduced in 1991, following an idea of the then minister of economy, Domingo Cavallo. For over a decade, the plan pegged the Argentine peso to the United States dollar at parity and required the Central Bank to back two-thirds of the monetary base with international reserves to bring down inflation and inflationary expectations. Combined with the full liberalization of capital flows and the structural adjustment program, among other policy reforms, the Convertibility Plan signalled the beginning of a new era in the political economy of Argentine society (Teubal 2004). State and society relations remained distant: Menemism—as implied by neoliberalism—relied on an increasing separation between them.

An anti-elite character marked the policy change (Sidicaro 1995). Coming from the provinces of the 'Interior', the president and his closest collaborators were not accepted by traditional elite groups. Being detached from the rules of the game, they could thus act much more autonomously and flexibly. However, large economic interests were intimately involved in the reform process and benefitted enormously. In the first place, Menem directly entrusted the handling of the economy to the managers of the Bunge & Born conglomerate, an active member of the Captains of Industry who further consolidated their economic leadership and political power during the decade. Second, individual business people from the largest companies were confidants of the president and prominent government officials. Thus, they attempted to influence decisions from the inside rather than criticizing from the outside (Viguera 2000).

Opportunities for similar dialogues with business associations were not available. Even if the Production, Investment and Growth Council had been set up as an official consultative mechanism bringing together business, labour and government, it worked merely as a forum for communicating already decided policies. Both business and government considered this mechanism as 'window dressing' (Teichman 2001:123).

Small and medium industrialists suffered this exclusion most and found it hard to bring up one of its major concerns: the negative impact of the fixed exchange rate on export competitiveness. The UIA, together with the SRA, celebrated free-market policies, the privatization of state enterprises, the attempts to fracture organized labour power and the reduction of state bureaucracy. Nevertheless, the interests of the most powerful groups within this organization, namely industrialists producing for the domestic market, were threatened. Liberalization was only positive for some export-oriented conglomerates and therefore strongly resisted by those economic sectors that had developed under protection and government contracts, and who were now left to face foreign competition on their own. To some extent, the sudden improvement of the economy after the implementation of the Convertibility Plan moderated the existing differences. In September 1991 the minister of economy, the CGE, UIA and other smaller industrialists associations signed a 'Productivity Pact'. Industrial associations thereby committed themselves to employment creation, to investment and to restraining price increases, whereas the government made different concessions, including lowering energy costs, special credit lines for small- and medium-sized enterprises (SMEs), a new foreign trade law and labour laws providing some flexibility (Manzetti 1994:101).

Market reform not only strengthened the process of *extranjerización* of the economic and business structure, but also entailed high costs for labour unions that had developed their political power under the wing of the ISI model. Whilst privatization and deregulation required labour restructuring and large layoffs, trade liberalization entailed more competition and increased differences among workers and sectors. In fact, the government's policy shift from populism to neoliberalism divided the CGT into three competing factions, which soon reunited under the most cooperative union leaders as the government offered selective positive incentives, namely guaranteed monopolies of representation and executive appointments. As the major trade union moved towards cooperation, it was rewarded with further concessions, including changes in the reform of pensions, social security, subsidies for health funds and the maintenance of legislation on collective bargaining and labour organization (Murillo 2001). Yet, labour unions were not invited to discuss trade liberalization.

During these years when business associations seemed to coalesce around a gradual, compensatory export model, they continued to work to slow liberalization and asked for exceptions and limitations. This was even the case with the more ideologically committed economic liberals in the business community, who also begged for protection as soon as imports threatened their profitability. However, as long as many business associations failed to build consensus, individual businessmen pursued their own interests and sought special consideration. Individual requests for exemption followed new policy measures. Business strategies were adaptive or reactive to government decisions, these being concentrated on trade policy implementation rather than on its formulation (Viguera 2000).

During the market reform process, particularly with regard to trade liberalization, business actors enjoyed only ad hoc access as no formal institutional mechanism was established. This prevented them from developing strong collective action and favoured discretion and private lobbying. More importantly, this relational pattern hindered the development of virtuous cycles involving important flows of information between state and business actors. The absence of such learning processes would become especially evident during the various trade negotiations launched in the following years.

### *Changing State-Society Relations: Bringing the State Back In? (1999–2005)*

In 1999, a centre-to-left coalition, the *Alianza*, took office with the promise of maintaining the economic model while combating corruption and addressing the social costs of neoliberalism. Once in office, they failed to fulfil either commitment. On the one hand, the government was too weak to resist external and domestic pressures to maintain the neoliberal economic agenda in general and the fixed exchange rate in particular. On the other, a severe institutional crisis arose in October 2000, resulting in the resignation of the vice-president and in the collapse of the ruling coalition. In an attempt to show its commitment to macroeconomic stability, the government appointed Domingo Cavallo as minister of economy and launched a 'Zero Deficit Plan' to curtail public sector wages, pensions and federal transfers to the provinces. Intense social protest rapidly followed. The institutional fragility and the government's weak relations with business and labour (Tedesco 2001:108), combined with the withdrawal of the IMF's support, were perfect ingredients for the explosive situation the country faced in December 2001.

The country defaulted on its financial obligations, and within two months the value of the peso dropped by more than a third—and even further in 2002—while demonstrations intensified, rallying behind the slogan, 'Throw everyone out' (*Que se vayan todos*). The political order collapsed, and during the next weeks, after De la Rua's resignation, four provisional presidents came in and out in rapid succession, until the Congress selected Peronist senator Eduardo Duhalde as a 'transitional president' in January 2002.

Duhalde put an end to the Convertibility regime, established a free-floating exchange rate and '*pesificación*' (pesification)—converting dollar-denominated accounts and debts to pesos; a policy decision that in the context of international isolation and widespread institutional collapse plunged the economy further into chaos. Economic activity was paralyzed, GDP contracted by 16 per cent in the first quarter of 2002 and the unemployment rate climbed to almost 25 per cent, and over five million people fell into poverty between October 2001 and June 2002 (Levitsky and Murillo 2003:155). The government's policy response entailed a break with neoliberalism and IMF-sponsored orthodox stabilization programmes. Moreover, it returned to some of the central ideas of the national development strategy in place before the 1980s and

1990s: a state active in some fundamental areas of the economy and the promotion of a new relation between state, business and civil society.

The *pesificación* showed the political influence of the so-called Productive Group (*Grupo Productivo*) made up of representatives from industrial sectors, including the UIA, the CRA and the Argentine Chamber of Construction (CAMARCO). The newly created—and short-lived—Ministry of Production was directly handed to the then president of the UIA, José Ignacio de Mendiguren, whose main task was to execute the pesification of the economy. Whereas the large conglomerates under the CEA were now excluded from the policy process, the Productive Group had the inside track. Indebted in dollars, the asymmetric pesification certainly helped these industrialists to face their debts. They also profited from the increasing costs of international products in the domestic market, while competitive tradeable goods benefitted from growing competitiveness in international markets. But, pesification had a negative impact on large societal groups, since deposits and savings were repaid in Argentine pesos. As the economy showed some signs of incipient recovery, the government also attempted to restore social peace through the promotion of effective policies.

In May 2003, a newly elected Peronist president replaced the interim administration. Néstor Kirchner (2003–2007) deepened the policy orientations initiated by his predecessor: the promotion of domestic industry, public works and services. This Post-Convertibility economic policy stimulated economic and industrial recovery, a fall in unemployment and an improvement in social indicators. At a time of more auspicious domestic and international conditions, maintaining relatively low salary costs and a high and competitive exchange rate favoured industrialization (Aspiazu and Schoor 2010).

By the end of 2004, the political scene had changed significantly. The state now had an active role in economic policy. In turn, this resonated with business, labour and civil society. There was communication between a politically mobilized labour movement, along with domestic industry and unemployed worker's organizations—the *Piqueteros*.[6] Labour unionists' support relied on favourable salary agreements and other policies intended to maintain real wages, i.e. sectoral agreements to control domestic prices for consumer goods and subsidies to compensate producers for the costs entailed. On the business side, the UIA backed the industrialist orientation and on many occasions expressed unreserved support for Kirchner's economic policies (Richardson 2009). Moreover, the government reestablished the old pattern of tripartite bargaining for collective contracts with the creation of the Minimum Wage Council. This brought together the government and the Peronist CGT, which under the lorry drivers' union had a strong presence in transport sectors, and the UIA, who were joined by the commerce, banking and construction associations, in systematic negotiations to contain inflation and excessive wage increases. Traditional rural organizations and the left-leaning and more belligerent Argentine Workers' Central Union (CTA) formed in 1992 to promote the interests of workers—employed and unemployed—and with a strong presence among state workers, opposed such an approach. Large conglomerates were also excluded from this tripartite dialogue. As the CEA lost its traditional economic and political influence, the Argentine Business Association (AEA) was created in 2002 and has since then advocated a free price system and the negotiation of wage increases for each sector.

The pattern of state-society relations changed under the first years of Kirchnerism. This was more the result of a strategy of 'bending and moulding' existing political institutions and the economic model rather than drastic reform (Panizza 2005).

## Chile: Between Technocratic and Consultative State-Society Relations

Compared with Argentina, Chile stands out for its stable political game during the years of the ISI model.[7] Yet, even if economic liberalism found little support in state and society before 1970 (Teichman 2001), Chile was the first country in the region to embark on a steep path towards market reform under the military government led by Augusto Pinochet (1973–1990). This path did not deviate after the restoration of democracy. Despite the fundamental change from a developmental to a subsidiary state that then took place, relations with non-state actors have maintained a specific pattern marked by the early development of a technocratic stratum, close collaboration with business actors, and the marginalization of labour and civil society actors from decision making.

### *Cooperative State-Society Relations Under the ISI Model (1930–1957)*

ISI began spontaneously after the 1929 crisis as a means to regenerate economic growth and employment in a country where export industries were still incipient (Silva 2007). However, business interests were already formally organized. Based on a national decree, the *latifundistas* had come together under the National Agriculture Society (SNA) as early as 1838. Twenty years later, the National Chamber of Commerce (CNC) was created. In 1883, the SNA established the Society for Promoting Manufacturing (SOFOFA) at the request of the minister of finance, who was interested in promoting industrialization. Under these same auspices, the SNA helped mining firms develop the National Mining Society (SONAMI). Even if the working classes were organizing by then, modern-looking labour unions came onto the scene only by the turn of the century, all of which impacted on their political clout: access to decision making was inhibited by violent repression (Collier and Collier 2002:72–75). In contrast, by the 1920s, business actors already relied on powerful sectoral peak organizations and provided technical advice and public officials to governments.[8]

Decision making increasingly included a public technocratic stratum that acted as a '*moderating mediator*' between competing social and political actors

(Silva 1994:282). This public technocracy played a key role in the functioning of the Chilean political system in the years to come and was central to the country's modernization and the consolidation of the entrepreneurial role of the state.[9]

Starting in the mid-1930s, state-led industrialization became a matter of government concern. The traditional clash within the ISI model—between industrial and agricultural actors—was absent in Chile: landowners actively supported industrial policy since this was a period of high unemployment and social unrest, and the agricultural sector could not absorb inactive labour quickly enough (Silva 2007). Even if discrepancies in trade liberalization persisted, they did not prevent cooperation among business leaders who formed a powerful and highly integrated group, which was deeply involved in right-wing political leadership (Drake 1978).

The Popular Front, an electoral and political left-wing coalition, provided the initial drive for developmentalism and for a kind of 'cooperative capitalism' (Muñoz 1986) or 'compromise state' (Barrett 1999). Nevertheless, business interests enjoyed institutionalized access to various public agencies, including the Chilean Economic Development Agency (CORFO). The government thus intended to mute political opposition to the new development strategy. In return for access to the decision-making process, business actors moderated their resistance to state intervention in the economy. Labour actors were then absent and remained largely excluded from policy making until the 1970s. Even if the deepening of industrialization triggered a rise in membership of industrial labour unions, labour legislation constrained their size, income and use of strikes, while also limiting industrial action by federations. Exclusion of labour from political power prompted two specific developments in Chile. First, the leaders were compelled to seek support from political parties to a greater degree than was usual in Argentina and other countries in the region. Second, a high degree of competition emerged among leftist parties for influence in the labour movement (Angell 1972, 1993). Again this was absent in Argentina after the emergence of Peronism in the 1940s.

By the mid-1950s, the ISI model was consolidated, but soon balance of payments difficulties, chronic inflation and irregular industrial growth signalled the limits of the easy phase of industrialization, while the international recession of the 1950s marked the beginning of stop-start economic growth. As different attempts at stabilization were unsuccessful and the government failed to meet popular expectations for reform, the solid social coalition supporting state interventionism and protectionism began to crumble. Rising tensions grew over who would pay the adjustment costs. The foundations of the compromise state thus eroded. Chilean society and politics became progressively polarized while the economy deteriorated, inflation rose and growth slowed down. Political factors, rather than economic constraints as in the case of Argentina, accounted for the end of the inward-looking development model and the later rise of a free-market strategy (Silva 2007).

### *Political Polarization and Democratic Governance (1958–1973)*

In 1958, Chile's political centre started to collapse. Changes in party alignments ushered in governments based on a single party. The right-wing president, Jorge Alessandri, a business person himself, triggered the 'revolution of the managers' (Pinto 1985). After being appointed to government positions, representatives of the emergent managerial elite succeeded thereby in transferring the burden of the adjustment costs onto labour. Yet, the illusion of a technocratic administration soon gave way to party and political interests. As the government initiated timid agrarian reform, business actors withdrew their support.

Until then, the four peak associations were voting members in several semi-autonomous financial institutions, such as the Central Bank, the State Bank that supervised credit and subsidies and CORFO. Additionally, they usually voted on the boards of specialized government economic committees dealing with their particular sectors[10] and participated in several public agencies such as the Council on Tariffs and the Advisory Commission for LAFTA. Business actors also played an active role in the legislature, where apart from the traditional lobbying strategies, they provided information and even drafted legislative proposals (Menges 1966). Informal channels with the Executive were also available. In all, their political leverage was a reflection of their institutional and informational abilities. They had permanent personnel and high public profiles, and assured representation for both regional and specialized producer members; there was a rather regular turnover of leaders who had been chosen from among the more successful executives. They also relied on technical staff to provide economic and regulatory information to their members, as shown by the Institute of Agrarian Studies (INTAGRO), created in 1960 by the SNA to develop sophisticated skills for participating in national political debates.

Starting in 1964, the new administration led by Eduardo Frei aimed to promote transition to the next level of industrial development, including attracting FDI and cutting protection for national industries. Whereas business interests managed to block this latest initiative through their lobbies in Congress (Silva 2007), the nationalization of the copper industry, which accorded compensation to foreign owners, faced less resistance. Agricultural policies included an agrarian reform program that expropriated large areas of land to form peasant cooperatives plus important transformations in the labour legislation allowing for the creation of rural unions. Combined with the mobilizing of rural unions and Marxist-left parties, this led to a quick increase in rural unionism, while at the same time negatively affecting landowners' interests. The mobilization of these previously excluded groups together with the government's agrarian reform threatened traditional economic elites and hence imposed severe strains on the existing institutional mechanisms of representation and intermediation.

These developments met with resistance from business associations. The SNA became the leader of the *gremialista* movement and promoted the revival of the Confederation for Production and Commerce (CPC) to respond to the government's reformist threats. Created in 1933 by the four major business associations in the wake of increasing worker mobilization and the spectre of socialism, the CPC had lain dormant during the first years of ISI as the perception of threats and menaces dissipated. The rightward shift of the Frei administration, which recommended the democratic participation of business actors in policy making (Schneider 2004), could not prevent the breakdown of the consensus about the role of the state in development strategy and the matter of property rights. Rising social and political polarization followed. Combined with the growing threat of violence and increasing economic pressures, this conflict would reach its apogee under the Popular Unity (UP) and the presidency of Salvador Allende.

The UP led a thorough process of agrarian reform, extensive nationalization and redistributive social policy. CORFO acquired 14 of the 17 existing commercial banks and by 1973 the government had expropriated 60 per cent of the country's agricultural land, while the number of state enterprises reached 596 (Larraín 1991). State expenditure stood at 40 per cent of GDP and the public deficit at 25 per cent, while both quantitative and tariff protection measures were devised for industry. Furthermore, the government reduced the number of SOFOFA representatives on the boards of public enterprises from 27 to eight firms, and even attempted twice to dissolve this organization on the grounds that business associations were banned from party politics (Drake 1978). Together with nationalization and expropriation policies, this approach galvanized property owners into strong anti-statist, deregulatory, pro-liberalization and anti-populist stances. As the new administration intensified the marginalisation of business and threatened property rights, once again business actors resorted to mass mobilization. At the same time, 17 years after its creation, the Unitary Workers Confederation (CUT) was finally granted legal status. The pronouncements and the pressure placed by business organizations on the government, on the one hand, and the strong moves of labour unions and students in support of the government, on the other, led to a spiral of polarization and radicalization that ran parallel to increasing fear and violence on both sides during this serious economic deterioration. All these different elements led to the collapse of democracy and the introduction of a harsh military government in 1973.

### *The End of Democratic Governance: Market-Oriented Dictatorship (1973–1989)*

The military government implemented the first market reform program in Latin America: one that radically transformed the Chilean economy, state, and society. However, the shift from ISI to a free-market strategy was not automatic; it evolved through three phases: gradual, radical and pragmatic neoliberal restructuring (Silva 1993).

The *gradual* approach to import liberalization and stabilization (1973–1975) entailed the progressive reduction of tariffs from an average rate of 94 per cent to 60 per cent in three years during which devaluations of a unified exchange rate provided further protection and allowed manufacturers to adjust to the increased competition that stemmed mainly from regional markets—namely, the Andean Community (CAN). The CPC and the four major business associations, including the SOFOFA, collaborated in the design of this policy change. Allende's nationalization policies had economically weakened the industrialists under the SOFOFA so that their negotiating power vis-à-vis other business and landowning groups was curtailed. Additionally, both the Allende experience and the labour-repressive military dictatorship destroyed the implicit alliance between domestic-oriented industrialists and organized labour. Finally, most of the elected members of SOFOFA were part of internationally competitive firms or had multiple economic interests (Silva 1993). In all, compromise appeared a more adequate strategy. Yet the gradualist coalition that mobilized against Allende[11] soon showed its lack of cohesion.

Whereas SOFOFA was still reticent about trade liberalization, the most radical internationalist groups that had been marginalized in 1973 gained increasing ascendancy in the business sector and over the government. Furthermore, as Pinochet consolidated his personal power within the military junta, he also nurtured tight links with a select group of neoliberal economists—the so-called Chicago Boys.[12] By the end of 1974, these technocrats rapidly extended their control over economic policy and over most of the strategic centres of economic decision making, including the Office of National Planning (ODEPLAN).[13] Based on the idea that consultation with business groups would contaminate their reforms, the representative arrangements, built over the previous decades to promote collective action in associations, were dismantled. The boards of already privatized core public agencies were reduced and replaced with military officers. The military dictatorship also actively intervened in business associations, imposing heavy controls on leadership selection until 1981—when the rule was finally lifted—thus freezing in place the leaders of 1973 who had supported the coup (Silva 1998).

Nevertheless, a few of the largest international conglomerates already in control of the most dynamic sectors of the economy did rely on informal ties with the government. At a time when the government was starved for foreign exchange, they eased access to international finance. This close alliance between Pinochet, ideologues and international corporations accounted for the emergence of a policy network, which offered key support to the *radical* economic liberalization and orthodox-IMF sponsored stabilization program implemented between 1975 and 1982. This included drastic deflation, an acceleration of tariff reductions, rapid privatization of public enterprises and services, and the total liberalization of the domestic economy to the extent that by 1979 Chile had a flat tariff of 10 per cent and a fixed exchange rate. The Direction for the Promotion of Exports (ProChile) was created in 1974 to strengthen the country's trade strategy. At first acting semi-autonomously, ProChile became part of the Ministry of Foreign Relations in 1979. Its remit was to help national firms explore unknown foreign markets, while special tax credits and favourable commercial credit for non-traditional exports were also established (Loveman 2001). This complex set of policies turned Chile into one of the most liberal countries in the world.

The economic shock and the subsequent financial crisis of 1982 dramatically altered this relationship between state actors, business and international conglomerates. As the economic collapse occurred and political protest against his rule escalated, Pinochet abandoned these economic interests and rather reluctantly embraced those within the moderate alliance that would promote important policy refinements, leading to a *pragmatic* approach to liberalization (1983–1988). These new model reflationary policies included grants to the industrial sector and thus improved the relevance of industrial policy (Silva 1993).

On the business front, international conglomerates were the first victims of the foreign-debt-led model, and their collapse galvanized the role of the CPC. Now led by business people and landowners with international economic interests—namely, in logging, fishing and mining—the CPC produced an alternative economic program. Without abandoning their commitment to a free-market economy, the plan included export promotion measures while protecting domestic market producers. Consensus building was not a difficult task given the relatively small number of participants and the consistent national-level interest (Silva 1998). Nonetheless, protection for industry turned out to be a thorny issue as it pitted SOFOFA's demand for differentiated tariffs against the SNA and SONAMI, which preferred flat rate tariffs. Once again, SOFOFA was standing alone.

The president of the CPC gave the sectoral organization an ultimatum: either SOFOFA dropped its demands and accepted uniform tariffs, or it would be excluded from drafting the CPC economic recovery plan. SOFOFA assented, as only joint action could promote policy change. Reconciliation and unity had its compensations. After 1983, the government rapidly adopted many of the CPC's proposals, together with the particular programs presented by the different top associations. Thus, the deep economic crisis of 1982–1983 led to the revival of Chile's prime encompassing business association. Moreover, after 1983, business organizations exercised more influence over policy making, and their leaders came to occupy most economic ministries—finance, economy, agriculture and mining. State actors worked closely with business leaders and reincorporated representatives from associations into various councils and commissions.[14]

Smaller firms organized several meetings in 1982 and issued declarations critical of the government's policy. Fearing that they might join the protests led by the left and labour, the government made some overtures to their demands and asked them to weather the protests. The Social and Economic Council (CES), an advisory board to Pinochet, brought together state, business and labour representatives to discuss demands and policy recommendations. This added to the two national commissions created by the Ministry of Economy to handle the negotiation of external and domestic trade. Finally, this Ministry established the National Commission of Foreign Trade to thrash out trade policy issues with non-state actors.

This enhanced participation might explain the gradual lowering of tariffs (1984–1985) to allow businesses to adapt to new market conditions and encourage exports. At the same time, most non-tariff barriers were eliminated in order to insert Chile aggressively into the international economy. These different forms of consultation and participation in decision making also had an impact on business associations, which underwent a deep process of professionalization. While in the early 1970s, only SOFOFA relied on a technical department capable of analysing and elaborating policy proposals, 10 to 15 years later, associations in all other sectors and even the CPC had organized their own technical units, but SOFOFA expanded its own department even further (Silva 1998).

This was a first step towards a relationship that deepened with time. By the end of the 1980s, the SOFOFA, the SNA and the CPC publicly advocated the maintenance of the pragmatic free-market economic model they had been building with the government since 1984, and supported the dictator during the plebiscite on his continued rule. After his defeat, business associations backed Pinochet's preferred candidate.

Labour and civil society actors lacked access to the decision-making process. Labour unions were repressed from the beginning of the military junta, the CUT was dissolved, collective bargaining was banned, the right to strike abolished, and the right to associate freely was curtailed. Government-sponsored surrogates replaced autonomous working-class mobilization (Drake 1978). Civil society organizations were also curtailed and persecuted. Nevertheless, the government became more vulnerable after the 1982 economic crisis and had to put up with increasing political opposition. Labour unions were central in reactivating and mobilizing opposition forces, including the Copper Workers Confederation (now Copper Workers Federation/FTC), the National Trade Union Coordinating Body (CNS), the Confederation of Private Sector Employees and the Workers' United Front (FUT). Given that political parties were outlawed and traditional political leaders were unable to assemble an effective opposition, labour leaders played a key coordinating role in the public demonstrations led by middle- and lower-class groups. Social opposition to the regime further increased in 1983 when political parties assumed a more active role. Under the lead of the Christian and Social Democrats, Radicals, and a section of the Socialist Party, they united to form the Democratic Alliance (AD) to demand Pinochet's resignation and a democratic transition. Political parties thus reoccupied the public space opened by labour and civil society (Pearce 2004).

### *Constructing Democratic Governance in a Free-Market Society (1990–2005)*

Democratic restoration was led by the centre-left coalition *Concertación de Partidos por la Democracia*. Formed in 1988 to oppose Pinochet's continuation in power, the coalition first won the democratic elections in 1990 and remained in office until 2010.

The Concertación yielded its broad economic reform in exchange for advancing political democratization (Barrett 2002). The coalition emphasized its commitment to moderation by stressing that market logic would drive its approach to redistribution and social and political reconciliation. To disperse the fear manifested by a powerful and highly distrustful private sector, the Concertación maintained close contact with business associations prior to the transfer of power to help smooth the democratic transition, which occurred during an economic boom, not the case for Argentina and most other Latin American countries. Whereas explicitly stating their commitment to pragmatic neoliberalism, business interests, landowners and conservative political parties accepted some degree of political change. This led to an accommodation between state and business and constituted the core of the implicit pact between them (Barrett 2002).

Once in power, the Concertación initiated close consultations with business organizations. There was a positive outcome to this relationship, as both sides gained mutual trust during the first two administrations (Patricio Aylwin, 1990–1994, and Eduardo Frei, 1994–2000). However, dialogue was limited to economic policy and international trade, whereas tensions and differences prevailed over more social and redistributive issues. Building on the Concertación's stated goal of reconciling growth with equity, the first two governments sought to introduce significant changes, such as reforming the tax system and the labour code. The CPC played an active role then, including as moderator when sectoral preferences differed. Business people resorted to extensive consultation with the administration.

Both the consensual approach to politics and the authoritarian enclaves retained in the 1980 Constitution account for this close dialogue (Silva 1998). On the contrary, labour remained politically marginalised. Its demands were thus not fully acknowledged,[15] and in time, this aggravated its internal divisions and weaknesses. Civil society also remained largely excluded from decision making.

In an attempt to balance this, Frei's administration summoned a National Forum for Productive Development to discuss regional economic integration, exchange rates, labour, taxation, technology and education, among other relevant policy issues. These meetings brought together government, business and labour representatives, though the latter had a rather subordinate role. Moreover, building on a joint initiative of the Ministry of Economy and the CPC, several long-term working commissions were established for government officials, the CPC and sectoral associations to meet and define an agenda for action, which would then be further elaborated by the relevant government agency and the research department of the most important corresponding association (Silva 1998). In all, despite these efforts to institutionalize the participation of other non-state actors, the dialogue mechanisms established by the military government during the last pragmatic liberalization phase remained largely unchanged.

Ricardo Lagos (2000–2006) faced fiercer confrontation from businesses and failed to reverse these practices. The business organizations' objective was to break up the government's attempt to construct a society-wide coalition in support of neo-structural economic policy and defeat its more 'socialist' policy proposals (Silva 2002). This confrontational stance brought to light underlying differences among business people. As the CPC had been traditionally led by more accommodating sectors than the SOFOFA and ones more willing to compromise with the Concertación, the industrial association had grown increasingly disappointed with its subordination to the former. In the late 1990s, the industrialists broke with the CPC, only to re-join it shortly afterwards and regain ascendancy within it. After the legislative struggle over the labour code,[16] the SOFOFA elected a more negotiation-prone president, who immediately approached the government with a new proposal: the creation of a joint commission to work on a pro-growth economic agenda that SOFOFA had already designed.

Under the Concertación, relations between business and government were largely harmonious. Even if the coalition cut off business representation through its appointments to top positions, democratic governments maintained close contact with businesses while at the same time they moved from dialogue with the CPC to consultation with sectoral associations, especially the SOFOFA. Whereas this consensus politics promoted greater stability in the relationship of state and business, labour access to decision making was not as easy as that of business. The establishment of a Table of Social Dialogue, which offered a formal system of interaction between state, business and labour for social issues, fell short of expectations (Silva 2002).

Although partly due to 17 years of repression and deprivation under the military dictatorship, this weakening was also a product of the Concertación's change in strategy and priorities. This further weakened the CUT, which also faced internal divisions. Even if the CUT could have done more to strengthen its fundamental social role, the labour legislation enacted during these years, rather than promoting the labour movement, hindered its development and made it difficult for trade unions to stand on an equal footing with business (Barrett 2001). On the civil society side, whereas fragmentation and limited capabilities might account for its loose interactions with the state, the absence of stable mechanisms for formulating demands and opinions was also implicated.

Finally, the Concertación accepted the principle that technical and not political skills were fundamental in decision making. Already in 1983, the political forces united by the opposition formulated common objectives through the creation of teams (*equipos técnicos*) made up of technocrats with expertise in specific policy areas and representing different political parties. Thus, after the democratic restoration, technocrats, especially those representing the Corporation of Studies for Latin America (CIEPLAN),[17] played a key role in the new government, which was maintained under successive Concertación administrations (Silva 1991). Moreover, democracy allowed for the return of exiles who had obtained specialized academic training abroad and who contributed to the high degree of technical expertise in policy making.

## Some Comparative Conclusions

Both Argentina and Chile pursued a development model based on ISI and the direct intervention of the state in the economy, especially from the 1940s onwards. This strategy was intended to include the interests of the working classes through a social reform programme. In this sense, it constituted both an economic and a political project, which reshaped these countries' economies, societies and institutions. The state became the locus of power over society and the battleground for all demands, and so it was overwhelmed by the scale and density of the demands.

By the 1960s, the model began to reach its limits, leading to profound economic and political crises, which finally triggered a wave of market-oriented reforms. These were mainly strategies intended to promote the retrenchment of the state, the enhancement of market activity and the increasing separation of the state, the market and the society. This new phase (*neoliberalism*) was henceforth embedded in a new political rhetoric, labelled 'anti political liberalism' (Hirst et al. 2009), which reflected a distrust in the growth of the state and its high levels of intervention (Ocampo 2001) and an effort to depoliticize society (Garretón 2002).

In Chile, market reform was implemented under a dictatorial regime, which gave the government a greater margin of manoeuvre. Still, as the liberalization process advanced and state personnel attempted to reduce their vulnerability, they sought alternative support from more international conglomerates and local industrialists. Consequently, while labour and civil society suffered persecution, business people enjoyed direct access to policymakers and even managed to place representatives in public institutions. This close relationship and participation in the policy-making process was not new. By the 1960s, business leaders had been appointed to top ministerial positions. However, even when institutionalized channels were available, relations between state and business proceeded through informal and highly personal channels.

Certainly, privileged access to decision making has in time given way to enhanced institutional leadership and capabilities among the business community. Moreover, it was fundamental to the adoption of the free-market credo by national industrialists. Liberalization led to important adjustments and adaptations, including the emergence of consensus on the fundamentals of the market economy—a consensus that extended to society and to left-wing political leaders under the Concertación as well. This contrasts with the relations with the labour movement and CSOs. They remained more dependent on party politics and thus developed weaker structures and institutional capabilities. Whereas the corresponding actors in Argentina lacked stable institutional access to the decision-making process, this obstacle was more striking in Chile, where business people have traditionally enjoyed privileged dialogue with the highest strata of political power.

In Argentina, the market reform program faced greater obstacles, as it was implemented at a time of political liberalization and democratization. Nevertheless, state-business relations remained highly informal—as in Chile—while the government resorted to different strategies to gain labour's acquiescence to the radical reforms stemming from the close ties between the Menem administration and the Peronist trade unions. In all, formal and stable access mechanisms for societal actors appear to have been absent throughout the twentieth century. Access was granted, though only sporadically, to business organizations in order to overcome particular perceived governmental vulnerabilities. Together with great political instability, this left little room for the institutionalization of business representation.

Transition to democracy in the 1980s saw the emergence of a new pattern: a direct relationship between public officials, including the president and senior ministers, and the representatives of large business conglomerates, such as the Captains of Industry. This new approach to business may be explained by the high degree of fragmentation and factionalism among business people in Argentina, partly induced by the highly politicized nature of state-business relations since Peronism. The lack of positive state incentives, combined with the rivalry among and within business organizations, hindered the development of their institutional capacity and leadership. Moreover, business operators have exhibited a more complex alignment with free trade. While staunchly supported by the largest economic sectors that, with the aid of various state mechanisms, had gone through a learning process and had thus become internationally competitive, trade liberalization was met only with ambivalence by the UIA. The emergence of a similar consensus on the benefits of free trade to that permeating Chile seems far from evident, given the complexity of interests.

Finally, the participation of academics and experts in the emergence of policy networks was a feature of the structural reform programmes implemented by both Pinochet and Menem, practices that succeeding governments would, to a certain extent, leave in place, though with quite different policy orientations. This 'knowledge politics' has been an extended practice in the case of Chile, where the idea of technical and apolitical policies flourished before inward-looking development strategies were put in place and has transcended both the military government of the 1970s and the democratic restoration.

This chapter has been dedicated to the task of laying out the particulars of national political economies and state-society relations in Argentina and Chile as a necessary foundation for the more detailed discussions of trade politics under the neoliberal age, which will feature in the following chapters. How did state and non-state actors form a relationship when dealing with the challenges and novelties brought about by the simultaneous trade negotiations Argentina and Chile faced from the 1990s?

## Notes

1 Between 1910 and 1943, five of nine presidents, over 40 per cent of all ministers, 12 of 14 ministers of agriculture, and roughly 15 per cent of all members of Congress belonged to the SRA (Smith 1969).

2 These included the immigrant-led Argentine Agrarian Federation (FAA), the Confederation of Rural Associations of Buenos Aires and La Pampa (CARBAP) and the Argentine Rural Confederations.

3 Those backing the electoral alliance opposing Perón in the 1946 presidential elections were excluded, i.e. the UIA, the SRA and the Argentine Chamber of Commerce (CAC).

4 These conglomerates emerged at two different moments. A first wave blossomed during the golden years of the agro-export model and concentrated on agribusiness. The second wave appeared during and after the Second World War in heavy industry, construction, oil production and services.

5 Argentina had developed a bureaucratized labour leadership willing to collaborate (Teichman 2001). Apart from jointly lobbying with trade unions to halt the restructuring economic project, military intervention in trade unions kept the old leaders as advisors (Gaudio and Thompson 1990).

6 The *Piqueteros* were new political organizations in Argentina, mainly because of declining public spending, mounting unemployment and the reduction of the formal wage-earning class in the 1990s. They played a central role starting in 1999 and resorted to direct action as a tactic (Svampa 2014).

7 In contrast to Argentina, where military coups were frequent, in Chile the military intervened only twice and for a few months in 1924 and 1931.

8 From 1873 to 1901, 25 to 33 per cent of members of Congress belonged to the SNA, whereas between 1883 and 1930, 36 per cent of the SOFOFA's executive council members served as congressmen, senators, public officials and even ministers of state (Loveman 2001:166).

9 This search for expertise and technical mediation also involved seeking technical advice from foreign investors. In 1925, the Kemmerer Mission conducted a far-reaching reform of the monetary, banking and fiscal systems. Argentina considered inviting it but finally did not do so (Drake 1989).

10 The SNA had two representatives on the board of the Corporation of Agrarian Reform (CORA), the state-planning agency for agrarian reform, and SOFOFA, on the Permanent Commission for Customs Reform.

11 The so-called Monday Club led this gradualist coalition, which included Chile's wealthiest business elites meeting over Monday lunches to organize opposition to the UP government.

12 The Chicago Boys was a group of young economists at the Universidad Católica de Chile who had received postdoctoral training at Chicago University by Milton Friedman through a program financed by the United States between 1955 and 1963. As part of the Monday Club, they designed a post-coup economic plan.

13 Created in 1967, ODEPLAN was a technical agency focused on national development planning. In 1990, it became the Ministry of Planning and Cooperation (MIDEPLAN).

14 Whereas the CPC had regular access to top economic policy makers to discuss macroeconomic policies—namely, interest and exchange rates, and monetary policy—sectoral associations and their technical departments had privileged access to commissions dealing with various issues, i.e. housing and construction, agricultural and mining prices, among others (Silva 1998).

15 The draft of labour code reform established that non-union employees would pay union dues if they benefitted from contracts negotiated by the unions, which fell short of the CUT's demand for mandatory enrolment (Silva 1998).

16 The Lagos administration managed to push through a labour code reform in 2001, which introduced improvements in conditions, working hours and unemployment benefits, and raised corporate income tax from 15 to 17 per cent.

17 Created in 1976 by a team of highly qualified academics, CIEPLAN was initially devoted to monitoring the economic policy of the Chicago Boys under Pinochet's regime and the elaboration of sophisticated technical studies. Later, it became a think tank for the Christian Democratic Party and worked an alternative socioeconomic model.

## References

Acuña, C. H. (1995). Business Interests, Dictatorship, and Democracy in Argentina, in E. Bartell and L. A. Payne (Ed.) *Business and Democracy in Latin America*. Pittsburgh, University of Pittsburgh Press: 3–48.

Acuña, C. H. (1998). Political Struggle and Business Peak Associations: Theoretical Reflections on the Argentine Case, in F. Durand and E. Silva (Ed.) *Organized Business, Economic Change, and Democracy in Latin America*. Coral Gables, FL, North-South Center Press: 51–72.

Angell, A. (1972). *Politics and the Labor Movement in Chile*. London, Oxford University Press.

Angell, A. (1993). *Chile: De Alessandri a Pinochet: En busca de la utopía*. Santiago de Chile, Editorial Andrés Bello.

Aspiazu, D. and M. Schoor (2010). La industria argentina en la posconvertilibilidad: reactivación y legados del neoliberalismo, *Revista Latinoamericana de Economía* 41(161): 111–139.

Barrett, P. S. (1999). The Limits of Democracy: Socio-Political Compromise and Regime Change in Post-Pinochet Chile, *Studies in Comparative International Development* 34(3): 3–36.

Barrett, P. S. (2001). Labour Policy, Labour-Business Relations and the Transition to Democracy in Chile, *Journal of Latin American Studies* 33(3): 561–597.

Barrett, P. S. (2002). Regime Change and the Transformation of State-Capital Relations in Chile, *Political Power and Social Theory* 15: 53–106.

Bisang, R. and B. Kosacoff (1995). *Tres etapas en la búsqueda de una especialización sustentable*. Buenos Aires, Comisión Económica para América Latina y el Caribe (CEPAL).

Brennan, J. P. (1998). Industrialists and Bolicheros: Business and the Peronist Populist Alliance, 1943–1976, in J. P. Brennan (Ed.) *Peronism and Argentina*. Wilmington, DE, Scholarly Resources: 79–123.

Bulmer-Thomas, V. (2003). *The Economic History of Latin America since Independence*. Cambridge, Cambridge University Press.

Canitrot, A. (1980). Discipline as the Central Objective of Economic Policy: An Essay on the Economic Programme of the Argentine Government since 1976, *World Development* 8(11): 923–928.

Cavarozzi, M. (2009). *Autoritarismo y democracia (1955–2006)*. Buenos Aires, Editorial Paidós-Ariel.

Collier, R. B. and D. Collier, Eds. (2002). *Shaping the Political Arena: Critical Junctures, the Labor Movement, and Regime Dynamics in Latin America (The Helen Kellogg Institute for International Studies)*. Notre Dame, IN, University of Notre Dame Press.

Damill, M. and R. Frenkel (1996). Democratic Restoration and Economic Policy: Argentina, 1984–91, in J. A. Morales and G. McMahon (Ed.) *Economic Policy and the Transition to Democracy: The Latin American Experience*. Ottawa, International Development Research Centre: 49–111.

Drake, P. W. (1978). Corporatism and Functionalism in Modern Chilean Politics, *Journal of Latin American Studies* 10(1): 83–116.

Drake, P. W. (1989). *The Money Doctor in the Andes: The Kemmerer Missions, 1923–1933*. Durham, Duke University Press.

Freels, J. W., Jr. (1970). Industrialists and Politics in Argentina: An Opinion Survey of Trade Association Leaders, *Journal of Interamerican Studies and World Affairs* 12(3): 439–454.

Garretón, M. A. (2002). La transformación de la acción colectiva en América Latina, *Revista de la CEPAL* 76: 7–24.

Gaudio, R. and A. A. Thompson (1990). *Sindicalismo peronista/gobierno radical, los años de Alfonsín*. Buenos Aires, Fundación Friedrich Ebert.

Hirst, P., G. Thompson and S. Bromley, Eds. (2009). *Globalization in Question*. Cambridge, Polity Press.

Kosacoff, B. (2000). The Development of Argentina Industry, in B. Kosacoff (Ed.) *Corporate Strategy under Structural Adjustment in Argentina: Responses by Industrial Firms to a New Set of Uncertainties*. Oxford, Macmillan: 36–64.

Larraín B. F. (1991). Public Sector Behaviour in a Highly Indebted Country: The Contrasting Chilean Experience, in F. Larraín and M. Selowsky (Ed.) *The Public Sector and the Latin American Crisis*. San Francisco, International Center for Economic Growth: 89–136.

Levitsky, S. and M. V. Murillo (2003). Argentina weathers the Storm, *Journal of Democracy* 14(4): 152–166.

López, A. (2006). *Empresarios, instituciones y desarrollo económico: el caso argentino*. Buenos Aires, Comisión Económica para América Latina y el Caribe (CEPAL)—Oficina en Buenos Aires.

Love, J. L. (1995). Economic Ideas and Ideologies in Latin America since 1930, in L. Bethell (Ed.) *The Cambridge History of Latin America*. Cambridge, Cambridge University Press, Volume 6: 391–460.

Loveman, B. (2001). *Chile: The Legacy of Hispanic Capitalism*. New York & Oxford, Oxford University Press.

Manzetti, L. (1994). Institutional Decay and Distributional Coalitions in Developing Countries: The Argentine Riddle, *Studies in Comparative International Development* 29(2): 82.

McGuire, J. W. (1997). *Peronism without Perón: Unions, Parties, and Democracy in Argentina*. Stanford, Stanford University Press.

Menges, C. C. (1966). Public Policy and Organized Business in Chile: A Preliminary Analysis, *Journal of International Affairs* 20(2): 343–365.

Muñoz, O. (1986). El papel de los empresarios en el desarrollo, *Colección Estudios CIEPLAN* 20: 95–120.

Murillo, V. (2001). *Labor Unions, Partisan Coalitions, and Market Reform in Latin America*. Cambridge, Cambridge University Press.

O'Donnell, G. A. (1973a). An Impossible 'Game': Party Competition in Argentina, 1955–1966, in G. O'Donnell (Ed.) *Modernization and Bureaucratic-Authoritarianism: Studies in South American Politics*. Berkeley, University of California Press: 166–200.

O'Donnell, G. A. (1973b). *Modernization and Bureaucratic-Authoritarianism: Studies in South-American Politics*. Berkeley, University of California Press.
O'Donnell, G. A. (1988). *Bureaucratic Authoritarianism: Argentina 1966–1973 in Comparative Perspective*. Berkeley, University of California Press.
Ocampo, J. A. (2001). A New Look at the Development Agenda, *Revista de la CEPAL* 74: 7–18.
Ostiguy, P. (1990). *Los capitanes de la industria: Grandes empresarios, política y economía en la Argentina de los años 80*. Buenos Aires, Editorial Legasa.
Panizza, F. (2005). Unarmed Utopia Revisited: The Resurgence of Left-of-Centre Politics in Latin America, *Political Studies* 53(4): 716–734.
Pearce, J. (2004). Collective Action or Public Participation: Contradictory or Complementary Democratisation Strategies in Latin America? *Bulletin of Latin America Research* 23(4): 483–504.
Pinto, A. (1985). Estado y gran empresa: de la precrisis hasta el gobierno de Jorge Alessandri, *Colección Estudios Cieplan* 16: 5–40.
Richardson, N. P. (2009). Export-Oriented Populism: Commodities and Coalitions in Argentina, *Studies in Comparative International Development* 44(3): 228–255.
Schneider, B. R. (2004). *Business Politics and the State in Twentieth-Century Latin America*. Cambridge, Cambridge University Press.
Schvarzer, J. (1986). *La política económica de Martínez de Hoz*. Buenos Aires, Hyspamérica.
Schvarzer, J. (1996). Una elite empresaria en la Argentina: la Unión Industrial Argentina, *Ensaios FEE (Fundação de Economia e Estatística Siegfried Emanuel Heuser)* 17(2): 123–151.
Sidicaro, R. (1995). Poder político, liberalismo económico y sectores populares en Argentina, 1989–1995, in A. Borón, M. Mora y Araujo, J. Nun, J. C. Portantiero and R. Sidicaro (Ed.) *Peronismo y Menemismo: Avatares del populismo en la Argentina*. Buenos Aires, Ediciones El Cielo por Asalto: 119–156.
Silva, E. (1993). Capitalist Coalitions, the State, and Neoliberal Economic Restructuring: Chile, 1973–88, *World Politics* 45(4): 526–559.
Silva, E. (1998). Organized Business, Neoliberal Economic Restructuring, and Redemocratization in Chile, in F. Durand and E. Silva (Ed.) *Organized Business, Economic Change, and Democracy in Latin America*. Coral Gables, FL, North-South Center Press: 217–252.
Silva, E. (2002). Capital and the Lagos Presidency: Business as Usual? *Bulletin of Latin America Research* 21(3): 339–357.
Silva, E. (2007). The Import-Substitution Model: Chile in Comparative Perspective, *Latin American Perspectives* 34(3): 67–90.
Silva, P. (1991). Technocrats and Politics in Chile: From the Chicago Boys to the CIEPLAN Monks, *Journal of Latin American Studies* 23(2): 385–410.
Silva, P. (1994). State, Public Technocracy and Politics in Chile, 1927–1941, *Bulletin of Latin American Research* 13(3): 281–297.
Smith, P. H. (1969). *Politics and Beef in Argentina: Patterns of Conflict and Change*. New York, Columbia University Press.
Smith, P. H. (1983). *Carne y política en la Argentina: los conflictos entre los trusts anglonorteamericanos y nuestra soberanía*. Buenos Aires, Paidós.
Smith, W. C. (1989). *Authoritarianism and the Crisis of the Argentine Political Economy*. Stanford, Stanford University Press.

Smith, W. C. (1990). Democracy, Distributional Conflicts and Macroeconomic Policy-making in Argentina, 1983–89, *Journal of Interamerican Studies and World Affairs* 32(2): 1–42.

Stokes, S. C. (2001). *Mandates and Democracy: Neoliberalism by Surprise in Latin America*. Cambridge, Cambridge University Press.

Svampa, M. (2014). Revisiting Argentina 2001–13: From "¡Que se vayan todos!" to the Peronist Decade, in C. Levey, D. Ozarow and C. Wylde (Ed.) *Argentina since the 2001 Crisis: Recovering the Past, Reclaiming the Future*. New York, Palgrave Macmillan: 155–173.

Tedesco, L. (2001). The 1999 Elections in Argentina: Change in Style or Substance? *European Review of Latin American and Caribbean Studies* 70: 105–113.

Teichman, J. A. (1981). Interest Conflict and Entrepreneurial Support for Peron, *Latin American Research Review* 16(1): 144–155.

Teichman, J. A. (2001). *The Politics of Freeing Markets in Latin America: Chile, Argentina, and Mexico*. Chapel Hill, University of North Carolina Press.

Teubal, M. (2004). Rise and Collapse of Neoliberalism in Argentina: The Role of Economic Groups, *Journal of Developing Societies* 20(3–4): 173–188.

Viguera, A. (2000). *La trama política de la apertura económica en la Argentina (1987–1996)*. La Plata, Ediciones Al Margen.

Waisman, C. H. (1987). *Reversal of Development in Argentina: Postwar Counterrevolutionary Policies and their Political Consequence*. Princeton, NJ, Princeton University Press.

# 4 Trade Politics in Argentina

Trade policies in Argentina have remained erratic and volatile, even after the far-reaching liberalization reform implemented in the 1990s. Swings and reversals have reflected the different degree of commitment of successive administrations. Consensus on free trade has thus remained elusive.

By the mid-1990s, unilateral liberalization was complemented with reciprocal trade strategies, leading to the reduction in tariffs and effective protection, and the elimination of import prohibitions and licenses.[1] Regional and multilateral agreements operated as lock-in-devices because they limited the scope for policy reversal, while at the same time confirming the country's commitment to reform. Starting with MERCOSUR, the regional bloc created in 1991 in tandem with Brazil to pursue deep integration, the trade strategy progressively included agreements with third countries—both developing and industrialized. At the same time, there was participation with the WTO; all of this presented new and challenging demands in the state and non-state sectors, which only recently had embarked on market liberalization.

## Going South in Regional Negotiations

Immediately after the creation of MERCOSUR, Argentina became involved in South-South trade negotiations. Directed at first towards neighbouring countries, as in the case of Chile, the strategy then broadened to include Mexico, and later on, even extra-regional countries such as India.

### *Trade Negotiations with Chile: A First Attempt at Expanding MERCOSUR*

Chile turned out to be the first and hence the most challenging case for the recently constituted bloc. Just 18 months after acquiring international legal status through the Ouro Preto Protocol (December 1994), MERCOSUR broadened its borders to include Chile. In 1991, Chile had been invited to join the Southern bloc as a full member but rejected the invitation since this would determine its trade strategy. In June 1994, negotiations were launched to establish an association agreement under a '4+1' scheme, which would grant Chile market access under preferential conditions over third countries without having to curtail its external trade policy. Two years later, Chile became the first associate member of MERCOSUR. Apart from establishing the creation of a free trade agreement (FTA) within the next 10 years, the agreement was intended to promote cooperation in many areas, economic, scientific and technological, and physical integration as established in a parallel protocol.

The launch of negotiations with Chile, and more generally the promotion of Argentina's foreign relations, was of especial interest to the Menem administration (1989–1999), which by 1992 implemented an institutional transformation to sustain these policy objectives. The reform granted to the Ministry of Foreign Relations[2] most of the responsibilities relating to trade promotion and the development of international trade negotiations, which until then had been under the Ministry of Economy. The latter was still responsible for the definition and implementation of trade instruments and other essential tasks related to international trade negotiations. Even if the reform had been intended to overcome existing rivalries among public agencies, especially between the Ministry of Economy, which was a well-equipped ministry of great ascendancy within the Executive, and the Ministry of Foreign Relations, in practice the division of labour remained rather blurred. It generated conflicts and struggles between both ministries and the various government departments and agencies. In turn, this vagueness allowed much room for manoeuvre. Thus, personalities and people in charge—the so-called the '*persona-grama*' (interview with former senior Economy and Foreign Ministry official)—turned out to be more relevant than the formal stipulations. Moreover, during the early years of MERCOSUR, the Ministry of Foreign Relations retained full responsibility for defining the country's position in the bloc's affairs.

Negotiations with Chile triggered divergent positions in the two leading ministries. Whereas the Ministry of Economy maintained a more pragmatic approach and argued that MERCOSUR was mainly an economic and commercial enterprise, the predominant stance within the Ministry of Foreign Relations was that the Southern bloc also included a social and political dimension. Thus, while the Ministry of Foreign Relations actively sought political support to deepen MERCOSUR and promote its enlargement, the then minister of economy, Domingo Cavallo, proposed delaying the establishment of a Common External Tariff (CET) that was already under negotiation with Brazil, to allow Chile's entry. Finally, the president swung the balance in favour of the agreement, since he was deeply interested in advancing the bloc's external agenda. By December 1995, when Carlos Menem became temporary president of the bloc, he insisted to public officials and negotiators that his six-month term of office should be recognized by MERCOSUR's involvement in external negotiations, which included not only Chile, but also Bolivia, the FTAA and negotiations with the EU as well.[3]

Public officials and negotiators in the Ministry of Foreign Relations showed significant informational weaknesses. The then secretary of international trade and economic relations, Jorge Campbell, who led Argentinian negotiators and had to confront the Chilean team under the direction of Carlos Mladinic during more than 50 meetings, acknowledged that Chilean officials were very good negotiators, and as a country Chile negotiated very well.[4] Official reports also suggested that the Chilean negotiating team was best equipped to deal effectively with the trade agenda and able to take advantage of the diverging interests between Argentina and Brazil (Campbell 1999).[5]

To overcome these informational disadvantages, several strategies were deployed, most of them drawing heavily on previous experiences. The first one was to canvass the preferences of public officials and the private sector in the provinces. However, consultations were not very fruitful, and responses came mostly from the more developed provinces, as in the case of the winery sector in Mendoza (interviews with senior trade diplomat and senior Foreign Ministry official).

The government also needed expertise about technical barriers to trade and protection measures from the Argentine Institute of Standardization and Certification (IRAM) (interview with IRAM representative). In 1991, during the process of creation of MERCOSUR, IRAM together with its three counterparts established the MERCOSUR Committee of Normalization (CMN), which laid the foundations of the joint management of voluntary regional normalization and standardization. Three years later, the government granted IRAM legal recognition as the national organization for normalization, thus it became the government's advisor on this and other related issues in international and regional fora.

From a business perspective, the Chamber of the Chemical and Petrochemical Industries (CIQyP) had a proactive role in the negotiation with Chile. Immediately after the launch of negotiations, the CIQyP, together with its MERCOSUR counterparts, namely, Brazil and Uruguay, offered the four national governments a proposal for the incorporation of the Chilean petrochemical and chemical industries. The four chambers thus spared national governments from having to perform this task for which they still lacked the necessary technical abilities (interview with CIQyP executive). The resulting document became part of the final agreement. The CIQyP's institutional leadership and expertise dated back to the 1980s, when the Latin American Petrochemical and Chemical Association (APLA) was established, based on the dynamic relationship between the Argentine and Brazilian industries within LAFTA and Latin American Integration Association (LAIA).[6] In 1986, during the negotiation of the Programme for Economic Integration and Cooperation (PICE), the CIQyP and its Brazilian counterpart drew up a document for the harmonization of regional tariffs.

The collaborative strategy deployed by the CIQyP and IRAM was the result of their expertise in areas that demanded sector-specific information. In turn, these abilities—reinforced by their link with regional counterparts—allowed them to develop a collaborative strategy with public officials and trade diplomats, even if relations with the latter were mainly ad hoc and irregular. The Coordinator for Food and Beverage Industries (COPAL) also deployed a collaborative strategy after the launch of negotiations with Chile, re-editing their role with the PICE.[7] However, they were exceptions.

The launch of the negotiations with Chile ran parallel to the definition of the CET. Industrialists, also under the UIA, viewed these processes with great scepticism and even speculated that deadlines would be missed (interview with UIA executive). A similar stance pervaded agricultural operators, who reacted with great disbelief when summoned by the secretary of agriculture. They believed these initiatives would never come to fruition and therefore would have no impact on their sector (interview with senior Economy Ministry official). The minister of economy's opposition to the agreement contributed to this perception.

Civil society remained largely detached from this negotiation. Several pressing domestic issues concentrated the attention of labour unions, such as labour reform and its impact on salaries, working conditions and rising unemployment. Moreover, after democratization, the agendas and strategies of CSOs and NGOs were related to national politics and promoting democracy (Jacobs and Maldonado 2005). But by the end of 1994, trade unions, consumers and environmental NGOs started debating the labour, social and environmental consequence of regional integration, including MERCOSUR's enlargement. Thus, for example, the CGT, the only trade union standing for the workers at both domestic and regional levels, highlighted the potential effects of new labour legislation on social rights. Within the negotiation process with Chile, this demand did not however lead to a defensive stance. In fact, regional networks—such as the Southern Cone Coordinator of Central Trade Unions (CCSCS)—promoted a positive agenda, given that with the exception of a few sectors, labour costs were rather homogeneous in the region (Portella de Castro 2000). Moreover, they expected regional integration to enhance and strengthen social and environmental standards and regulations (Botto 2004).

### *Trade Negotiations with Mexico: When Going South Is Going North*

While negotiating with Chile, MERCOSUR launched negotiations with Mexico to substitute the existing bilateral agreements in place with a '4+1' scheme. Negotiations turned out to be more complicated than expected. After having languished for almost two years, dialogue was resumed on 28 August 1996, but one year later, differences emerged among MERCOSUR member countries as to how the costs and benefits of market access would be distributed. Even though the four member countries then took different paths regarding the negotiation of previous bilateral agreements,[8] in 2002 all parties signed the Economic Complementation Agreement (ECA 54). This established a legal framework for trade relations between MERCOSUR and Mexico, and bilateral negotiations between the five countries. Whereas this agreement led to the signing of an FTA between Mexico and Uruguay, and the extension of the scope of the ECA with Argentina and with Brazil, in 2005 formal negotiations for an FTA were launched. Mexico still has privileged bilateralism when dealing with MERCOSUR.

Unstable and fractious coordination between the Ministries of Economy and Foreign Relations predominated in Argentina when negotiating with Mexico. Nevertheless, as the Ministry of Economy's capacity to define and provide technical support to trade policy declined, Foreign Relations assumed a more active role in the definition of trade policy and the implementation of negotiation strategies with both MERCOSUR and third countries.

A recurrent pattern in trade decision making was the division between office holders and a small but stable technical cadre, this being especially striking in the case of the Ministry of Economy, in areas such as the Secretariat of Industry and the Secretariat of Agriculture, which in the mid-1990s became actively involved in international trade negotiations. In these areas, personnel under professional services contracts—'*contratados*'—were the coordinators between state and business. Despite its informal and ad hoc character, this liaison was fundamental when formulating the country's position in international negotiations such as those with Mexico. The gap between office holders and the *contratados* deepened when negotiations gained in complexity and when those politically responsible for trade negotiations lacked such expertise. Complexity and lack of expertise became particularly significant in North-South trade negotiations, as detailed in the next section.

To overcome this informational weakness, in the mid-1990s the then secretary of industry, Alieto Guadagni, created the Centre for Production Studies (CEP). Financed through the United Nations Development Programme (UNDP) and the Inter-American Development Bank (IADB), the CEP aimed to reproduce the experience of the Ministry of Foreign Relations' in-house technical unit, the Centre for International Economy (CEI). Established in 1987, the CEI is an economic think tank that develops economic and international trade studies to provide up-to-date information and technical support to officials, and collaborate in the design and implementation of trade policies. In contrast, the CEP has developed a more sector-based approach and promotes industrial activity by stimulating its performance and integration with regional and international markets.

Even though both think tanks were in charge of undertaking specialized studies to support trade negotiations, the persistence of underlying conflicts and competition between the two ministries hindered a more fluid relationship between them and the public officials and negotiators. The lack of an adequate prioritization of demands, the absence of proper links among agencies, and competition for funds, reinforced the competition (Botto and Bianculli 2009).

This fragmentation did not offer a fertile terrain for establishing an extensive institutional architecture. Led primarily by the Secretariat of Industry within the Ministry of Economy, and to a lesser extent by the Secretariat of Trade and International Economic Relations of the Ministry of Foreign Relations, the consultations with the private sector remained highly informal and ad hoc.

They consisted mainly of surveys and meetings—both formal and informal—with business industries, including associations, and even companies. This strategy, which had been especially evident in the Ministry of Foreign Relations since the mid-1990s, was a '*divide and rule*' policy (Gargiulo 2003:50). However, this approach was to a certain extent justified by industrialists, since the negotiation with Mexico, and South-South negotiations, entailed granting reciprocal fixed tariff preferences or partial ones, and the government had to consult with sector-based organizations to elaborate these preferences.

Large businesses came together under the Mexican-Argentine Group created in November 1996 when the Mexican president, Ernesto Zedillo, visited Argentina. However, this bi-national group was limited to large multinational companies, such as the iron and steel Techint, and leading business associations, including the UIA, the SRA and the CAC.[9] Second, once again, particular representatives took the lead and elaborated joint sectoral proposals, as in the case of the chemical, petrochemical and the dairy sectors. At the domestic level, the CIQyP led this initiative; thus, the association revamped previous experiences in negotiation and further deepened its expertise and leading role in advising trade diplomats and public officials.

While CIQyP and COPAL were already developing strong relations with public officials and, to a lesser extent, with negotiators, the UIA as such was only just initiating its path towards enhanced professionalization. In 1993, it created the MERCOSUR Department, which turned out to be a by-product of the regional process of which the industrial association was not a strong supporter in its initial phase because they thought MERCOSUR would never be established (interview with UIA executive). This department was to represent industrial interests within MERCOSUR and was responsible for monitoring negotiation processes. Leaders in the sector now acknowledged the need to develop specific abilities if they were to have an effective role in regional and international negotiations.[10] Nevertheless, the most active participants in its weekly plenary sessions were the 'usual suspects': the CIQyP, the COPAL, the Chamber of Industrial Food Products Manufacturers (CIPA), the Argentine Association of Metallurgical Industry (ADIMRA) and the Centre of Iron and Steel Industrialists (CIS) led by Techint; most of which were already participating in the Mexico-MERCOSUR negotiations. In all, this was evidence of the fragmentation within the UIA. Only a few sectors—the petrochemical, food, dairy, automotive and steel and iron sectors—supported regional and international liberalization, in contrast to the defensive stance of most of UIA's members, a rather recurrent pattern during these first trade negotiations.

Institutional mechanisms to allow civil society input in trade policy making were almost negligible. The mobilization of trade unions and NGOs during negotiations with Mexico was rather weak. The narrow scope of the agreement and the traditional collaborative stance of these actors towards South-South integration processes as a way of enhancing social and labour norms certainly account for this limited mobilization.

### *Trade Negotiations with India: A South-South Extra-Regional Agreement*

Negotiations with India were launched on 17 June 2003 and were part of the multipolar trade strategy encouraged by the then vice-counsellor and minister of foreign relations and international trade, Martín Redrado (2002–2004). Aimed at opening multiple and simultaneous negotiation scenarios, this strategy promoted two different, connected objectives: the search for new markets and the development of existing markets—or 'trade intelligence'—to detect new opportunities for Argentina's products in international markets (Redrado 2003). The assumption was that Argentina had failed to develop a consistent export model during the four previous decades. The 2001 crisis and the consequent devaluation opened a window of opportunity for developing a more aggressive trade policy. This entailed going beyond false antinomies—MERCOSUR vs. FTAA, or FTAA vs. EU— and replacing the 'vs.' with 'and'.[11] Furthermore, MERCOSUR was to work as the springboard for integration into the world economy, including all ongoing negotiations: WTO, FTAA, EU, the CAN, China, India, Mexico, South Africa and Thailand.

The aim of the agreement with India, a first step towards the creation of an FTA, was to strengthen existing trade relations and promote trade expansion by granting reciprocal fixed tariff preferences. Furthermore, it included provisions on trade measures, namely rules of origin and safeguarding measures to conform to WTO rules. A Joint Administration Committee was also created to evaluate the process of trade liberalization among the parties and to propose further strategies in the path towards an FTA. Trade negotiations with India, as part of this new multipolar strategy, led to the signing of a preferential trade agreement (PTA) in January 2004, which was the first deal between MERCOSUR and an Asian country.

The Ministry of Foreign Relations introduced relevant changes to promote its leadership and institutional capacities and to engage with non-state personnel as a way of ensuring this new approach to international negotiations.

The CEI gained prominence. In 2002, it launched a Series of Studies, which was funded by the Secretariat of Trade and International Economic Relations, the UNDP and the IADB and provided technical support for the new multipolar trade strategy. In 2004, a study discussed the opportunities and threats that South-South trade entailed for Argentina, only to conclude that out of the 45 developing countries included within the Global System of Trade Preferences, India was among the six countries offering the most important market opportunities (CEI 2004).

Nevertheless, conducting multiple and simultaneous negotiations demanded not only technical expertise but also enhanced coordination abilities to assure institutional leadership in every case. First, the Ministry of Foreign Relations became stronger in trade negotiations because these—and more markedly the negotiation of the FTAA—involved new issues in which neither the Ministry of Foreign Relations nor the Ministry of Economy could act on their own.

Second, the 'empathy' and personal commitment of Martín Redrado and the then minister of economy, Roberto Lavagna, reinforced this attempt at coordination and information sharing among ministries. Third, diplomats were now holding important posts in the Ministry of Economy, i.e. secretary of industry and under-secretary of agriculture. Finally, this empathy and good personal relations resulted in meetings being called on a bimonthly basis. Ministers and the secretaries of agriculture and industry and trade attended. At a time when internal divisions predominated, given the fragility and low institutionalization of trade policy making, once again the *persona-grama* turned out to be crucial.

The Ministry of Foreign Relations also implemented different mechanisms to promote dialogue with business and civil society, though with varying success. The National Council on International Trade (CNCI) intended to grant more visibility to international trade negotiations, traditionally imbued with a secretive atmosphere. Of a strictly consultative nature, the CNCI brought together business representatives and academics and offered a space for the discussion of ideas and proposals with public officials and trade diplomats. Nevertheless, neither the CNCI nor the more recently created Civil Society Consultative Council (CCSC), which comprised trade unions, academics and a wide range of NGOs, together with businesses, altered the prevailing relationships. As evidenced by the negotiation with India, these channels proved to be merely informational and rather irrelevant for business people, who still relied on informal but more effective channels.

The secretary of trade in the Ministry of Economy carried out formal consultations with the largest business chambers, the UIA, the Argentine Chamber of Exporters (CERA), and ADIMRA, among others. Again, the limited negotiation agenda and the small portion of trade covered accounts for this restricted consultation (interview with middle-ranking trade diplomat). Nonetheless, differences soon appeared.

For agribusiness interests gathered under the SRA and the Argentine Oil Industry Chamber (CIARA), trade negotiations with India did not entail major benefits given India's high protection of the agricultural sector, especially oilseeds and edible oils. Even if there was not much to struggle for, business operators developed a collaborative strategy because they still expected to achieve greater market access in the wider agricultural sector (interview with SRA representative). This contrasted with competition among the industrial groups.

Within the UIA, and as was the case in most South-South negotiations involving fixed trade preferences, consultations were devolved to second-degree and sector-based chambers (interview with UIA executive). The latter—namely, the textile, footwear, clothing and pharmaceutical sectors—openly opposed the agreement and asked either for exemption or ad hoc protection measures (interview with senior Economy Ministry official, 2). Within the realm of the SMEs, and given the high fragmentation of the sectors, discussions were bilateral and with companies (interview with middle-ranking trade diplomat).

## Conclusions

The creation of MERCOSUR in 1991 triggered relevant changes in domestic trade policy procedures. However, whereas some dimensions of the policy making showed continuity with the processes of the ISI model, the intense intra-regional activity, combined with the country's external agenda, posed new challenges and demands on both the government and societal actors (state and non-state), which still showed relevant weaknesses in their institutional and trade capacities.

In the public sector, responsibilities for trade policy formulation and negotiations were fragmented and dispersed among several ministries and agencies, which also held conflicting views regarding the country's international strategy. Lack of coordination and leadership and fragile public institutions were then the main traits of trade policy making.

The institutional changes introduced both in the Ministry of Economy and of Foreign Relations were intended to enhance the institutional leadership and abilities of state representatives, with the latter being sharper after the launch of the multipolar trade strategy. Apart from the establishment of in-house think tanks to provide more information, new consultation mechanisms were inaugurated mainly to overcome these perceived disadvantages. These entailed significant improvements in the visibility and transparency of the trade policy process as public officials and negotiators reached out to more non-state actors, especially from the 2000s. However, whereas in the case of businesses, formal mechanisms complemented pre-existing informal channels and personal relations with public officials and negotiators, thus building an extensive institutional architecture; the participation of labour unions and CSOs remained formally confined within the limits of the CNCI and the CCSC. Furthermore, substantial issues were discussed outside the formalities of these institutions. In all, the different institutional structures led to different patterns of trade politics as depicted in Table 4.1.

South-South negotiations mobilized those already involved in regional and international trade dynamics. They viewed these negotiations as a way of enhancing their competitive advantage and deepening already established trade flows. Included in it were national business sectors, which in some cases exhibited similar structures and importance to transnational companies as they deployed a collaborative strategy with public officials and trade diplomats. On the contrary, those still focused on the domestic market distrusted South-South agreements while SMEs, after the negative impact of structural reforms, were still scrutinizing the new window of opportunity these offered.

More importantly, most of these divergent positions coexisted within the UIA, where the inability to reconcile divergent interests prevented it from speaking with one voice. In terms of its institutional ability, starting with the MERCOSUR Department and its later transformation into the Department of Trade and International Negotiations, the UIA showed an interest in developing its expertise. However, even in the case of the negotiations with India,

*Table 4.1* South-South trade negotiations in Argentina

| | | *State actors* Institutional architecture | *Non-state actors* Strategies | *Trade politics patterns* |
|---|---|---|---|---|
| **Chile** | *Business* | Extensive | Collaborative: CIQyP, COPAL, large firms | Cooperative |
| | | | Competitive: UIA | Pressured |
| | *Civil society* | Limited | Collaborative: trade unions, NGOs | Subordinated |
| **Mexico** | *Business* | Extensive | Collaborative: CIQyP, COPAL, large firms | Cooperative |
| | | | Competitive: UIA | Pressured |
| | *Civil society* | Limited | Collaborative: trade unions, NGOs | Subordinated |
| **India** | *Business* | Extensive | Collaborative: CIARA, SRA, large firms | Cooperative |
| | | | Competitive: UIA, sectoral associations (clothing, footwear, textiles, pharmaceuticals) | Pressured |
| | *Civil society* | Limited | Collaborative: trade unions, NGOs | Subordinated |

Source: *Author-created*

which involved only a limited portion of trade, the UIA still exhibited little competence for effective involvement in trade negotiations. Though also enjoying extensive institutional access, industrialists assumed defensive postures and resorted to traditional lobbying strategies to demand protection or ad hoc measures to reduce competitive pressures. Institutional channels did not offer a strong incentive to overcome their intrinsic fragmentation and weak expertise in trade politics.

Civil society actors remained largely detached from these South-South negotiations, and mainly resorted to a collaborative strategy after the launch of the processes, which were perceived as further deepening relations with their counterparts. With these limitations, their input into trade policy making was negligible and resulted in a subordinated pattern of trade politics.

## North-South Trade Negotiations and the Search for Northern Partners

Argentina was already involved in two trade negotiations with industrialized countries when the multipolar trade strategy was established. These included negotiations at the FTAA and with the EU. Although launched in 1998 and 1999 respectively, both dated back to the early 1990s and were fundamental parts of the country's international agenda.

### *The FTAA: A Long and Winding Road to No Free Trade*

Promoted by the United States, and somehow recapturing the 'Initiative for the Americas' proposed by George H. W. Bush, the FTAA was intended to bring together all countries in the region—with the unique exception of Cuba—with the primary goal of liberalizing trade and investment. As the Summits of the Americas advanced, trade negotiations moved to centre stage and became pivotal. After a four-year preparatory phase, during which the institutional procedures and structures were defined via a dense round of meetings, formal negotiations for the FTAA were launched at the Second Summit of the Americas in Chile in April 1998.

Negotiating Groups—[12] subsidies, antidumping and countervailing duties, market access, agriculture, government procurement, investment, competition policy, IPRs, dispute settlement, and services—were to draw up draft texts for their respective chapters to be presented for a preliminary deal at the Summit of Quebec (April 2001). However, marked differences about access to the United States market, especially for agricultural products, hindered substantive agreements. Furthermore, the United States refused to negotiate this within the FTAA and accorded the privilege to the WTO instead. The draft finally presented in Quebec was still far away from what should have been the final version of the agreement. After 2001, the pace of negotiation decelerated because of these diverging preferences and priorities. Some steps were taken to revive the process in 2002, and a year later, after the first exchange of market access offers, countries agreed to what was termed an 'FTAA *à la carte*' or an 'FTAA light', which implied a two-tier framework intended to allow greater flexibility in negotiations. Whereas a common tier of mutual but minimal obligations focused on market access, an upper and voluntary tier centred on strengthened obligations in various trade-related disciplines. This new strategy also fell victim to the unresolved differences among countries. As hemispheric negotiations lagged, the United States pursued bilateral trade agreements with Latin America, i.e. Peru and Colombia, and the Dominican Republic-Central America FTA (CAFTA-DR). The FTAA project finally collapsed during the Mar del Plata Summit in 2005.

In 1998, negotiations began in auspicious circumstances, reflecting the widespread consensus on the benefits of economic (and political) liberalization. At the domestic level, the institutional changes introduced in the early 1990s were already showing fruit. The transfer in 1992 of the responsibility for trade from the Ministry of Economy to that of Foreign Relations was compounded by the increasing technical trade expertise of diplomats: the National Foreign Service Institute (ISEN)—the official Diplomatic School—now provided specialized training in trade. Additionally, given that so far negotiations in the regional arena through MERCOSUR and the conclusion of the UR at the multilateral level had failed to produce the expected results, businesses were now more actively knocking on the government's doors.

The broad and complex trade agenda of the FTAA elicited a quick response from the private sector. First, business associations and chambers were now developing their own studies or commissioning them from consulting firms. Second, at least once a month, they invited public officials and negotiators to meetings to gather information on the latest developments in trade negotiations. Later on, the Ministry of Foreign Relations devised different mechanisms to provide updated information on negotiations to businesses and civil society. However, only in 2002 did they become effective.

Until then, state-business relations relied on informal meetings convened by the largest business associations. The establishment of the CNCI and the CCSC did not put an end to these informal encounters, which still took place when negotiations required the elaboration of more sector-specific proposals (interview with senior trade diplomat).

Whereas after 2002 formal and informal channels coexisted, when the FTAA was launched in Santiago, domestic consultation mechanisms remained highly informal, with the sole exception of the Advisory Council on Foreign Trade (CACE) in the Ministry of Economy. Created in 1988, the CACE had a marginal role in trade policy making since only lower rank officials participated; in time, it lost power and simply faded away. Félix Peña, the foreign trade undersecretary, revived the CACE in 1998 to promote closer relations and coordination with private companies. Even so, this mechanism could not overcome the inertia in trade policy making. The CACE was dissolved when Peña left office in 1999, and both public officials and businesses went back to the usual ad hoc and informal practices.

By then, the division between the Ministries of Economy and Foreign Relations came to a happy accommodation. The former was responsible for the technical dimension of trade negotiations, whilst the latter focused on the diplomatic aspect. Still, this division was far from optimal given that in order to negotiate effectively trade diplomats also needed to understand the technical specificities of the agendas at stake. Moreover, this exacerbated the isolation of the Foreign Office: liaison with businesses remained in the hands of the Ministry of Economy, which was in charge of elaborating the national position (interview with senior trade diplomat). Additionally, coordination among public agencies was still pending. To this end, in 2000 the government created an Inter-Ministerial Commission of International Trade (CICI), which included representatives from all the relevant agencies and operated under the authority of the secretary of the presidency. Its main objective was to coordinate trade policy making and implementation and to set international trade strategies. However, the initiative had limited impact.

Business was actively involved in the FTAA throughout the process. At the regional level, the UIA and the SRA, together with CERA, CIQyP, Industrial Chamber of Argentine Pharmaceutical Laboratories (CILFA), Acindar and Techint adhered to the Business Network for Hemispheric Integration (BNHI). Made up of a small but powerful number of globally operating businesses, the BNHI had supported the negotiation process since the first trade ministerial meeting in 1995, and just one year later, its participation in the Americas Business Forum (ABF) was institutionally integrated within the FTAA. These business people were responsible for summoning the most representative businesses for the ABF's meetings that ran parallel to each ministerial meeting, and for elaborating policy recommendations. Participation in this regional network triggered increased coordination among businesses, leading in turn to common proposals at the national level and enhanced collaboration with the government, in particular with the Ministry of Foreign Relations, although such collaboration remained informal (interview with UIA executive).

Despite this close relationship, industrialists still displayed a marked division between those more linked to the domestic market, which in general terms sustained a competitive strategy, and large economic interests for whom the FTAA secured market access to the United States. By contrast, positions within the agricultural sector were uniform. Furthermore, together with the government, they demanded the liberalization of the highly subsidized agricultural sector in the United States. To this end, associations pursued a collaborative strategy with the government, while at the same time they sought consensus with their MERCOSUR partners, as in the case of the COPAL that worked closely with its Brazilian counterpart to develop a common regional position (interview with COPAL trade consultant). The CIQyP had already developed solid trade negotiation skills and followed a similar strategy, just as CILFA did to oppose the United States' proposal to include a WTO-plus chapter on IPRs, based on its experience during the UR (interview with CILFA representative). Information underlay the nexus between the government and IRAM, which was actively involved in the working group on norms and technical barriers to trade (Group 4) as the government's main advisor (interview with IRAM representative).

The FTAA brought fresh challenges and raised the interest of a larger number of business people. However, when it came to industrial interests, only those already showing sound technical ability and negotiating expertise, and capable of speaking with one voice, managed to develop a close dialogue with public officials and negotiators. The UIA was a prime association yet had limited resources in both dimensions. The difficulties still present in 2003 during the exchange of market offers question to what extent this novel involvement and interest enabled industrial interests to learn anything of value. Moreover, SMEs remained excluded from these informal talks with public officials and diplomats, and from the ABF and other regional fora. Their chief demand was for inclusion in decision making since theirs would be the most affected sector if the FTAA prospered; labour unions' demands were along the same lines.[13]

Civil society's response to the launch of the FTAA was fragmented. A division among CSOs slowly emerged. Whereas by the time negotiations were formally launched, business people had had four years of learning by doing, only two NGOs stood out for their collaboration with the regional process: Asociación Conciencia and Poder Ciudadano. Because of their advocacy of democracy, transparency and information access, they were dynamically involved in the Summits of the Americas concerning civil society participation. Still, this did not entail the elaboration of alternative proposals, even less to the trade agenda. As in the case of other insider groups, their contributions remained in the procedural arena and managed to deepen their role and to raise the support of peer associations. In contrast, outsider groups slowly began to emerge in relation to the recently created Hemispheric Social Alliance (HSA). Based on its rejection of the regional project, given the pre-eminence of trade and investment liberalization, the HSA intended to use the regional process as an opportunity to promote an alternative, democratic model of development. In Argentina, Diálogo 2000, a network of organizations and social movements led by the Peace and Justice Service of Argentina (SERPAJ), attempted to open a public debate on the FTAA and mobilize opposition. The declarations of the *Alianza* minister of foreign relations, Adalberto Rodríguez Giavarini, raised further opposition. In a meeting with several CSOs, he asserted that even if society had the right to be informed and to participate, FTAA negotiations were secret (interview with senior trade diplomat).

Hence, by the end of 2000 and more particularly after the VI Trade Ministerial Meeting that took place in Buenos Aires in 2001, the FTAA gained more visibility. While businesses engaged in organizing the parallel ABF, the city of Buenos Aires was flooded with street protests to proclaim civil society's rejection of the FTAA ('*No al ALCA*'). Interestingly, for the first time since 1998, trade unions adopted an explicit and common stance regarding the FTAA. Both the CGT and the CTA rejected the project but still mobilized in different ways. In so doing, the CTA counted on the support of the FAA, social and human rights organizations, and trade unions in Brazil, Chile, Cuba, Paraguay and Uruguay.[14]

Rejection of the FTAA deepened after the 2001 crisis and the political and institutional collapse that followed. At a time of rapid impoverishment, the economic crisis led to a complete rejection of neoliberal policies and market-led developments, of which the FTAA was perceived as the stellar example. The '*No al ALCA*' gained new and heterogeneous adherents.

Following a mandate of the III Summit of the Americas in Quebec, between 2002 and 2003 the Ministry of Foreign Relations created new channels for the participation of civil society in the design of the new trade strategy. The CCSC, established in 2003, was to give more transparency to trade negotiations and thus brought together public officials and negotiators, a broad range of CSOs—including trade unions, consumers and environmental organizations, among many others—with business associations, such as the UIA, the FAA and the Assembly of Small and Medium Entrepreneurs (APYME). Even though those concerned with society valued this mechanism positively as it enabled access to public officials and negotiations, even to Martín Redrado, it was, nevertheless, perceived as mere window dressing. It was just a *one-way street*, with no opportunities to discuss substantive issues. As opposed to businesses, which apart from the CNCI still had informal access to public officials, civil society and SMEs were denied such dialogue. Moreover, after 2003, business representatives participated in the room next door during FTAA meetings—a mechanism which was also implemented when negotiating with the EU and at the WTO.

Certainly, the institutionalization of these mechanisms responded to the government's urgent need to reestablish domestic governance by canalizing protests and demands within formal procedures. While organizations under the Diálogo 2000 firmly refused to attend meetings at the Foreign Relations Ministry, other organizations such as Citizens' Justice and Human Rights Forum (FOCO) and the Centre for Human Rights and Environment (CEDHA) took part in these discussions and debates. In spite of the shortcomings identified above, the creation of the CCSC, to include over 400 organizations, certainly altered the traditional landscape of the elegant San Martín Palace (headquarters of Foreign Relations), at least in form, though not in content. Moreover, much of the essence of its creation vanished over time as the agenda no longer directly focused on trade negotiations.

### *The EU-MERCOSUR Negotiations: A First Attempt at Interregionalism*

Although the idea of creating what would be the first ever case of interregionalism was certainly prior to that of the FTAA, the EU had to wait until the creation of the MERCOSUR customs union in 1994 to formalize this proposal. The I EU-Latin America and Caribbean Summit that took place in Rio on 28 June 1999 was the scene for the launch of trade negotiations between the EU and MERCOSUR, and was preceded by long years of dense and legally driven relations across the Atlantic. In fact, EU-MERCOSUR relations are based on the Interregional Framework Cooperation Agreement signed in 1995 to promote trade liberalization, cooperation and political dialogue.

In Rio, based on the European Commission's limited negotiating mandate, both partners agreed to begin the discussion of information and identification of the Non-Tariff Barriers (NTBs) immediately, whereas custom duties and market access for goods and services would have to wait until 1 July 2001. These issues would only be debated in light of the Third WTO Ministerial Conference to be held in Seattle in 1999. Market access negotiations were formally inaugurated in Montevideo in 2001, with the actual exchange of negotiating texts for goods, whilst in 2003–2004, proposals in the areas of services, investments and government procurement were exchanged.

The EU offer included all sectors—namely, fishing services, industry and agriculture—but came with important restrictions. First, the proposal involved a gradual liberalization schedule of 10 years—very compatible with the WTO—with no immediate change in the Common Agricultural Policy (CAP), and second, the liberalization program included 100 per cent and 90 per cent of industrial and agricultural goods, respectively. MERCOSUR members' disappointment was reflected in their counter-offer, which involved a 10-year gradual liberalization program, covering 86 per cent and 90 per cent of manufactured and agricultural goods, respectively, and which excluded the automotive industry, one of the sensitive areas for these countries, but a priority for the EU. By the end of 2003, when the deadline for concluding bi-regional trade negotiations had already been missed, a new and certainly ambitious working program was established. This included five negotiation rounds and two ministerial meetings intended to close all talks by October 2004. Nevertheless, difficulties in coming to an agreement soon became evident. Each regional partner failed to agree on the other's final offer. Since then, the interregional process has been characterized by spasmodic and bilateral attempts to achieve an agreement. Discussions were resumed in 2005, but once again, the deadline proposed by the EU was missed.

Six years earlier, the launch of trade negotiations with the EU in Rio had been met with high expectations by the government. Yet asymmetries between partners became evident. Argentinean public officials and negotiators faced large and well-trained working teams made up of lawyers and economists, following established routines and procedures, and who had clear objectives and relevant financial resources (interview with senior Economy Ministry official).

To make up for the disadvantages caused by lack of information, the secretary of agriculture consulted widely with business associations; the resulting format was nevertheless elastic and depended on the specific sector and product. For example, when consultations involved loosely organized sectors—namely, wine or potato producers—invitations to participate were forwarded to individuals. The government also required businesses to collect crucial technical information, which public agencies could not do since they lacked the necessary time and human resources. A working relationship was thus established with institutions such as the SRA and COPAL, which, based on their strong export-oriented profile, had by the end of the 1990s developed solid technical abilities through the creation of specific departments devoted to international trade negotiations and by the hiring of trade experts and consultants. Moreover, the SRA and COPAL established a working relationship based on their interest in gaining stable market access to the EU and the large experience of the COPAL in trade negotiations. Consequently, summoned by either the Ministries of Economy and Foreign Relations or COPAL, they actively participated in meetings with public officials and negotiators. Interactions with the Ministry of Foreign Relations gained in intensity, especially after the 2002 launch of the new multipolar trade strategy.

This more active attitude contrasted with that of the potential losers who, fearing the negative impact of the EU-MERCOSUR agreement, contacted high-ranking government officials to ask for protection (interview with senior Foreign Ministry official). Industrialists put on more pressure during the regular meetings held with public officials and negotiators, which were inaugurated just after the launch of negotiations with the EU as the government attempted to establish a new working scheme with the private sector to be repeated during the various negotiation rounds. Textiles, clothing and footwear strongly resisted trade liberalization (interview with senior Economy Ministry official, 2). In contrast, the CIQyP and CILFA just re-edited previous proposals and elaborated a joint proposal that was presented as the MERCOSUR position (interviews with CIQyP and CILFA representatives), showing that the collaborative strategy had matured over the years and across negotiations.

Interestingly, both those who were pro-free trade and those against it were part of the MERCOSUR-EU Business Forum (MEBF), which dated back to 1997 with the intention of consolidating trade and inter-business relations at the interregional level. Building on an initiative by large European companies, mostly in the area of services, the MEBF also included big companies in Argentina, most of them multinationals and '*multilatinas*', together with business associations such as the UIA and SRA. Despite discrepancies among members, in practice the MEBF managed to speak with a single voice on behalf of EU and MERCOSUR business interests, except for one occasion in which European and MERCOSUR versions were produced because of contradictory views on agriculture (interview with SRA representative).

Talks at the regional level through the MEBF did not block domestic communication channels. Whereas the regional forum assumed a more political role, technical aspects were discussed with sector-based associations. Moreover, businesses resorted to these channels when putting forward their demands. This was especially evident in the case of agriculture, since the SRA lacked an EU counterpart in the MEBF (interview with SRA representative).

The activation of trade unions came at a rather late stage. By the time this negotiation found a place on their agenda, trade unions were already suffering the negative consequences of structural reforms and increasing unemployment. However, their mobilization was more a response to the FTAA and the role of regional networks, namely the position of the HSA.

In the case of EU-MERCOSUR negotiations, Northern actors took the initiative. In the mid-1990s, European trade unions contacted their Latin American partners, including those in MERCOSUR, about the EU's trade strategy in the region. In May 1998, before the launch of bi-regional negotiations, the European Trade Union Confederation (ETUC), the International Confederation of Free Trade Unions (CIOSL) and the Inter-American Regional Workers' Organization (ORIT) organized the 'Trade Union Conference on the Social Dimension of MERCOSUR and the European Union'. The intention was to demand the democratic integration of the regions. Despite these early developments, it took three years to establish the 'First EU-Latin America and the Caribbean Trade Union Summit'. Organized by the ETUC and the ORIT, this meeting was then followed by other encounters in Buenos Aires and Mexico, where the CCSCS had an active role.

Given their fragmentation and organizational weaknesses, trade unions valued these networks as a means of bridging the informational and financial gaps with their developed partners. Still, they regretted the lack of a mechanism similar to the MEBF (interview with CGT representative), whose policy proposals fed directly into the Bi-regional Negotiating Committee, the formal body which was in charge of the EU-MERCOSUR negotiations.

As negotiations gained momentum, trade unions had more incentive to get involved, and so they created technical departments to deal with the complexities of regional and international negotiations. By developing networks and in-house working groups, trade unions started a learning process. Still, differences between the CGT and the CTA deepened as the latter rejected the FTA model, irrespective of the specific industrial counterpart (interviews with CGT and CTA representatives). This was particularly shown in the dialogue with state representatives.

Members of trade unions and civil society were invited to participate within the CCSC at the Ministry of Foreign Relations after 2003. Before that, participation was limited to the regional level, mainly through informal consultations between the European Commission and CSOs in Brussels. Participation was confined to European organizations, whereas similar initiatives were not present in MERCOSUR.

In sum, the role of trade unions and CSO representatives was almost nil after the launch of trade negotiations with the EU. Only between 2002 and 2004 did their participation become more meaningful, though the limited character of the channels provided by the government resulted in a subordinated pattern of trade politics. Interestingly, unlike the FTAA, negotiations with the EU did not spur massive street protests.

Asymmetries in institutional access deepened in 2003, when businesses were invited to participate in the room next door. Given the complexity and technicality of the issues at stake, large companies and leading businesses were thus consulted constantly during the negotiations and asked to assess proposals. More than 40 years later, what had been a rather common procedure within LAIA and LAFTA was revisited. Though not institutionalized, the practice gradually became routine (interview with UIA executive). However, in the late 1990s and early 2000s, to the extent that this system was not formally enshrined in the legislation, it left businesses room to manoeuvre. Hence, as the interchange of offers gained momentum, especially after 2004, even if they were not formally invited, private representatives attended EU-MERCOSUR government meetings to contact their own counterparts. This business initiative resulted in agreements between particular groups beyond the negotiation table, though they did not prosper as negotiations decelerated and finally came to a halt until 2010.[15]

## Conclusions

Preceded by the preparation of procedures and standards common to all the relevant countries, North-South negotiations thus revealed the importance of coordination and technical expertise for both governments and societal actors from the inception. The increasing breadth and complexity of the trade agenda raised the demand for coordination in policy making and exacerbated the need to develop trade strategies and expertise even further, but the follow-up was slow.

The lack of coordinating mechanisms and technically prepared trading teams in public agencies became more apparent after the launch of North-South negotiations. The CICI's precise intention to enhance coordination between the two main ministries responsible for trade and international negotiations made only a modest impact. Consultation with societal representatives, namely businesses, remained concentrated in the Ministry of Economy. To this end, the CACE offered a formal channel for business people to interact with public officials in that ministry, which thus became the main interlocutor for the private sector. After the closing down of the CACE, the *contratados* assured the stability of these contacts and relations, which were then mainly informal again. To make up for this asymmetry, to a certain extent in response to the strong demands from business organizations, the Ministry of Foreign Relations devised a series of formal mechanisms. These became effective only in 2002. In all, whereas formal consultation mechanisms showed their limitations, businesses still relied on the more traditional informal and personal channels, thus enjoying an extensive institutional architecture, which contrasted with the limited mechanisms available to the broader civil society. In turn, these different institutional designs triggered much more varied patterns of trade politics as depicted in Table 4.2.

Businesses became actively involved in the FTAA and the dealings with the EU even before the launch of negotiations. In both cases, regional networks became a focal point for the definition of preferences and strategies. However, this did not entail a sharp transformation in the strategies deployed, which, in the case of industrialists, were more defensive than offensive. Industrial actors showed a division between those more linked to domestic markets, which in general terms sustained a competitive strategy, and large economic interests for whom these negotiations meant securing market access. For this reason they needed to collaborate in order to speak with one voice and stand up for the preferences of their sectors, and even of their regional counterparts.

*Table 4.2* North-South trade negotiations in Argentina

| | | *State actors* Institutional architecture | *Non-state actors* Strategies | *Trade politics patterns* |
|---|---|---|---|---|
| **FTAA** | *Business* | Extensive | Collaborative: COPAL, CILFA, COPAL, SRA | Cooperative |
| | | | Competitive: UIA, FAA | Pressured |
| | *Civil society* | Limited | Collaborative: Asociación Conciencia, CEDHA, FOCO, Poder Ciudadano | Subordinated |
| | | | Competitive: CGT, CTA, FOCO, SERPAJ | Resistant |
| **EU** | *Business* | Extensive | Collaborative: CILFA, CIQyP, COPAL, SRA | Cooperative |
| | | | Competitive: UIA, sectoral associations (clothing, footwear, textiles) | Pressured |
| | *Civil society* | Limited | Collaborative: trade unions, NGOs | Subordinated |

Source: *Author-created*

Furthermore, this strategy relied on the provision of solid technical expertise, proving that these were fundamental resources for gaining access to trade negotiations, especially those involving deeper agendas such as North-South initiatives. Moreover, these resources constituted the basis of a new form of working relationship with public officials and trade diplomats. Though not fully formalized, the arrangement led to a pattern of cooperative trade politics. Clearly, these coordination and technical resources were not evenly distributed across the business community and even less in civil society.

Trade unions and civil society became involved at a rather late stage in both negotiations, especially when compared with businesses. Still, their role and strategies varied between the FTAA and the initiative with the EU. Both agendas aimed at promoting trade liberalization and advancing harmonization and convergence towards WTO-plus commitments. However, whereas the FTAA became a site of public debate, contestation and heated controversy, negotiations with the EU did not spur massive protests. Hence, the FTAA crystallized a division between insiders and outsiders. In time the limited institutional architecture devised for the participation of civil society further deepened this cleavage. Whereas outsiders firmly refused to debate and resorted to a competitive strategy, insiders attended the meetings summoned by the Foreign Relations Ministry and collaborated with the government even when it might compromise their demands. Despite being a novelty, the creation of formal mechanisms, as in the case of the CCSC, had limited practical impact. In all, North-South trade negotiations stand out for the highly diverse and complex collective strategies deployed by non-state representatives.

## Multilateral Trade Negotiations under the WTO

Unilateral trade liberalization was already completed before the conclusion of the UR. Hence, WTO commitments did not affect tariffs, which were at about 35 per cent. Rather, they locked in previous reforms. Moreover, multilateral undertakings entailed new commitments. They included the reform of intellectual property laws according to the Agreement on the Trade Related Aspects of Intellectual Property Rights (TRIPs), and this directly impinged on services, investments, government procurement, among other matters. In addition measures incompatible with the Trade-Related Investment Measures (TRIMs) were eliminated and subsidies reduced. Together with the legal formalization of the trade regime through the WTO dispute settlement mechanism, these changes put strong pressure on decision making. In addition, at this time of active regionalism, the new multilateral trade regime entailed an important shift in the country's priorities and guidelines regarding the WTO.

The WTO Agreement on Agriculture mandated a new round of multilateral negotiations to be launched in Seattle in November 1999, but the delegations failed to reach consensus on the agenda. Massive street protests led to the negotiations being postponed until the following Ministerial Conference two years later. The EU recommended that this should be called the 'Doha

Development Round' to emphasize the leading role of less developed countries in these talks, which were designed to put development and poverty reduction at the centre. Although they were initially intended to be completed by 31 December 2004, negotiations remain stalled because of marked divergences across global South and global North countries and major obstacles about farming trade liberalization.

The end of the UR and more prominently the commitment to reopen negotiations on agriculture introduced important transformations within the public sector and its relationship with the private world, which deepened in the aftermath of the failure of the III Ministerial Conference in Seattle and after the launch of the Doha Round.

First, the acceptance of WTO conflict resolution procedures led to the creation of a quasi-independent body: the National Commission of Foreign Trade (CNCE). Under the aegis of the Ministry of Economy, the CNCE was responsible for handling business petitions for trade relief against unfair foreign practices affecting the domestic market. Even if technically independent, the Ministry of Economy was responsible for appointing the CNCE board, which left the agency often subject to pressure, power and politics. The CNCE also established a rather fluid relation with the private sector. Besides responding to industrialists' requirements regarding protectionist measures, it provided technical assistance on international trade policy.

Second, in 2002, as the multipolar trade strategy was taking off, Argentina became enthusiastically involved in the Doha Round.[16] During the UR, Argentina's participation was aimed at consolidating domestic economic reforms and the Ministry of Economy was thus mainly responsible (Bouzas and Soltz 2002). In contrast, the country's strategy was now based on diversified and reciprocal criteria. Moreover, the Marrakesh WTO agreement included a commitment to reopen services and agricultural negotiations to improve market access and reduce trade-distorting subsidies. In 2001, these issues became part of the Doha agenda. Public agricultural agencies, including the Ministry of Economy, undertook important measures to deal effectively with it.

The Secretariat of Agriculture became immersed in a process of capacity building. A small group of young economists was trained in state-of-the-art impact assessments with the aim of leading technical discussions within the WTO in relation to formulas that could lessen trade distortions in agriculture. Interestingly, some of these economists had attended the ministerial institute that Domingo Cavallo created in 1994 to train professionals for the Ministry of Economy. Funded by the WB, this program was an attempt to reproduce the ISEN model, which had been in place within the Ministry of Foreign Relations since 1963. Now, as the country's strategy placed greater emphasis on reciprocity in assessing concessions, public officials were compelled to deepen their technical work.

The Ministry of Foreign Relations undertook a similar process. To improve its technical ability, after 2002 the CEI focused strongly on multilateral negotiations. Apart from more general research papers, it produced negotiation documents to develop the strategy of the then director, Néstor Stancanelli, one of Argentina's negotiators during the UR. In time, CEI's experts were part of the delegation to WTO Ministerial Meetings to offer direct technical support to trade diplomats (interview with CEI expert).

Collaboration with the private sector was also part of this learning process. Moreover, business interest in the multilateral arena grew after the launch of the Doha Round, which contrasted with their rather modest participation during the UR. Still, the degree of engagement varied across sectors.

Industrial sectors imbued with a short term perspective viewed the WTO negotiations as tedious because they had no immediate impact on their activities (interview with CERA representative). They also assumed that multilateral talks were largely resistant to their influence, given that Argentina represented only a small portion of world trade and had to negotiate with 150 other countries. The lack of transparency and information also contributed to this perception, while traditional lobbying strategies were no longer of use in demanding such information. Finally, discussions at the WTO were highly technical and abstract (interview with middle-ranking trade diplomat), which required expertise and technical abilities that many business people still lacked.

Industrial interests in the UIA deployed a defensive strategy that contrasted with that of other actors. Given its interest in promoting their members' competitiveness by offering specialized advice regarding exports and international trade, CERA frequently consulted with public officials on trade rules and commitments and their impact on exports (interview with CERA representative). Other chambers were also actively involved in the definition of a negotiating position or at the negotiation table itself. Again, through their cooperative relationship with the Secretariat of Trade and the Foreign Office, the CIQyP was part of the official ministerial delegation, providing technical support to negotiators and participating during the negotiations of the Non-Agricultural Market Access (NAMA) 11 (interview with CIQyP executive).

The failed WTO Ministerial Conference in Seattle was certainly a turning point for agriculture. Moreover, it offered an important incentive to invest in its own leadership and institutional abilities.

In 1999, the Buenos Aires Grain Exchange, the Rosario Board of Trade and the Bahía Blanca Grain Exchange created the International Negotiation on Agriculture Institute (INAI), an initiative that then gained the support of other sectoral associations, including CIARA and the Chamber of Grain Exporters. The objective was to develop strong advocacy structures based on adequate technical abilities to match the enhanced sophistication of the multilateral trade agenda (interview with CIARA representative).

Just after the Seattle conference, the INAI began to work steadily with the Secretariat of Agriculture and also with the Ministry of Foreign Relations in the assessment of negotiating proposals, the analysis of standards, the provision of technical input in legal controversies and the presentation of detailed information on the CAP, among others (interview with CIARA representative). In time, it developed a cooperative relationship with the technical and professional experts in the Secretariat of Agriculture. As interaction with public officials deepened, the INAI expanded its research agenda to other sectors and implemented an in-house training scheme through the so-called 'Working Tables', where agribusiness representatives and public officials from various agencies discussed sectoral proposals.

This collaboration with the public sector was further strengthened when the INAI became the leader of the agribusinesses and coordinated a common stance for the WTO Ministerial Conferences (Cancun 2003 and Hong Kong 2005). Additionally, the INAI was part of the room next door arrangement to make sure no agreement was made unless their main demands were accepted. They also attempted to coordinate a common position with industrialists but with no success.

In fact, the Doha Round revived the traditional cleavages between industry and agriculture. The former assumed a defensive attitude based on the idea that the negative costs of this negotiation round would be borne by medium countries such as Argentina. While they asked the government for a more active industrial policy and a clearer international strategy, public officials highlighted the fact that the sector usually failed to take a unified position regarding negotiations on tariffs or on market access for non-agricultural products (interviews with UIA executive and senior Economy Ministry official, 2).

In contrast, agriculture had a positive and monolithic vision of WTO negotiations and pushed for further reforms. It thus deepened its cooperative relationship with public officials, especially in the Secretariat of Agriculture. In time, the INAI and the sectoral associations behind it had further incentives to invest in their organizations and promote their institutional leadership and capabilities. However, this close and active relationship was still based on informal channels and mechanisms, the same informalities that existed between public officials and industrial actors.

Finally, civil society's involvement in multilateral trade negotiations was limited and focused on issues relating to trade liberalization in services, including health and education among others. NGOs developed different activities aimed at raising awareness about the impacts of trade liberalization on daily life and organized meetings and seminars to develop technical capacity and to produce a common stance on these issues (interview with FOCO representative). Only a few NGOs assumed more direct participation, as in the case of CEDHA, which was present at the Doha Ministerial Conference. Unlike other countries, the Argentine government did not include NGO representatives in the official delegation. Furthermore, NGOs and civil society lacked frequent and ready access to discussions of multilateral issues, and their participation was restricted to the more general discussions within the CCSC. Thus, they valued the fact that during the Doha Ministerial Conference, they had the chance to discuss some issues relating to trade, human rights, and development with one of the public officials. However, this was merely a presentation of their proposals and suggestions rather than an interchange of ideas and positions (interview with CEDHA representative). Trade unions had practically no relationship with public officials regarding multilateral negotiations. Nevertheless, during the launch of the Doha Round and in other meetings where the WTO agenda included a particularly relevant issue, the International Trade Union Confederation (ITUC), the main worldwide trade union organization, acted in representation of both the CGT and the CTA (interview with CGT representative).[17]

## Conclusions

The launch of the Doha Round presented state and societal actors with an agenda that required enhanced coordination and coherence and highly technical competence. Furthermore, multilateral negotiations confronted public officials and trade diplomats with solidly equipped counterparts, both in number, capabilities and expertise. Business representatives also had to fulfil such requirements if they intended to participate effectively in the domestic trade policy process.

Argentina's strategy at the WTO and the Doha Round demanded analytical and informational capacities. Apart from the creation of the CNCE, the Ministry of Economy now relied on a group of young economists trained at their in-house postgraduate institute. The Ministry of Foreign Affairs initiated a similar learning process, as the CEI focused on multilateral negotiations and provided technical studies and direct input in policy making by attending WTO negotiation rounds.

Additionally, in order to develop their technical expertise further, public officials pursued a closer relationship with the private sector, though with varying success. Whereas officials and *contratados* in the Ministry of Economy established a mutually beneficial close working relationship with agricultural organizations, a similar liaison proved difficult to achieve with industry under the UIA and other sectoral associations that developed a more competitive strategy and failed to provide the technical information needed by state representatives. However, again differences emerged in the industrial sectors. Those already integrated into regional and international flows and closely collaborating with the government were part of the national delegation and had access to negotiations.

One of the biggest changes to trade politics was the new, non-traditional emphasis on the developmental dimension of trade as established during the Doha Round. However, trade unions and civil society lacked access to the domestic policy process. Furthermore, they were not part of the national delegation. Given their limited resources, both informational and organizational, their participation was more strongly influenced by their adherence to international networks.

The relationships between state, labour and civil society representatives hence remained thin and largely informal, the limits of the institutional architecture being especially striking when compared with the mechanisms—both formal and informal—on which businesses could rely to promote their claims and demands. All of this led to different patterns of trade politics, as detailed in Table 4.3.

*Table 4.3* Multilateral trade negotiations under the WTO in Argentina

| | | *State actors* Institutional architecture | *Non-state actors* Strategies | *Trade politics patterns* |
|---|---|---|---|---|
| **Doha Round** | *Business* | Extensive | Collaborative: CIQyP, INAI, SRA, sectoral associations (automotive) | Cooperative |
| | | | Competitive: UIA, sectoral associations (textiles, footwear) | Pressured |
| | *Civil society* | Limited | Collaborative: trade unions, NGOs | Subordinated |

Source: *Author-created*

## Notes

1 In 1991, the National Meat Board and the National Grain Board, created after the 1930 crisis to regulate meat and grain export trade respectively, were dissolved.
2 This reform changed the name of the Chancellery to 'Ministry of Foreign Affairs, International Trade and Worship'.
3 'Menem quiere liderar el MERCOSUR' and 'Días claves para un acuerdo', Economía, La Nación, 25 March and 17 June 1996, respectively.
4 'Comienza a regir la asociación de Chile con los países del MERCOSUR', Economía, La Nación, 30 September 1996.
5 For Argentina, the agreement with Chile was a means for consolidating peace, getting access to the Pacific and strengthening MERCOSUR's position within the FTAA, while also balancing Brazil's influence in MERCOSUR. Brazil, on the other hand, perceived it as a way of consolidating the bloc that it aspired to lead, especially when facing future negotiations in the region.
6 Created in 1980, LAIA replaced LAFTA and was intended to promote the gradual and progressive establishment of a common Latin American market. For further details on this first phase of regionalism, see Bianculli (2016).
7 Signed in 1986, the PICE was the first step towards integration with Brazil. It entailed the negotiation of sectoral agreements to stimulate bilateral trade on the grounds of complementarities and political symmetry, to foster efficiency in key economic sectors through bilateral investment flows, and to promote cooperation in areas of critical importance for joint economic development.
8 'Menem intentará atraer a México', Política, La Nación, 26 November 1997; 'México-MERCOSUR se firma en diciembre' and 'México no entrará en el MERCOSUR', Economía, La Nación, 13 June and 12 December 1997.
9 'México quiere aumentar el intercambio comercial', Economía, La Nación, 13 November 1996.
10 'Negocian un acuerdo con Chile', Economía, La Nación, 27 November 1996.
11 'ALCA: las cartas sobre la mesa', Opinión, La Nación, 14 November 2002.
12 Whereas ultimate decision-making authority over the FTAA rested with the heads of state and their governments, substantive negotiating took place within the Negotiating Groups, a Consultative Group and different Special Committees.
13 'Discrepan el MERCOSUR y Estados Unidos', Economía, La Nación, 14 May 1997.
14 'El gremialismo se une en la protesta', Economía, La Nación, 6 April 2001.

15 The suspension of trade negotiations in 2004 did not bring a loss of EU interest in the region. Relations continued through ministerial and informal technical meetings intended to deepen the agenda on political dialogue and cooperation (Botto and Bianculli 2011). Negotiations were then re-launched at the EU-Latin America and the Caribbean (EU-LAC) Summit (Madrid, May 2010), and in 2015, during the EU-MERCOSUR Ministerial Meeting that took place in the margins of the recently created EU-CELAC (EU-Community of Latin American and Caribbean States) Summit, both parties exchanged general information on their respective market access offers. In April 2016, the EU and MERCOSUR agreed to exchange fresh market access offers in the second week of May.

16 Such activism showed ups and downs. Argentina had confirmed one of the vice-presidencies of the Doha meeting that would elaborate the negotiating mandate of the new round, but failed to send representatives given the economic, social and political turmoil of December 2001.

17 Collaboration between trade union confederations of the NAMA 11 countries, which deals with negotiations for the reduction of tariffs of non-agricultural products, resulted in the creation of the NAMA 11 trade unions. This alliance includes organizations in Argentina, Brazil, India, Indonesia, Namibia, Philippines, South Africa and Tunisia, and have made several proposals regarding the potential impacts of trade liberalization on the industrial development and employment prospects of their economies (Busser 2007, Hilary 2015).

## References

Bianculli, A. C. (2016). Latin America, in T. A. Börzel and T. Risse (Ed.) *The Oxford Handbook of Comparative Regionalism*. Oxford, Oxford University Press: 154–177.

Botto, M. (2004). Los nuevos regionalismos y la acción colectiva transnacional, *Perfiles Latinoamericanos* 25: 9–41.

Botto, M. and A. C. Bianculli (2009). The Case of Argentine Research in the Building of Regional Integration, in D. Tussie (Ed.) *The Politics of Trade: The Role of Research in Trade Policy and Negotiation*. Leiden, Brill Academic Publishers: 83–120.

Botto, M. and A. C. Bianculli (2011). Comparative Asymmetric Trade Negotiations in the Southern Cone: FTAA and EU-MERCOSUR, in S. Bilal, P. De Lombaerde and D. Tussie (Ed.) *Asymmetric Trade Negotiations*. Aldershot, Ashgate Publishing: 83–120.

Bouzas, R. and H. Soltz (2005). Argentina and GATS: A Study on the Domestic Determinants of GATS Commitments, in P. Gallagher, P. Low and A. L. Stoller (Ed.) *Managing the Challenges of WTO Participation*. Cambridge, Cambridge University Press: 38–52.

Busser, E. (2007). Why NAMA Is a Trade Union Issue: Negotiations, Policy Implications and Trade Union Responses, *Labour, Capital and Society* 40(1/2): 160–189.

Campbell, J., Ed. (1999). *Mercosur: Entre la Realidad y la Utopia*. Buenos Aires, Centro de Economía Internacional-Grupo Editor Latinoamericano.

CEI (2004). *Oportunidades y amenazas para la Argentina en el comercio sur-sur: Estudios del CEI N° 8*. Buenos Aires, Centro de Estudios Internacionales.

Gargiulo, G. (2003). *Estudios sobre el sector agroalimentario: Componente B: Redes agroalimentarias. Tramas. B-5: La cooperación público-privada en la política agroalimentaria. Situación actual y perspectivas*. Buenos Aires, Comisión Económica para América Latina y el Caribe (CEPAL).

Hilary, J. (2015). European Trade Unions and Free Trade: Between International Solidarity and Perceived Self-Interest, in A. Bieler, B. Ciccaglione, J. Hilary and I. Lindberg (Ed.) *Free Trade and Transnational Labour*. New York, Routledge: 47–57.

Jacobs, E. and M. Maldonado (2005). Civil Society in Argentina: Opportunities and Challenges for National and Transnational Organisation, *Journal of Latin American Studies* 37(1): 141–172.

Portella de Castro, M. S. (1999) Brasil: informe sobre a questão laboral e as estratégias sindicais. Research Report for the Project 'Estrategias sindicales frente a los procesos de globalización e integración regional: un análisis comparado TLCAN-MERCOSUR.' São Paulo, mimeo.

Redrado, M. (2003). *Exportar para crecer*. Buenos Aires, Editorial Planeta.

# 5 Trade Politics in Chile

Chile is notable for its stable trade policy and the rapid negotiation of trade agreements with countries and regions all over the world. At the time of writing, it has 24 agreements with 63 countries that cover 94 per cent of the country's total exports (DIRECON 2015).[1] Trade policy has remained constant through time but especially across regimes and governments. The dictatorship of Augusto Pinochet introduced radical deregulation and increasing liberalization on a unilateral basis while also participating in multilateral negotiations under the GATT.

Since 1990, the Concertación committed to this liberalization and export-led strategy, which was then complemented with multilateral negotiations and bilateral and plurilateral agreements under the label of so-called 'open regionalism'. Apart from achieving further preferential liberalization while also widening sectors, issues and countries (Sáez and Valdés 1999), the objective has been to bring Chile back onto the regional and international arena. Consequently, Chile has become involved in numerous trade negotiations since 1990: first, in South-South initiatives, given that the United States rejected its attempt to enter negotiations for an FTA, and later on in North-South agreements, while simultaneously negotiating at the WTO.

## The '*Barrio*' and South-South Regional Negotiations

After 17 years of isolation, the Concertación viewed trade agreements as a key instrument for opening new markets, but mainly for strengthening political ties. Despite underlying differences within the Executive, under the auspices of the first democratic government led by Patricio Aylwin (1990–1994), Chile veered towards trade agreements with Latin American countries to reinstate the country in '*el barrio*' (the neighbourhood).[2] Agreements included ones with Mexico and MERCOSUR in the 1990s and China 15 years later.

### *Trade Negotiations with Mexico: A Stepping-Stone towards Regional Reengagement*

In 1990, Chile launched negotiations with Mexico to establish a broad agreement as part of the second export phase, which entailed productive reconversion, development policies and compensation measures for sensitive sectors. However, the most relevant objective was to deepen recently reestablished diplomatic relations between the countries.[3]

Negotiations turned out to be more complex and challenging than originally expected, given strong business opposition and the limited abilities of public officials and trade diplomats. Despite these hindrances, Chile and Mexico signed an ECA in 1991, which quickly showed positive results in terms of trade and investment dynamics. Chilean and Mexican businesses then demanded that the Administrative Commission accelerate the tariff reduction schedule (Porras 2003).

Despite this 'happy ending', the launch of negotiations with Mexico seriously challenged the government. First, the Executive needed to overcome differences among ministries regarding the orientation of the trade strategy to build its institutional leadership over trade policy and regional and international negotiations.

The Ministry of Foreign Affairs was the leader in this rush towards the diversification of trade relations and, together with the Ministry of Economy, advocated negotiations with *el barrio*. In contrast, the Ministry of Finance prioritized an FTA with the United States and Chile's incorporation in NAFTA, even if this entailed relegating Latin America to a lower priority.[4] The president tilted the scales in favour of agreements with Mexico and the region. Moreover, just after the launch of negotiations, the Executive established a complex division of labour across ministries. The Ministry of Foreign Affairs was responsible for negotiations with Latin America, together with the Ministry of Economy, which was also in charge of Asia-Pacific and the EU, whereas the Ministry of Finance was to focus on North America. Coordination became a priority. Until then, international trade policy had been the shared responsibility of the ministries of Finance, Economy, and Foreign Relations—a situation inherited from the dictatorship. Within the latter, the General Directorate for International Economic Relations (DIRECON) was responsible for negotiating trade agreements, including those under LAIA in the 1980s, and ProChile supported the diversification of national firms into new export products and markets.

Second, as the then minister of finance, Alejandro Foxley Rioseco (1993:50), noted, the ambitious and multifaceted trade strategy required large numbers of public officials to develop technical abilities. To this end, the DIRECON hired young and well-educated economists, thus further promoting economists as '*a new dominant class*' (interview with senior trade expert) within the public administration as these reached ministerial positions, including highly political ones. However, and since most of these young professionals had no practical experience, the government retained some of the key negotiators from the past dictatorship who had a leading role during negotiations with Mexico (interview with SOFOFA executive). Thus, the DIRECON combined the expertise of old public officials with the knowledge of young professionals.

Finally, the government established new organizational procedures to enhance participation and transparency in trade policy decision making. By 1990, the newly set up Bilateral Council for Trade and Investment brought together state, business and labour to debate the new trade agenda and to look for consensual policy options. Still, the new democratic administration was more attentive to businesses as it had to respond to a double imperative. First, it had to gain business confidence by showing commitment to the market-based economy, and second, it needed to rally their support for the new trade strategy. As negotiations advanced, however, these various mechanisms proved insufficient.

Businesses exhibited weaknesses, despite their experience during the 1980s when they enjoyed access to trade decision making. The DIRECON not only consulted private groups extensively about the concession exchanges within LAIA, but business was then part of Chile's delegation. Rather than sitting in the room next door, two representatives of the CPC sat at the negotiating table next to public officials (interview with SOFOFA executive).

In contrast, in the early 1990s the private sector was not capable of responding to the government's requirements (interview with SOFOFA executive). Consultations were mainly with the CPC, which showed two important limitations. First, the CPC provided a nucleus for second-degree organizations and had no direct contact with industrialists and producers. Second, it relied on limited human resources and expertise to elaborate proposals, suggestions and even reports on vulnerabilities and sensitivities in due time and manner. Furthermore, private actors strongly opposed negotiations with Mexico. Based on an over-estimation of the negative impact the agreement could have, especially on agriculture, they presented a list of 224 products (representing 30 per cent of Mexican exports to Chile) to be excluded from the agreement. Yet disagreements between business and government went well beyond this particular negotiation. Businesses were still suspicious of the centre-left coalition and felt that the new trade strategy distorted unilateral liberalization.

The SNA was one of the more fervent opponents. Not only did the strategy distort the tariff policy, but it also exposed Chilean products to unfair competition in subsidizing countries. The CPC seconded the SNA, though with less intensity, and called for investments in infrastructure, human resources and state institutions before signing new agreements (Montero and Federici 1999). Only non-traditional exporters took a positive stance.

Trade unions were then part of the recently created Bilateral Council for Trade and Investment. Still, they were not actively involved in the formulation of trade policy. After the launch of negotiations with Mexico, Chile was undergoing democratic restoration, which entailed greater expectations regarding civil society participation. However, trade unions and CSOs were recovering from the 17-year dictatorship. Whereas business associations had enjoyed access to decision makers during the dictatorship, trade unions were subjected to all kinds of legal prohibitions and persecutions that affected their activities and level of affiliation. CSOs, with their non-conformist and anti-establishment attitudes during the 1980s, now had to reorient their discourse and activities to adapt to the new political times. Consequently, the various forms of social organization and mobilization focused on the reestablishment of rights within the process of democratic restoration (Rojas Aravena and Pey 2003). In all, trade policy formulation and negotiations with Mexico did not rank high on the agendas of trade unions and CSOs in the early 1990s.

### *Trade Negotiations with MERCOSUR: A Long and Highly Debated Process*

Relations between Chile and MERCOSUR evolved gradually over a number of years. By 1991, the bloc invited Chile to sign the Treaty of Asunción, an offer that raised opposing views within the government. The Executive emphasized—just as in the case of Mexico—the political and economic relevance of this agreement, which would contribute to Chile's political re-integration in the region and enhance the move towards a second export phase. Opposition came from the Ministry of Finance, which viewed the agreement as conditioning unilateral trade liberalization, especially regarding access to third countries. Economists, having an increasing ascendency within the government, resisted this deal because of the high economic instability of MERCOSUR countries and the dubious prospects for the new bloc (Porras 2003). The Ministries of Foreign Affairs and Economy responded rather timidly to these objections despite advocating deeper relations with neighbouring countries. Finally, considerations of economic autonomy prevailed over political ones, and Chile declined the invitation to join MERCOSUR.

Economic factors dominated again when Chile agreed to negotiate in June 1994. First, the new administration led by Eduardo Frei (1994–2000) feared that the creation of the MERCOSUR customs union would negatively affect the economy because of the elimination of LAIA preferential tariffs. Second, the trade balance had grown immensely (from 2,100 million dollars in 1991 to 4,500 million dollars in 1995), and Chilean FDI had expanded in the four countries, especially in Argentina. Finally, MERCOSUR appeared solvent at the time and well on track to consolidation and therefore a potential ally in the restructuring of international trade alliances. Although Chile's proposal was limited to a less encompassing ECA, the initiative had to pull down domestic economic resistances and protectionist barricades. Pressures from within and from below put the institutional structure and procedures for mediation to severe test.

Frei's administration was committed to stimulating the new regionalism model further,[5] thus promoting the consistency of the formulation, negotiation and implementation of trade liberalization. This certainly demanded greater coordination among public agencies but also stronger abilities. Dealing effectively with businesses was another priority.

Based on this diagnosis, the government made DIRECON responsible for the coordination of negotiations. Hence, DIRECON underwent essential institutional transformations, including the creation of different regional departments (MERCOSUR, EU, Asia-Pacific), together with thematic ones, e.g. market access, IPRs and environmental issues. Changes within the organization were part of a more extensive reform program resembling the Mexican Secretariat of Commerce and Industrial Promotion (SECOFI) and the office of the United States Trade Representative (USTR) (Jara 2001). Three new mechanisms were created to promote further coordination among state actors.

First, the Inter-Ministerial Committee on International Economic Negotiations brought together the ministers of foreign affairs, finance, economy and the Ministry General Secretariat of the Presidency (SEGPRES)[6] as it attempted to enhance trade policy coordination while also advising the president and making policy proposals. Two other committees were to support the work of the Inter-Ministerial Committee.

Second, at a more technical level, the Committee of Negotiators was in charge of examining the evolution of trade negotiations. This Committee interacted with chief negotiators, trade diplomats, public officials and non-state personnel, including consultants, experts, academics and businesses. Third, though excluded from this mechanism, trade unions were part of the Committee for the Private Sector Participation, which was composed of the ministers of economy, foreign affairs, finance, agriculture and the SEGPRES. Certainly, the inclusion of the Ministry of Agriculture showed the relevance of this agenda in regional and international negotiations, as was the case with MERCOSUR. Two business and labour delegates from the CPC and the CUT respectively were involved, together with three people of recognized expertise in international negotiations who had been directly appointed by the president.

These institutional transformations aimed at strengthening and consolidating the institutional leadership and capabilities of the government, on the one hand, and its relations with society, mainly business people, on the other. Still, the launch of negotiations with MERCOSUR revealed the fragility of existing institutional mechanisms, but also businesses' weak abilities.

Broad sectors of businesses were rather sceptical. Even if the negotiation agenda did not restrict Chile's independence with respect to trade policy, large companies advocated deepening unilateral liberalization. Moreover, they preferred an agreement with the United States. Yet this dubious stance failed to overcome the enthusiasm of industrialists under the SOFOFA and the Association of Manufacture and Services Exporters (ASEXMA), who resorted to informal and traditional lobby strategies to promote the agreement even before negotiations were formally launched. Their strategy, seconded by the agro-industry, some niches of the fishing industry, the mining sector and other traditional manufacturers, including textiles and shoes, aimed at avoiding a partial agreement, as was the case with Bolivia, where SNA preferences predominated at the expense of more broadly based exporters (Porras 2003).

The service sector under the National Corporation for Exporters (CNE), which was created by ASEXMA to include the representation of non-industrial exporters, and the Services Committee within the CNC also favoured far-reaching integration with MERCOSUR, together with the Chilean Construction Chamber (CChC) and the Chilean Association of Banks and Financial Institutions (ABIF). In all, as these sectors acknowledged the irreversibility of the new trade strategy, they were now interested in promoting their own preferences and agendas.

Opposition stemmed from agriculture, though with nuances. Non-traditional agricultural exporters proposed the creation of complementary programs to compensate for the negative effects of the agreement and to modernize and improve the sector's competitiveness. The SNA highlighted the potentially massive economic and social costs for traditional agriculture and demanded the exclusion of all traditional products, which represented most of MERCOSUR exports to Chile. Moreover, it refused to participate through available institutional mechanisms, which included representation by the CPC at the Committee for the Private Sector Participation and direct access to the Ministry of Agriculture through the National Council for Agriculture Development. In fact, the SNA resorted to lobbying the Congress with public demonstrations and even protests through the media.

The SNA gained the support of the CPC, which proposed the creation of compensating measures and phasing-out schemes, while still backing the agreement with MERCOSUR. To counter the CPC attempt at balancing the protectionist concerns of agriculture with the more aggressive stance of SOFOFA and ASEXMA, the latter two resorted to informal mechanisms to promote their free trade agendas. However, only ASEXMA exhibited relevant institutional leadership and capabilities given that since its creation in 1985, it had deployed a strong export-oriented strategy. As Chile faced the first South-South negotiations, ASEXMA attempted to reach agreements with its regional counterparts before the formal launch (Bull 2008). This more open and aggressive attitude towards free trade led to frequent clashes with SOFOFA, which only recently had adopted the FTA canon and lacked relevant expertise. Negotiations with MERCOSUR revealed the significance of the CPC in harmonizing opposing sectoral views and to overcoming businesses' technical limitations. The SOFOFA then acknowledged that they had to develop and enhance their technical skills if they were to become the government's major interlocutor on trade negotiations (interview with SOFOFA executive). The SNA also became aware of this requirement, even if it managed to get compensatory funding from the government after the MERCOSUR agreement.

The participation of labour and civil society was low after the launch of negotiations with MERCOSUR. Despite being part of the Committee for Private Sector Participation, the role of labour in trade policy making was negligible until the late 1990s. Different elements account for this. First, the movement of labour suffered from structural problems after years of proscription and repression. Second, unions were then deeply involved in domestic debates, about such matters as labour reform, which businesses strongly opposed, since they resisted the idea of modernizing labour relations. Finally, labour lacked the technical abilities to participate effectively in trade policy decisions. However, both trade unions and NGOs—mainly, consumers' and environmental organizations—valued the agreement with MERCOSUR as this could impact positively on SMEs and thus on employment, whereas environmental and consumers' organizations thought it would promote and enhance domestic regulations and the domestic visibility and legitimacy of these agendas. Moreover, the agreement could open a window for working with similar organizations in MERCOSUR countries, promoting collaboration and information sharing (Carnevali 1999).

### *Trade Negotiations with China: A Pioneer Agreement*

In January 2005, Chile launched negotiations for an FTA with China. Some months earlier, prior to the Asia Pacific Economic Cooperation (APEC) Summit (Santiago, November 2004),[7] both countries expressed their desire to strengthen bilateral trade relations. In 1970, under Allende's presidency, Chile was the first Latin American country to establish full diplomatic relations with the Asian giant, which were maintained during the dictatorship. In 2002, they announced their interest in establishing a wide cooperative relationship. Thus Chile became the first country in the region to seal an agreement with China, which had become one of its top five export markets by 2000. Through extensive experience in trade negotiations combined with the simplicity of the bilateral FTA, which mainly focused on goods and mutual tariff reductions, Chile was able to complete the agreement in less than one year.[8]

Bilateral trade negotiations with China took off 15 years after the negotiation with Mexico. By then, Chile's strategy was well on track. Public officials, trade diplomats and business interests publicly acknowledged its benefits. Furthermore, this active engagement in international negotiations had improved the negotiating capabilities of the state and businesses and to a lesser extent, those of trade unions and civil society.

Ricardo Lagos (2000–2006) led negotiations with China. Shortly after coming into office, he issued an executive resolution recommending the establishment of institutional mechanisms to promote citizen involvement in decision making, to enhance transparency and accountability. Though not binding, the Presidential Guidelines for Citizen Participation triggered different participatory initiatives at the national and local levels. The Ministry of Foreign Affairs introduced various mechanisms to promote the participation of institutions other than business, which already relied on extensive institutional access.

However, negotiations with the largest world economy of the twenty-first century went almost unnoticed and did not attract the attention of the media or others for whom they might have been relevant. Furthermore, the Congress approved the agreement unanimously after a rather short debate, compared with the high controversies triggered by other agreements such as the one with the United States, which required 27 Congressional sessions (interview with former senior trade official).

Businesses had also undergone transformations since negotiations with Mexico and MERCOSUR. Leading business associations had assumed a firm free trade stance except for some particular sectors, which were mostly within the world of SMEs. These played a very active role just after the launch of negotiations with China. By then they were part of the Public-Private Council for Export Development (CPPDE), which was created in 2003 after negotiations with the United States and as a response to the private sector, which demanded formal dialogue (Sáez 2005).

To a certain extent, the CPPDE was to replace the Committee for the Private Sector Participation that lay dormant after 2000. The CPPDE offered a space for information exchange on Chile's export strategy and worked through thematic groups dealing with trade facilitation, product promotion, international penetration, export promotion, investment and tourism. Both state and business valued this mechanism as it allowed key governmental branches in the economic and foreign relations areas and private companies linked to exports and foreign investment to formulate policy recommendations (interviews with former senior trade official and with SOFOFA executive). However, as the CPPDE further strengthened relations between state and businesses, as represented by SOFOFA, it excluded the National Confederation for Medium Sized, Small and Micro Industry, Service and Craftsmen of Chile (CONUPIA), trade unions and civil society. In sum, formal channels turned out to be insufficient. Moreover, the high resistance and strong opposition of sectors that until then had openly advocated free trade overwhelmed the institutional mechanisms.

Negotiations with China reversed the dominant business logic. Whereas previously almost all businesses demanded an open market for all imports, when negotiating with the Asian giant, about 30 per cent or 40 per cent now called for protection (interview with DIRECON official). Furthermore, this negotiation pitted industrialists against agriculturists, and so SOFOFA faced serious internal disagreements.

Whereas sectors that had traditionally maintained a free trade position—i.e. textiles, footwear, iron and steel—were now demanding protection, agricultural interests under the SOFOFA refused to be used as bargaining chips in the bilateral negotiations and urged the association to look after their preferences as well. This was the case with the SNA, the Federation of Chilean Fruit Growers (Fedefrutas), SONAMI, together with the Chilean Association of Fruit Exporters (ASOEX) and the Chilean Association of Poultry Producers (APA), who favoured the FTA, as it would lower trade barriers and transport costs. In contrast, industrialists argued that they had already paid heavily to sustain traditional agriculture, for example through the variable price band system for sugar, wheat and oil. Hence, demanding the exclusion of some particular and strategic goods from the tariff reduction scheme was fair (interview with SOFOFA executive).[9] The media were important battlegrounds for business disputes and for petitioning the government (interview with SOFOFA executive).

Torn between protectionism and free trade, SOFOFA thus failed to come up with a unique proposal, and the DIRECON had to contact sectoral associations to elaborate preference lists. The final agreement catered for some of businesses' sensibilities. While the final deal might have affected market access for agricultural and agro-industrial products,[10] in the end it involved establishing trade rules and disciplines. Consequently, it enhanced Chile's protection vis-à-vis Chinese competition in areas relevant for industrialists (interview with SOFOFA executive).

CONUPIA strongly opposed an agreement with China, as overall they rejected the Concertación's trade diversification strategy, which responded to large businesses' preferences. They advocated, instead, an approach focused on Latin America and *el barrio*, which would most directly cater for SMEs (interview with CONUPIA executive).

SMEs were consulted after the launch of negotiations with China, but they were then too weak to influence the government. Being systematically excluded from trade decision making, organizations representing SMEs appeared impermeable to the professionalization process that the SOFOFA and other peak sectoral associations had undergone since the 1990s. This exclusion, together with the high fragmentation of the sector, negatively affected their institutional leadership and trade abilities. These asymmetries were especially evident when visiting the premises of these organizations. The offices of the SOFOFA in the Industry Building (*Edificio de la Industria*) were located in Las Condes, Santiago's new business district in an area inhabited primarily by upper-mid to high-income families; in contrast, CONUPIA occupied a less fashionable and rather run-down building in the city centre.

Trade unions also resisted negotiations with China, though their involvement came at rather a late stage. First, the CUT criticized the agreement in view not only of the violations of human rights in that country—based on a report by Amnesty International—but also regarding the impact of the agreement on particular sectors, namely, textiles, footwear, metal industries, and small and medium agricultural producers.[11] Second, without fully rejecting the agreement, the recently created National Union of Workers (UNT) led by Diego Olivares, former director of international relations of the CUT, demanded the inclusion of an additional protocol on labour issues. To voice their demands, both trade unions had personal—though separate—interviews with the DIRECON director, Carlos Furche. The UNT called for these meetings, which took place just a few days before the end of the last negotiation round. It was then agreed that labour commitments would be part of an additional protocol and not a chapter in the final agreement, which had been the case in the agreement with the United States. To develop the scope of this protocol further, the DIRECON director participated in a council meeting at the UNT. While admitting their limited ability to influence the government's intention of signing an agreement with one of the largest world economies, the president of the UNT, Diego Olivares, admitted that their objective was that the government acknowledged labour unions' position regarding negotiations with China. The CUT manifested similar demands, since they had concerns over the negative impact of free trade on employment.[12]

## Conclusions

The first South-South negotiations that were pursued reflected the Concertación's need to reintegrate Chile into the regional and international arenas. Thus, apart from the economic objectives underlying such initiatives, these had a clear political aim. The government's strong commitment accounts for the agreements with Mexico and MERCOSUR in the 1990s. Fully developing this strategy required enhancing institutional leadership and trade abilities. To this end, relevant institutional transformations attempted to improve coordination among the various public agencies involved while also promoting the principles of transparency and accountability within the democratic canon. The incorporation of young professionals was intended to develop the technical expertise of public officials, negotiators and trade diplomats.

By then, however, two factors hampered dialogue with businesses. First, the government lacked experience in connecting with them and also in dealing with a more complex trade strategy. Second, given businesses' lack of technical expertise, they failed to provide sound proposals and resorted to a competitive strategy as they distrusted the government's approach to trade.

In time, the conciliatory and moderate leadership style of the centrist Christian Democratic Party that dominated the first two administrations of the Concertación helped in building confidence between state and business (Silva 2002). Policymakers sought the collaboration of the private sector, which thus relied on an extensive institutional structure, whereas the participation of others remained limited, as depicted in Table 5.1.

Formal channels coexisted alongside traditional informal pathways whose prominence increased when the formal ones proved insufficient or inadequate for transmitting businesses' demands, as shown by the Committee for the Private Sector Participation where only the CPC was invited to participate in the 1990s and by the SNA's radical strategies after the launch of negotiations with MERCOSUR. Lack of institutional and trade capabilities still hindered businesses' active participation in trade negotiations. ASEXMA was then the only exception to this rule.

Certainly, access to policy makers affected the incentive structure and the dynamics of businesses in general. These mechanisms encouraged associations such as the SOFOFA and the SNA to invest in their institutional and trade capacities. Hence, whereas negotiations with Mexico were opposed, a mixture of competitive and collaborative strategies predominated after the launch of negotiations with MERCOSUR and China. Interestingly, even if 15 years lay between these negotiations, both processes reveal the strong cleavages between industrialists and agriculturists. In this sense, China was to agriculture

*Table 5.1* South-South trade negotiations in Chile

| | | *State actors* Institutional architecture | *Non-state actors* Strategies | *Trade politics patterns* |
|---|---|---|---|---|
| **Mexico** | *Business* | Extensive | Competitive: SOFOFA, SNA | Pressured |
| | *Civil society* | Limited | Collaborative: CUT | Subordinated |
| **MERCOSUR** | *Business* | Extensive | Collaborative: ABIF, ASEXMA, CChC, CNC, CNE, SOFOFA | Cooperative |
| | | | Competitive: SNA (*outsider*) | Pressured |
| | *Civil society* | Limited | Collaborative: CUT, NGOs | Subordinated |
| **China** | *Business* | Extensive | Collaborative: ASOEX, APA, Fedefrutas, SNA, SONAMI | Cooperative |
| | | | Competitive: CONUPIA, SOFOFA | Pressured |
| | *Civil society* | Limited | Collaborative: CUT, UNT | Subordinated |

Source: *Author-created*

what MERCOSUR was to industry.[13] The press was the perfect battleground for these disputes.

Regarding dialogue with labour and civil society, this remained constrained within a limited institutional architecture. Institutional mechanisms were mainly formal and insufficient, and they did not offer enough incentives for trade unions and NGOs to invest in their own institutions. In turn, this may account for their narrow collective action and the low quality of their institutional leadership in trade policy issues. This was especially relevant when dealing with China, since previous South-South agreements were valued for enabling cooperation rather than conflict with regional counterparts. A similar stance pervaded SMEs.

## North-South Negotiations: A Long-Awaited Goal

Agreements with both the US and the EU had long gestations. By 1990, Chile was among the first countries to express interest in the 'Initiative for the Americas' proposed by President George H. W. Bush, which did not flourish. In 1994 Chile was invited to join NAFTA, though bilateral negotiations soon stalled because of difficulties with the renewal of the Trade Promotion Authority (TPA). Even if interests and stakes had always been high in the case of an FTA with the United States, in 1995, when the Clinton administration was forced to close this mode of entry, Chile opted for an agreement with Canada in an attempt to enter NAFTA through the back door.[14] Moreover, in 1998, the ECA with Mexico was transformed into an FTA following both the NAFTA model and the bilateral agreement with Canada signed in 1996 (DIRECON 2014).[15] Finally, in 2000, the United States and Chile agreed to start negotiations for an FTA with or without TPA. Simultaneously, from 2000, Chile intensified negotiations with the EU. By then, the FTAA already involved active, ongoing negotiations with all countries in the Americas—except for Cuba. Chile was part of the negotiation since its inception in December 1994. The mid-1990s and early 2000s were thus years of intensive and simultaneous North-South negotiations.

### *The FTAA: From Activism to Disillusion*

The Frei administration was actively implicated in the FTAA and hosted the launch of negotiations in 1998. Both the government and businesses were enthusiastic, as they viewed the FTAA as a desirable goal and a large project for a country that already had FTAs with almost all the countries involved in the regional project.

The agreement was to achieve three objectives. First, it would grant market access to 33 countries and broaden and deepen already existing trade agreements, namely the ones with MERCOSUR and the Andean Community, in the areas of services, investment and government procurement. Second, it would promote clear and transparent rules and regulations together with a good dispute settlement mechanism (Frohmann s.d.). Finally, as argued both by the government and businesses, the FTAA would simplify the operation and administration of trade: the private sector would rely on one comprehensive agreement based on common regional regulations, as in the case of rules of origin (interviews with DIRECON official and with SOFOFA executive). However, as explained in the previous chapter, FTAA negotiations lingered on with no concrete results. In 2000, President Lagos set an FTA with the United States as his main trade policy objective.

A strong and strategic alliance between state and businesses emerged after the launch of the FTAA in 1998 (interview with DIRECON official). The private sector '*aligned with the government*', and bilateral meetings were organized to define a joint strategy as they sought to build together '*a strategic position as Chile*' (interview with SOFOFA executive).

Two main transformations within the private sector account for this alliance. First, business associations had already developed strong trade policy abilities. While in the early 1990s ASEXMA seemed to monopolize trade expertise and an aggressive approach to FTAs, by the end of that decade, SOFOFA assumed the role of coordinator for the entire business community. It was based on the institutional changes and learning processes underlying this new leadership (interview with SOFOFA WTO expert). The CPC had led negotiations with Mexico and MERCOSUR. Now, as the trade agenda diversified and gained in complexity, sectoral issues gained prominence, and dealing with them required enhanced institutional leadership and trading skills. SOFOFA undertook several institutional changes to strengthen its focus on international trade and on FTA negotiations. First, in 1995, a former DIRECON director was hired to lead the recently created Department of Foreign Trade, together with an expert on the WTO from the same institution, and a former director of ProChile as a second general manager with responsibility for strategic issues. These incorporations not only strengthened SOFOFA's technical capabilities, they also provided the foundations for a closer relationship with public officials and trade diplomats. Second, when the CPC established the International Commission on Foreign Trade, SOFOFA's Department of Foreign Trade became its technical secretariat. As power and expertise became centralized in SOFOFA, the organization provided the government with a new institutional channel for dialogue and information exchange: the Commission of International Negotiations and Exports, which organized monthly meetings to discuss the different negotiations with the DIRECON director. Finally, various non-industrial sectors became members of SOFOFA, and this further promoted its representativeness. These included businesses providing foreign trade services—e.g. the Chilean Chamber of Customs and the Chamber of Maritime Transport and Ports (Camport)—together with logistics companies and courier services. Moreover, Chilefood and ASOEX, one of the oldest associations representing agricultural export sectors, joined the industrial association (interview with SOFOFA executive). Consequently, by the end of the 1990s, SOFOFA presented itself as the main business interlocutor with the government. Since then, it has led the private sector participation in international negotiations.

A second important change was the restructuring of business elites. Until the end of the 1990s, the private sector had acted as an 'ideological bloc' based on opposition to the UP government and scepticism about state intervention and public regulation. Moreover, their strict and rather fundamentalist adherence to neoliberalism promoted a new cultural *ethos*, whereby business people were seen as the 'protagonists' of development. In turn, they firmly defended the neoliberal model and rejected any change or alteration to it (Campero 2003). This identity principle guided their relations with state officials after democratic restoration. Still, by the end of the first democratic decade, political, economic and social changes required significant adaptations if business was to maintain a leading role. An important change in leadership then occurred. New leaders gaining ascendancy shared this cultural identity in which businesses were fundamental and irreplaceable participants. Still, their professional and academic backgrounds allowed a better understanding of the challenges ahead and also a more fluid dialogue with the government. This rupture between old and new business leaders was illustrated by the appointments of Juan Claro and Andrés Concha in the SOFOFA, of Andrés Vicens in ASEXMA, and of Ricardo Aritzia—a successful exporter—as president of the SNA (Campero 2003). These business leaders would now deploy a more flexible and consultative approach towards the government. Nevertheless, this did not preclude differences among businesses, especially when facing particular negotiations.

The launch of the FTAA revealed that as Chile advanced in its liberalization strategy and in the negotiation of new trade issues, SOFOFA had to come to some accord with businesses that intended to assert their own sectoral interests, i.e. services and exports.

Created in 1996 under the aegis of the Santiago Chamber of Commerce (CCS), the Coalition of Service Exporters (CES) aimed at promoting the participation of the sector in trade negotiations. The CES represented over 30 firms and associations interested in the incorporation of trade liberalization in services in the FTAA agenda and was very active both at the domestic and regional level. Whereas in the domestic arena the CES maintained direct and fluid relations with various public agencies, including ProChile, CORFO and the DIRECON,[16] at the regional level it played a dynamic role within the BNHI, where it stood for services exporters, whereas the SOFOFA was left with representing industrialists. Similarly, but with a focus on exporters at large, between 1994 and 2000 and without being a member of the CPC, the CNE managed to group together the main 23 exporting associations, including mining, fishing, and land and sea transport. This multi-sectoral representation allowed the CNE important access so that it could challenge the role of the SOFOFA. Interestingly, ASEXMA, which acted as the voice of small- and medium-sized export-oriented manufacturers, also sought to become more independent of the SOFOFA during these years and participated in the CNE. The CNE was also a part of the BNHI. Still, it did not take long for differences to emerge among these various associations and companies. As divergences widened, vital exporters' associations left the CNE, which hence lost representativeness and finally dissolved. As a result, the SOFOFA absorbed the CNE, strengthened its leadership and reinforced its role as business interlocutor.

Despite these cleavages and realignments, the private sector supported the FTAA process without fully abandoning hope of a bilateral agreement with the United States. The SNA, on the contrary, did not support the FTAA. They argued the initiative was not a powerful multilateral mechanism for trade liberalization and favoured the agricultural commission established with the United States, which provided a stepping-stone towards a bilateral FTA (interview with former SNA executive). The fishing sector under the National Fishing Society (SONAPESCA) did not find the regional initiative very attractive but did not object to it. Its participation was still only minor (interview with SONAPESCA executive).

After the launch of the FTAA, dialogue between state and business proceeded formally and informally at both domestic and regional levels. Participation at the regional level was based on an ex ante coordination mechanism. Apart from the formal channels in place, public officials and businesses involved in the FTAA negotiating groups held informal meetings. The objective was to reach a consensus on the agendas at stake and to elaborate the position of the country vis-à-vis its regional counterparts, which SOFOFA was to communicate and discuss internally. Domestic informal mechanisms persisted, as businesses could rapidly activate them when interested in transmitting their demands and proposals. Hence, the private sector relied on having dual access to policy makers: it could resort to these bilateral meetings with DIRECON officials and the various formal and informal mechanisms at the domestic level, which were complemented by the channels devised at the regional level, namely through the ABF.

For the private sector, the regional arena turned out to be a productive space for relating with Northern partners and constructing regional networks. However, the presence of Chilean representatives at the ABF remained modest (Rojas Aravena and Pey 2003). Businesses preferred bilateral relations, as shown by the increasing links established with United States' companies through the American Chamber of Commerce (AmCham), which then led the United States-Chile Free Trade Coalition comprised of more than 250 companies and business organizations advocating a bilateral FTA. In contrast, civil society lacked easy and constant access to domestic decision makers; hence, access to regional networks and alliances was vital.

Civil society led two initiatives during the FTAA launch in Santiago. First, Corporación Participa, a dynamic participant during the democratic transition, was then actively promoting new agendas and international alliances. During the FTAA, they worked closely with the Ministry of Foreign Affairs and the DIRECON, and were responsible for the organization and coordination of the regional consultative process with CSOs that preceded the Santiago Summit and the follow-up consultations implemented for the Third Summit of the Americas in Quebec in 2001.

For outsiders, the launch of the FTAA ran parallel to the First Summit of the People, where Chilean CSOs gained momentum as hosts of this massive counter meeting that gathered over 2000 representatives from the Americas. Led by the emerging HSA, the summit gave a prominent role to the Chilean Alliance for Fair and Responsible Trade (ACJR). Also formed after the democratic restoration, the ACJR brought together a range of social groups critical of the neoliberal model in place in Chile since the dictatorship. After the launch of the FTAA, it became a strong advocate of the inclusion of social and environmental clauses as a way to mitigate the negative effects of trade liberalization.

By 1998, a division between insiders and outsiders was thus established. In time, this cleavage split even further because of the different relational patterns established with the government. As those under the aegis of the HSA fragmented and reorganized around new cleavages, the ACJR gained new prominence and finally constituted the Chilean Chapter of the HSA until 2016.[17] Led by Coral Pey, this organization brought together academics, CSOs and activists and attempted to overcome the traditional division between NGOs and trade unions. Still, this was rather difficult to achieve because labour resisted an alliance with NGOs and social movements.

Under its then president, Diego Olivares, who had just returned to Chile after being Assistant Deputy at ORIT, the CUT immersed itself in a process of change. This included the creation of a department of international affairs to promote a learning-by-doing process and adapt the organization's trade expertise to the government's strategy. The CUT also developed a more elaborate discourse on Chile's trade policy, emphasizing social and labour clauses as being instrumental in sustainable development (Porras 2003). In all, Olivares attempted to imbue the CUT with a new and more pragmatic approach to free trade. However, it failed to speak with one voice as more radical and left-wing forces within the organization held opposing views. These divergent understandings, combined with modest professionalization, hampered the role of the CUT after the launch of the FTAA. Indecisiveness between a desire to participate and a total rejection of FTAs prevented the organization from speaking with one voice and impeded its role as a counterpart to the state. Relations with labour unions in the region then allowed access to technical expertise and resources that were fundamental to being able to voice their demands and influence a trade-led agenda. Nevertheless, differences persisted.

Strong social mobilization surrounded the formal initiation of FTAA negotiations during the Second Summit of the Americas in Santiago. The American Federation of Labour-Congress of Industrial Organizations (AFL-CIO) and its Latin America affiliates in the ORIT had proposed the organization of a summit jointly with social and environmental NGOs and movements under the HSA. The CUT rejected the proposal because of two different, though related, factors. First, its more pragmatic approach to trade negotiations, which were perceived as a mechanism for reinforcing national labour regulations, and second, the close and long-standing ties with the Concertación, which were strengthened during negotiations with the United States. Overall, the high specificity and technicality of the topics under discussion, and certain deficits in institutional leadership, together with the opposing views maintained vis-à-vis other trade unions and social organizations, held back their active involvement and participation in trade negotiations.

Despite showing strong opposition to the FTAA and the signing of trade agreements at large, the ACJR accepted some of the invitations to participate that the government offered after 2000. Building on their own research on trade issues, the ACJR aspired to have an informed role in trade decision making in order to promote the inclusion of social (gender equality, labour rights) and environmental clauses, together with IPRs, in the FTAA agenda. ACJR representatives held several meetings with public officials and negotiators, and submitted written presentations and proposals on FTAA topics. Yet their competitive strategy contrasted with the more collaborative approach of organizations like Corporación Participa.

After the Santiago Summit, civil society demanded opportunities to present their own ideas on the FTAA and also on the official international trade strategy. The Executive established a series of instruments to respond to this demand, including the creation of a working group on the FTAA to bring together social organizations and the Ministry of Foreign Relations. This working group held meetings, seminars and conferences to deliver information on the FTAA process but also to receive contributions and comments in an attempt to facilitate dialogue with more heterogeneous societal groups. These procedures were developed as negotiations advanced and were not integrated into a formal, institutionalized framework. Within the structure, organizations, like Corporación Participa, assumed a more executive role by fulfilling the assigned tasks, because the government attempted to promote transparency and democracy in decision making, while at the same time complying with the regional mandate raised by the Northern partners. The vast majority of CSOs found it difficult to have access to and discussions with government officials, and when invited, it was only to agree on matters already decided. The lack of technical expertise to elaborate sound proposals also hindered their participation, to the extent that their contributions to the national position were almost negligible. Under these circumstances, bridging regional networks allowed them to voice their demands and proposals. Together with Northern counterparts, they would then claim '*another integration is possible*' (interview with Organization of Consumers and Users of Chile/ODECU representative).

### *Trade Negotiations with the EU: From Political Dialogue and Cooperation to Trade*

Relations with the EU progressively consolidated after democratic restoration, when both parties started rebuilding their political contacts while also strengthening commercial links (Van Klaveren 2000). In 1994, the EU formally invited Chile to increase bilateral political dialogue, cooperation and trade liberalization agendas. Two years later they signed the Framework Cooperation Agreement—known as the Florence Agreement—aimed at establishing a political and economic association. Negotiations towards a Chile-EU Association Agreement were launched in the EU-Latin American Summit in Rio de Janeiro in 1999, and the negotiation was then part of the congested international agenda of Ricardo Lagos.

The EU had initially resisted bilateral negotiations and favoured a joint agreement with MERCOSUR—with Chile as an associate member—given Europe's strong support for regional integration in Latin America. Nevertheless, as the bi-regional process began to lose pace, the EU acceded to Chile's request. The first bilateral negotiation round took place in Santiago in April 2000. Negotiations proceeded rather smoothly except for some disagreements that arose during the seventh round in 2001. After quickly resolving these, in November 2002 Chile and the EU signed the Association Agreement, which covered the main dimensions of bilateral relations: political dialogue, trade liberalization and cooperation. In economic terms, the agreement created a free trade area in goods, services and government procurement; liberalized investment and capital flows; and strengthened the IPRs' protection—beyond WTO commitments—and foresaw further liberalization in agricultural goods and services.

Negotiations with the EU came at a time when public officials and trade diplomats, mainly those in the DIRECON, had already developed strong trade expertise. Still, dealing with multiple negotiation arenas simultaneously put these abilities to the test. Even if the DIRECON was the main agency responsible for trade, given the complexities of the agenda at stake, it had to consult with other ministries and agencies on specific issues. However, these consultations remained informal, as in the case of the Ministry of Finance and the Central Bank jointly discussing financial services.

Negotiations with the EU turned out to be the most difficult Chile faced, and the ones where the government and businesses established a solid alliance even before talks were launched. As the government acknowledged the difficulties MERCOSUR and the EU would face in trying to come to an agreement, public officials invited businesses to be part of a shared strategy. This was a joint public-private effort to differentiate Chile from the MERCOSUR and to persuade EU leaders that Chile was a suitable candidate for an FTA (interview with SOFOFA executive). Furthermore, the preferences and expectations of state and the private sector were now very close as they both intended to show the robustness and solvency of Chile's economic model and trade liberalization strategy by signing an agreement with the EU.

Businesses became part of the Advisory Council created within the Ministry of Foreign Affairs to deal with this negotiation. Political leaders, both from the party in government and from the opposition, former ambassadors to EU countries, businesses and academics were all invited because of their knowledge and expertise in Europe. This 'wise council' met on a bi-monthly basis to exchange information on the negotiation's progress and to analyse the agenda and trade offers. Overall, the Advisory Council intended to broaden the base of political support for the government's position in this pivotal negotiation. Additionally, the private sector communicated informally with the DIRECON, whereas the monthly meetings of the Commission of International Negotiations and Exports at the SOFOFA brought together businesses with the DIRECON director, who directly collected their suggestions and proposals.

In fact, the private sector's engagement in trade negotiations reached its peak during this negotiation. Over 30 business people participated in the last rounds, including representatives of the SOFOFA, ASEXMA and the CNE, together with others from organizations directly involved in the most controversial issues, e.g. in the wine industry (interview with DIRECON official).

With the SOFOFA leading, businesses strongly supported an agreement with the EU (interview with SOFOFA executive). The technical secretariat of the SOFOFA, now showing enhanced institutional leadership and trade expertise, coordinated the private sector offers and proposals, and identified and reconciled differences among sectors in order to speak with a strong, unified voice. Public officials and trade diplomats also encouraged businesses to resolve their internal discrepancies in advance. Otherwise, they would have to reconcile business preferences, and this would have hampered the expression of the national position (interviews with former senior trade official and with DIRECON official). Those sectors having particular demands directly accessed negotiators and public officials at the DIRECON, as in the cases of the SNA and SONAPESCA. However, these differences did not affect the strategic alliance and the deep conviction that an agreement with the EU was crucial for the private sector and for Chile. Furthermore, sectoral organizations, more prominently the SNA, had undergone important transformations in their institutional leadership and capabilities.

The agreement with MERCOSUR was a turning point for the SNA as they acknowledged that their limited trade expertise had negatively affected their role in the negotiation process (interview with former SNA executive). The SNA therefore embarked on an ambitious restructuring process. First, it managed to overcome the marked atomization of agricultural interests and achieve representation of the whole sector. Second, it created a technical department to provide professional support to help elaborate the sector's position in trade negotiations, and finally, the SNA established a close relationship with the Agrarian Research and Policy Office (ODEPA). Rather than a political task, this was mainly a technical undertaking to build consensus and a common agricultural position, on the one hand, and to gain leverage vis-à-vis other sectors, such as the agro-industrialists under the SOFOFA, on the other (interview with former SNA executive). Unlike their role during negotiations with MERCOSUR, the SNA became an active player in all trade initiatives.

SONAPESCA directly accessed public officials and negotiators while also resorting to mediation by the SOFOFA and even the media to express its concerns regarding the EU proposal to obtain access to Chilean maritime zones for EU fishing boats (interview with SONAPESCA executive). Finally, the EU-Chile agreement excluded fishing, although the Chilean government had never intended to include it despite strong demands from Portugal and Spain (interview with senior academic).

This fluid and constant relationship with businesses stood in sharp contrast to the interaction with trade unions and civil society. First, the Committee for the Private Sector Participation, which brought together public officials, business, labour and other societal actors, was barely summoned during this negotiation. Second, despite the regional acknowledgement of the importance of civil society input to the trade negotiations as expressed during the First Meeting of the European Union-Chile Negotiations Committee,[18] the opening of domestic channels became effective only in the early 2000s, following the Presidential Guidelines on Citizen Participation. These recommended, among other points, holding consultative seminars with civil society representatives to discuss the foreign relations agenda at least once a year and incorporating civil society representatives in presidential delegations to third countries. In all, the Lagos administration was convinced that gathering civil society support for trade policy was a sensible strategy for a small country with a very open economy. This support would not only grant legitimacy to policy decisions but would be fundamental when dealing with Northern partners, namely the EU and the United States (interview with senior ProChile official).

Nevertheless, after the launch of negotiations with the EU, the CUT still showed limited institutional abilities and failed to conciliate differences among factions. Whereas the leading group headed by Diego Olivares maintained a pragmatic approach based on the notion that social and labour clauses could be instrumental in the country's sustainable development, more radical and left-wing forces opposed such a strategy. The CUT had a positive attitude towards the EU and its approach to social and labour policies and acknowledged that its economic agenda did not differ substantially from the United States'. The CUT leadership had maintained close contacts with labour unions in Spain and valued their role in European regional integration (interview with UNT executive). In time, and as negotiations advanced, the relationship between the CUT and public officials and trade diplomats became closer. Moreover, and for the first time, a CUT representative was part of 'the room next door' during the last negotiating rounds, thus inaugurating a practice that had been common with businesses dating back to the first negotiation with MERCOSUR. Nevertheless, the selective incentive offered by the inclusion of labour representatives in the negotiations was too weak to allow the CUT to speak with one voice and to constitute a unified front. Internal differences and fragmentation persisted in 2002. Whereas Diego Olivares showed his support for the EU-Chile agreement, the CUT did not favour it and explicitly stated that they did not back the government either.[19] Finally, Olivares left the CUT and founded the UNT in 2004.

Civil society showed a similarly positive attitude towards EU negotiations. Based on the regional and domestic commitment to promote civil society participation in trade policy making, the DIRECON organized several seminars to promote information dissemination and also discussions between DIRECON officials and CSOs, including environmentalists and academics among others. Still, dialogue with these people was hampered by their rather radical stance and opposition to FTAs, which contrasted with the more conciliatory approach of trade unions (interview with former senior trade official). In any case, the negotiations with the EU did not spur strong opposition strategies or public demonstrations as in the case of the FTAA.

## Conclusions

In the late 1990s and early 2000s, Chile's agenda became more diverse and crowded as the country became immersed in two North-South initiatives: the FTAA and the negotiations with the EU.

To face these processes adequately, the government placed further coordination and leadership in the hands of the DIRECON. When it came to businesses, negotiations within the FTAA did not introduce major changes in the relationship between the state and the private sector, which relied on both formal and informal mechanisms, also covering, in the case of the FTAA, the regional arena. Domestic mechanisms were further reinforced as dealing with the EU required a joint public-private effort because both the government and business people intended to draw the bloc's attention to the need for a bilateral trade agreement. Being the leader in trade negotiations, the DIRECON and its highly professional staff sought closer relations with business even before the launch of negotiations with the EU.

In both negotiations, informal and ad hoc channels firmly complemented formal ones. The business leadership had undergone a significant process of renovation and modernization, and had together thus developed greater expertise in trade negotiations. These two factors then combined with the strong conviction that coming closer to the United States and the EU was crucial. In all, it provided an opportunity for consensus and common effort and thus strengthened a public-business pattern of relations that had already grown and consolidated. Moreover, by then, and after almost 10 years of continuous trade negotiations, a close working relationship had emerged between the DIRECON and businesses, based on expertise, learning and information exchange, but equally importantly on mutual trust (Bull 2008).

The pace at which channels were opened up to civil society showed relevant differences. Even if the Chilean democratic governments that took office after the military rule attempted to legitimize the same economic model by making room for extended participation, the opportunities remained limited to the private sector. Only under the socialist administration of Lagos were stronger efforts made to establish links with wider civil society. At the regional level, the FTAA pushed Latin American countries to open dialogue; Chile was in this respect a pioneer. The government developed different activities to enhance its relationships with trade unions and civil society, though these mechanisms entailed a limited institutional architecture, unlike the extensive formal and informal mechanisms in place for the private sector, as depicted in Table 5.2. The low level of formality and institutionalization attached to this dialogue contrasted with that between the state and business representatives, who could also rely on informal channels and mechanisms.

The limited mechanisms in place offered different incentives for civil society. Outsider groups advocated the inclusion of social and environmental clauses in the FTAA, and in FTAs at large. For example, ACJR used these channels while also actively resisting the agreement at the regional level. Insider groups used

*Table 5.2* North-South trade negotiations in Chile

| | | *State actors* Institutional architecture | *Non-state actors* Strategies | *Trade politics patterns* |
|---|---|---|---|---|
| **FTAA** | *Business* | Extensive | Collaborative: ASEXMA, CCS, CES, CNE | Cooperative |
| | *Civil society* | Limited | Collaborative: Corporación Participa | Subordinated |
| | | | Competitive: ACJR, CUT | Resistant |
| **UE** | *Business* | Extensive | Collaborative: ASEXMA, CNE, SOFOFA, SNA, SONAPESCA | Cooperative |
| | *Civil society* | Limited | Collaborative: CUT, NGOs | Subordinated |

Source: *Author-created*

institutional mechanisms to promote their goals of participation, transparency and access to information by opening up access mechanisms to decision making, e.g. Corporación Participa. In time, as the FTAA process was derailed, the gap between insiders and outsiders widened.

## Multilateral Trade Negotiations under the WTO

Multilateral trade negotiations were also essential components of the Concertación's trade strategy. Whereas differences emerged regarding which partner should be a priority when pursuing trade agreements, especially in the early 1990s, all three administrations supported multilateral liberalization through the WTO.

Actively involved in the UR negotiations, Chile deemed participation at the WTO to be crucial for its liberalization agenda. Together with bilateral and plurilateral agreements, this was intended to expand economic openness and at the same time draw the country in the international arena. Later on, however, Chile's interest in this multilateral forum took a slightly different turn, which emphasized more prominently the role of the WTO as a forum for the creation of rules rather than for achieving greater market access (interview with DIRECON official).

Chile regarded two issues as particularly relevant in the Doha Round: trade in services and agriculture. Progress at the multilateral level had not met the country's expectations regarding market access in agriculture. Nevertheless, as long as the belief was that agricultural liberalization would not advance at the bilateral level unless consensus was reached at the WTO, the latter was then a pertinent arena for pursuing further market access. Additionally, the country prioritized the broadening and strengthening of multilateral rules and was hence part of several committees, including the WTO Safeguards Committee (interview with DIRECON official).[20] From a government perspective, multilateral rules regarding trade defence mechanisms were important to protect a small economy like Chile's from arbitrary rulings. Accordingly, its proposals focused on three main areas: further trade liberalization in agriculture and services, stricter disciplines in antidumping and safeguards, and finally, a more effective dispute settlement mechanism.

Additionally, from an institutional perspective before the launch of the Doha Round, Chile had already deemed relevant the introduction of channels—both at the domestic and international level—to allow for the participation of society and promote constructive dialogue with state officials.[21] Despite the government's interest in establishing such links, at least at the level of discussion, capturing the attention of both the private sector and civil society turned out to be a difficult task.

The DIRECON organized a relatively large number of seminars to discuss and explain developments at the WTO, only to find that the private sector showed little interest in events in Geneva, unlike United States or European businesses (interview with DIRECON official).

Viewing it as distant and having no immediate impact on their interests and activities, businesses were less likely to participate in WTO negotiations. Furthermore, when compared with bilateral FTAs, the *tempo* of multilateral liberalization had always been slower than Chile's (interviews with senior ProChile official and with former senior DIRECON official). Finally, tariff levels in Chile's WTO scheduled consolidation were well above the average and hence the private sector did not feel menaced by the eventual multilateral commitments (interview with DIRECON official).

Even if businesses responded less enthusiastically to the launch of the Doha Round, the SOFOFA attempted to keep up with multilateral initiatives. In 1995, the organization hired a WTO expert from the DIRECON and since then, the SOFOFA has improved its technical abilities in areas such as those related to dumping actions and dispute settlement. In an effort to generate a spillover effect among its associates, the organization offered advice and consultancy on these issues, since its leaders perceived that member companies were not fully aware of the results of the UR and the new Doha Round. Moreover, the SOFOFA maintained direct and constant dialogue with DIRECON officials through the Commission of International Negotiations and Exports and the meetings at the DIRECON, where they analysed and discussed the evolution of the multilateral trade agenda. However, as argued by public officials, SOFOFA leaders found it difficult to promote stronger involvement in the Doha Round by the business sector (interview with SOFOFA WTO expert). This was also the case in ASEXMA, which did not attach a high priority to it because it did not impinge on their interests and activities (interview with ASEXMA representative). This contrasted with their extensive participation in FTAs and their early commitment to free trade. Hence, when it came to the WTO and the Doha Round, interaction with public officials and trade diplomats relied mainly on the seminars organized by the DIRECON (interview with ASEXMA representative). Relations between ASEXMA and the DIRECON and the Multilateral Director remained minimal. However, the WTO did have an impact on ASEXMA: by 2003, in order to comply with multilateral rules the Chilean government dismantled existing promotion mechanisms for industrial exports.[22]

Chile's strategy at the Doha Round included achieving greater access in services—professional services, sea and air transport—as well as information technology. Once again, trade officials and diplomats found that the private sector lacked the necessary technical abilities to deal with this new trade agenda. Businesses had difficulty in understanding the scope of the trade commitments in an area in which Chile had gone beyond WTO requirements (interview with DIRECON official).

After the launch of the Doha Round, and in the realm of agriculture, Chile strived towards the elimination of export subsidies, substantial reductions in trade-distorting domestic support measures, and the dismantling of tariffs and other barriers to market access. At the domestic level, the governmental strategy included the creation of a trade policy branch in ODEPA, reinforcing its role in negotiations. Additionally, the latter developed a strong working relationship with the SNA, which under the lead of Gustavo Rojas, undertook a process of institutional and capacity building. Apart from the creation of the technical department to provide support in elaborating the association's trade strategy, the SNA established a collaborative approach towards ODEPA and DIRECON. This entailed frequent consultations and the technical support of SNA's experts at WTO gatherings. Still, relations between the SNA and public officials and diplomats had upsets due to the institutional changes and political reshuffles the organization underwent, which in turn affected its trade expertise.

The DIRECON extended the invitation to WTO seminars and conferences to civil society. Nevertheless, as in the case of businesses, trade unions and NGOs did not manifest a strong interest in the WTO (interview with senior ProChile official). In contrast with this negligible presence at the domestic level, Chilean CSOs—as in the case of consumers' organizations—participated in WTO debates through umbrella organizations and networks. With a base in Northern countries, these organizations and networks provided their Southern counterparts with fundamental resources, namely information and access to specialized and technical knowledge that CSOs in the South lacked. More importantly, being part of these networks allowed the latter to be present at regional and international forums, as in the case of the WTO. Otherwise, they would not have had a say in multilateral trade negotiations (interview with ODECU representative). Interestingly, this appeared to be common to labour and consumers' organizations. In the case of trade unions, the UNT was part of the ITUC, whose main objective was to promote and defend workers' rights and interests through international cooperation between trade unions and advocacy within the most relevant international institutions, including the WTO (interview with UNT executive).

## Conclusions

As Chile broadened its 'lateral' trade strategy, the UR gave rise to the WTO and introduced regulations about issues that until then had been exempted from trade policy, as in the case of IPRs. Chile actively supported the launch of the Doha Round as the multilateral system complemented its bilateral initiatives, all of which had an impact on the country's new path of international integration. Furthermore, the Doha agenda included topics that bilateral initiatives had not been able to address, such as agricultural subsidies and the use of anti-dumping measures. Thus, despite the large number of FTAs already signed, the country attached great importance to the Doha negotiations and took several proposals to the multilateral arena.

In so doing, state representatives sought business input and cooperation through the various formal and informal mechanisms already in place. However, public officials and trade diplomats found it increasingly difficult to rely on the private sector as providers of technical contributions. Two factors seem

*Table 5.3* Multilateral trade negotiations under the WTO in Chile

| | | *State actors* Institutional architecture | *Non-state actors* Strategies | *Trade politics patterns* |
|---|---|---|---|---|
| **Doha Round** | *Business* | Extensive | Collaborative: SNA and SOFOFA | Cooperative |
| | *Civil society* | Limited | Collaborative: trade unions, NGOs | Subordinated |

Source: *Author-created*

to explain business responses. First, businesses had become more specialized in the negotiation of FTAs, where their active involvement contrasted with their limited engagement at the multilateral level. Second, WTO negotiations took a long time and had a more uncertain outcome. The positive incentives provided by the extensive institutional architecture in place seemed insufficient when facing long and complex negotiations that imposed significant demands in terms of businesses' institutional abilities. Overall, Chilean businesses have shown only marginal interest in WTO negotiations and commitments, all of which combined with the discredit that delays and disagreements in the Doha Round brought to the WTO.

The SNA was an exception though. This organization had been involved in a serious learning process to provide technical support to its demands. Moreover, in the case of agriculture, it was then clear that consensus at the multilateral level was fundamentally necessary for removing obstacles to further liberalization in this sector. Hence, although both the SOFOFA and the SNA deployed a collaborative strategy, as depicted in Table 5.3, the SNA provided better technical input.

Whereas specialized information and expertise seemed to escape both labour unions and CSOs, international networks worked as palliatives for Southern organizations. The limited institutional architecture at the domestic level did not offer incentives for developing institutional and technical capabilities. Their involvement in international networks acted as a counterbalance since they provided indirect access to the multilateral arena. This was especially evident in the case of consumer organizations, which played a significant role in the definition of standards at the WTO, although this was not reflected nationally.

## Notes

1 For a complete list of FTAs, see www.direcon.gob.cl/en/trade-map/, last accessed 6 June 2015.

2 Returning to the neighbourhood was also fundamental because Chile, a founding member of the Andean Pact in 1969, had withdrawn from the regional organization in 1976 because of the latter's protectionist policies that stood in sharp contrast to

those implemented under the dictatorship. In 2006, Chile became an associated member of the now Andean Community.

3 Mexico condemned the coup d'état and finally broke off diplomatic relations with Chile in November 1973.

4 Differences also emerged regarding the implementation of the second export phase, which the Ministries of Economy and Agriculture supported, whereas the Ministry of Finance preferred uniform tax reductions (Silva 2001).

5 In fact, during the presidency of Eduardo Frei, Chile became known for its trade diplomacy, for which the Ministry of Foreign Affairs gained overall responsibility in 1994 (Tussie 2013).

6 The SEGPRES is a strategic body responsible for the political agenda of the Presidency government and its relationship with Congress.

7 Chile became part of APEC in 1994, one year after the accession of Mexico. Since then, it has attempted to become a bridge between the Asia-Pacific region and Latin America (Oyarzún 2013).

8 Two supplementary agreements on trade in services and on investments were signed in 2008 and 2012, respectively (DIRECON 2009).

9 'Chile no descarta excluir textiles de TLC con China', El Mercurio Online, Economía y Negocios, 23 June 2005.

10 Declarations by Rodrigo Contreras, DIRECON-Head of Market Access Department, in 'Agro da batalla para ser gran ganador del TLC con China', El Mercurio Online, Economía y Negocios, 22 September 2005.

11 This was part of the document prepared by the CUT-International Relations Department, 'Tratado de Libre Comercio con China', available at www.choike.org/documentos/cut_tlc.pdf, last accessed 8 March 2016.

12 'Temas laborales del TLC entre Chile y China serán incluidos en protocolo' and 'China: los compromisos laborales que trae el TLC', El Mercurio Online, Economía y Negocios, 19 and 20 October 2005, respectively.

13 'Gobierno enfrenta polémica SOFOFA-SNA por TLC con China', El Mercurio Online, Economía y Negocios, 20 October 2005.

14 The Canada-Chile Free Trade Agreement (CCFTA) covers trade in goods and services, telecommunications and investments. Environmental and labour accords were incorporated as side agreements, just as NAFTA did. Signed in December 1996, the agreement was the first comprehensive FTA concluded with a Northern country.

15 In September 2004, Chile and Mexico launched negotiations towards a Strategic Association Agreement that included three pillars, thus replicating the structure of the agreements pursued by the EU in the region: trade, political dialogue and cooperation.

16 In 2004, ProChile and the CES jointly created the portal 'Chileexportservices' (Chilexportaservicios) to support the sector.

17 ACJR had to close down in 2006 because of lack of funding for projects and activities (interview with Coral Pey in von Bülow 2010:136).

18 First Meeting of the European Union-Chile Negotiations Committee, Conclusions, available at www.sice.oas.org/TPD/CHL_EU/Negotiations/Round1_e.pdf, last accessed 15 March 2016.

19 'Malestar en la CUT por respaldo de uno de sus dirigentes al acuerdo con la UE', EMOL, Nacional, 20 May 2002.

20 The WTO Safeguards Committee is responsible for monitoring and overseeing the use of the Agreement on Safeguards and member states' compliance with the procedural specifications.

21 For further details on Chile's proposals, see Statement by H.E. Mr. Juan Gabriel Valdés, Minister of Foreign Affairs, available at www.wto.org/english/thewto_e/minist_e/min99_e/english/state_e/d5253e.pdf, last accessed 18 March 2016.

22 'Presupuesto no incluiría US$ 20 millones para el sector: ASEXMA reclamó incumplimiento de compromisos del gobierno', El Mercurio Online, Economía y Negocios, 27 October 1999.

## References

Bull, B. (2008). Policy Networks and Business Participation in Free Trade Negotiations in Chile, *Journal of Latin American Studies* 40(2): 195–224.

Campero, G. (2003). La relación entre el gobierno y los grupos de presión: el proceso de la acción de bloques a la acción segmentada, *Revista de Ciencia Política* XXIII(2): 159–176.

Carnevali, I. (1999). *MERCOSUR-Chile: temas emergentes y posiciones de los actores chilenos*. Santiago, FLACSO-Chile.

DIRECON (2009). *20 años de la evolución del comercio exterior chileno.* Santiago de Chile, Departamento de Estudios e Informaciones, Dirección General de Relaciones Económicas Internacionales, Ministerio de Relaciones Exteriores de Chile.

DIRECON (2014). *Evaluación de las relaciones comerciales entre Chile y México a 15 años del tratado de libre comercio.* Santiago de Chile, Departamento de Estudios e Informaciones, Dirección General de Relaciones Económicas Internacionales, Ministerio de Relaciones Exteriores de Chile.

DIRECON (2015). *Informe Anual Comercio Exterior de Chile 2014–2015.* Santiago de Chile, Departamento de Estudios, Dirección General de Relaciones Económicas Internacionales, Ministerio de Relaciones Exteriores.

Foxley Rioseco, A. (1993). *La economía polítca de la transición: El camino del diálogo.* Santiago de Chile, Ediciones Dolmen.

Frohmann, A. (s.d.). *ALCA ¿De qué se trata?* Santiago de Chile, DIRECON.

Jara, A. (2001). Aspectos institucionales y económicos en las negociaciones comerciales de Chile. Parte 1: Aspectos institucionales, in A. Estevadeordal and C. Robert (Ed.) *Las Américas sin barreras: Negociaciones comerciales de acceso a mercados*. Washington, DC, Banco Interamericano de Desarrollo: 187–199.

Montero, C. and J. Federici (1999). La inserción comercial de Chile en el mundo: un caso de cooperación entre empresarios y gobierno, in M. García (Ed.) *Inserción internacional de Chile y participación ciudadana*. Santiago de Chile, Corporación de Estudios de Políticas Públicas y Relaciones Internacionales (CEPPRI): 65–98.

Oyarzún, L. (2013). When Trade Policy Is Not Enough: Opportunities and Challenges for Chile's International Insertion, *Journal of Iberian and Latin American Research* 19(2): 268–285.

Porras, J. I. (2003). *La estrategia chilena de acuerdos comerciales: un análisis político*. Santiago de Chile, Comisión Económica para América Latina y el Caribe (CEPAL).

Rojas Aravena, F. and C. Pey (2003). La sociedad civil en el proceso de integración comercial, in D. Tussie and M. Botto (Ed.) *El ALCA y las Cumbres de las Américas: ¿una nueva relación público-privada?* Buenos Aires, FLACSO-Argentina-Editorial Biblos: 215–233.

Sáez, S. (2005). Implementing Trade Policy in Latin America: The Cases of Chile and Mexico. Working Paper 54. Santiago de Chile, ECLAC-Division of Trade and Integration.

Sáez, S. and J. G. Valdés S. (1999). Chile and Its "Lateral" Trade Policy, *CEPAL Review* 67: 85–99.

Silva, E. (2002). Capital and the Lagos Presidency: Business as Usual? *Bulletin of Latin America Research* 21(3): 339–357.

Silva, V. (2001). *Estrategia y agenda comercial chilena en los años noventa*. Santiago de Chile, Comisión Económica para América Latina y el Caribe (CEPAL).

Tussie, D. (2013). Trade Diplomacy, in A. F. Cooper, J. Heine and R. Thakur (Ed.) *The Oxford Handbook of Modern Diplomacy*. Oxford, Oxford University Press: 625–641.

Van Klaveren, A. (2000). Chile´s International Integration, in E. Lahera and C. T. Toloza (Ed.) *Chile in the Nineties*. Stanford, CA, Stanford University Libraries: 119–161.

von Bülow, M. (2010). *Building Transnational Networks: Civil Society and the Politics of Trade in the Americas*. Cambridge, Cambridge University Press.

# Part III

# When Policy Creates Trade Politics

# 6 Trade Politics in Comparative Perspective

The analytical framework presented in Chapter 2 focuses on trade politics as the result of state and societal relations and strategies. A state's perceived vulnerabilities when facing trade negotiations influence the institutional architecture deployed to relate to society and thus strengthen its informational and legitimacy capabilities. The extensive or limited character of these mechanisms, which in turn yield different political opportunity structures, affect the ways in which business and civil society respond to states' requirements. Their responses and collective strategies, however, also interact with their institutional leadership and capabilities, and the uncertainty of policy outcomes. Chapters 4 and 5 apply this framework to unravel the political dynamics in the context of three different types of negotiations in two countries. This chapter puts together all the pieces of the puzzle in a cross-negotiation and cross-national comparison of South-South, North-South and WTO trade negotiations in Argentina and Chile.

## Comparing Trade Negotiations

To contribute a cross-negotiation perspective to the literature on trade politics, the comparative analysis first focuses on the general assumption guiding this book, namely, that variations across the agendas promoted by South-South, North-South and WTO negotiations are important. This approach emphasizes the specific characteristics of the agendas at play and attempts to unravel whether and how these different types of negotiations promoted diverse patterns of trade politics at the domestic level. This means that variation can be comprehended by lineally looking into the state-society dynamics elicited by South-South, North-South and WTO agendas. However, by exploring the similarities and variations across countries in the context of various trade negotiations, the differences in the impact on trade politics also become apparent. In this case, they are similarities explained by the specific type of negotiation the country faces.

### *South-South Trade Negotiations*

To analyse the effect of South-South trade negotiations in Argentina and Chile, I have focused on those agreements where the primary emphasis was on gaining market access and not on pushing for rulemaking in the new trade agenda, i.e. services, investment, government procurement and IPRs. This pattern, which is valid for both the agreements signed in the early 1990s and those pursued a decade later with China and India, seem to have been superseded by later negotiations—as with developing countries—intended to deepen trade relations by promoting new policy areas, as in the case of services. Leaving the negotiation of these later agreements out of the analysis was fundamental to assuring comparability.

These first negotiations stemmed from the governments' clear leaning towards Latin America and were then complemented with the expansion of existing FTA networks and the effective renewal of South-South relations in the twenty-first century. Based on this commitment, when differences emerged regarding the priorities of public agencies, which could be reinforced in the absence of concrete mechanisms for promoting coordination, presidents played a fundamental role in hitting the balance among discrepant agencies that could ultimately influence the effectiveness of their governments' strategies. Political will was hence central in the early 1990s.

South-South negotiations did not impose stringent requirements on public officials and agencies with regards to their information and legitimacy capabilities. When promoting institutional mechanisms for the inclusion of societal representatives, these were not directly related to the negotiation itself. Actually, they responded to the need to adapt institutional structures and decision making to the democratic canon. Public agencies and officials had then to submit to a quick and intensive process of learning-by-doing to deal with this new phase of trade liberalization while also adapting to the democratization of domestic policy processes, as shown by the Chilean experience of negotiating with Mexico and MERCOSUR.

Regarding state-society relations, whereas the private sector had access to policy making through an extensive institutional architecture, dialogue with labour and civil society was through a process of limited inclusion.

Even when formal mechanisms were in place—as in the case of the CACE in Argentina or the Business Advisory Mechanism in Chile—dialogue with the private sector also relied on informal channels and ad hoc procedures. The limited and sectoral character of South-South agreements required the more traditional, informal and ad hoc consultations between public officials and sectoral associations and even individual companies to elaborate product lists, with no need to discuss deep technical issues as when negotiating the liberalization of trade in services or the regulation of IPRs. Though governments attempted to formalize relations with businesses, informality still prevailed. Informal channels and mechanisms were fundamental to assessing sectoral demands and needs.

Second, within this political structure, business sectors threatened by future imports more prominently sought protection and ad hoc measures to offset the effects of trade liberalization. Others even took an extreme position in demanding exclusion from the agreement. In all, uncertainty was low, and businesses were quite certain about the negative effects of these agreements. Hence, based on a competitive strategy, a pressured pattern of trade politics most frequently emerged. Businesses in Chile largely opposed the agreement with Mexico and MERCOSUR,[1] whereas in Argentina, opposition to these first trade agreements was also deeply imbued with scepticism.

Only a small group of the business elite deployed a collaborative strategy. Based on their economic weight, institutional leadership and sound trade abilities, multinational and large firms already immersed in increased commercial interactions with the negotiating partners supported these agreements. They intended thus to consolidate and expand their market access opportunities. This collaborative strategy was even reinforced in the case of businesses capable of representing their sector and reconciling the different underlying positions at the domestic level but also with their regional partners, as shown by the various initiatives led by the CIQyP. In brief, the emergence of a cooperative pattern of trade politics relied on the affinity of economic preferences between the government and specific business organizations, although rather few in number, and on the provision of sectoral information and technical reports.

Across the spectrum of South-South negotiations, the definition of agricultural preferences under the SNA and the collective action strategy deployed during Chile-MERCOSUR negotiations deserve special attention. In what turns out to be an exception in terms of business strategies, at least in this study, the SNA assumed a radical and outsider stance. Even if both formal and informal mechanisms were in place, the agricultural association did not only ask for the exclusion of the sector from the agreement. SNA leaders fully rejected participating within the established channels of dialogue with trade officials. Moreover, they advocated a more anti-establishment strategy as outsiders. Being highly critical of economic integration with MERCOSUR, the SNA opted for exercising external pressure through the media and mass mobilizations. Based on a competitive strategy from an outsider standpoint, a pressured pattern of trade politics emerged, though this was an exceptional case.

The participation of trade unions and CSOs was negligible and confined to invited spaces, which were scarce. There was little encouragement for a wide variety of civil society voices to discuss the negotiation agenda. Informal access to public officials and trade diplomats also remained low. These institutional barriers constituted a pattern of limited inclusion. Leaving aside these constraints, South-South negotiations did not trigger a strong social demand either. The primary focus of the negotiations was on market access, and hence, rather than fearing the imposition of foreign standards and regulations, trade unions and NGOs expected that these regional initiatives would enhance and strengthen social and environmental rules. The core idealist interests of those involved were compatible with the governments' intention to foster cooperation with regional neighbours. Hence, despite the limited character of the institutional offer, trade unions and NGOs—mainly, consumers' and environmental organizations—opted for a collaborative strategy, leading in turn to a subordinated pattern of trade politics. The lack of a strong social demand for inclusion and influence during the negotiation of South-South agreements in the early 1990s was reinforced by distinct domestic variables, including the reorganization of civil society entities, in the aftermath of dictatorship and in the context of deep structural reforms.

Later on, even when society representatives feared the negative impact of free trade on labour standards, as in the case of the FTA between Chile and China, rather than opposing and assuming a radical, outsider strategy, they presented their demands to the governments through the limited institutional channels available, thus pursuing again a collaborative strategy. In this sense, negotiating with China introduced an important novelty, not so much because of the economic agenda, which was still restricted to market access, but mainly because Chinese domestic labour regulations and the protection of human rights challenged labour unions' material and idealist interests. Both the CUT and the UNT feared the agreement could affect workers' interests negatively given the low labour standards in China. Still, rather than rejecting the negotiation process, their demands focused on the incorporation of labour issues in the final agreement.[2]

### *North-South Trade Negotiations*

By the end of the 1990s, North-South negotiations burst onto the scene. Within the Southern Cone, the launch of the FTAA and the negotiation process with the EU reshaped the regional political economy, transforming the North-South architecture in the process. These restructuring forces also impacted on the domestic patterns of trade politics.

Public officials and trade diplomats perceived these negotiations as complex and demanding because they included a wide variety of issues, which ranged from the more traditional trade agenda to investments, services, government procurement and IPRs, among others.

Dealing with these deeper agendas required mechanisms for coordination and information sharing among ministries and agencies, on the one hand, and enhanced specialized information and technical knowledge, on the other. Achieving the broadest possible base of support was also important to attain a high level of legitimacy but also to create greater commitment among all those involved. Thus, in practice, North-South negotiations more decisively triggered regular exchanges among public officials and trade diplomats through informal coordination procedures, which, in some cases, complemented the formal mechanisms already in place.

However, the institutional architecture offered to society to make up for these informational and legitimacy vulnerabilities showed marked differences across social groups. In all, the political opportunity structure available to business and civil society differed, and this certainly affected the ways in which they mobilized and organized after the launch of North-South negotiations.

Governments most actively sought the support and active engagement of business both through formal and informal mechanisms. Even in Chile, where public officials and trade diplomats were better trained and more numerous, the state constantly attempted to integrate the private sector input into decision making to attain consensus and channel the information and expertise of a larger number of sectors, as in the case of the Advisory Council. Thus, they expected to reinforce the national position in these more complex negotiations. The strategy towards business led to an extensive institutional architecture immediately after the launch of trade negotiations as well as during the preparatory phase, since public officials and trade diplomats were aware of their resource and technical constraints as they faced better-equipped and more solid counterparts. This contrasted with the reticence towards providing a similar institutional framework to trade unions and CSOs, whose political opportunity structure was then seriously limited. In turn, these different mechanisms of access to political authorities triggered diverse patterns of trade politics.

One of the novelties of these negotiations was the upsurge in business interest, which turned out to be more marked in those countries where the transformation to trade liberalization was recent, as in the case of Argentina. However, business strategies and involvement were sifted through their technical abilities and expertise, which were then unevenly distributed, on the one hand, and the uncertainty of policy outcomes, on the other.

North-South negotiations brought to light the learning process already undergone by leading sectors, which had acknowledged that they needed to develop their abilities if they intended to have an effective role in trade negotiations. The congested trade agenda and governments' commitments to negotiated liberalization reinforced this perception. Additionally, through involvement in previous negotiations, these sectors had already established links and networks with regional and extra-regional counterparts. These included the close relations between Chilean businesses and the AmCham and the APEC Business Advisory Council (ABAC), and the chemical and petrochemical sector in Argentina through the establishment of APLA already in the mid-1980s. These private sectors quickly assumed a leading role and thus deepened their learning process in the context of North-South negotiations. Given that the latter involved issues that had remained largely out of the scope of South-South agendas, uncertainty and lack of knowledge prevailed. Their strategies to cope with uncertainty relied on searching systematically for additional information, allowing business to counteract uncertainty individually or in cooperation with others. Moreover, with dependable links to policymakers already, interactions and exchanges with public officials and trade diplomats relied on expertise, learning and informational give-and-take. As this collaborative strategy consolidated, it laid the basis for a close working relationship between leading sectors and public cadres as shown by the alliance established between the Chilean government and the SOFOFA during the negotiations with the EU.

Nevertheless, important parts of the business community were then only embarking on such organizational and institutional learning processes. Their strong protectionism had hindered any active involvement in these new regional and international trade dynamics, as in the case of the UIA in Argentina. After the launch of North-South negotiations, on the contrary, they showed a stronger interest in participating. Business people then pursued constant contacts and interactions with public officials and trade diplomats as they intended to make use of all possible mechanisms to press their governments to comply with the demands of their particular sector, on either a free trade or a protectionist basis. To a certain extent, these sectors acknowledged that traditional lobbying techniques were no longer useful and were not producing the expected results in terms of either protection or liberalization. Furthermore, the complexity of the issues at stake under North-South agendas and the associated uncertainty about the implications of prospective outcomes required constructing a well-informed basis equipped with the necessary skills and information for effective involvement in these initiatives. However, a strong protectionist sentiment still operated among many industrial and agricultural leaders and members. Hence, even if some attempts at collaboration were made, these coexisted with the traditional pressure from those sectors seeking protection and compensation.

North-South negotiations also triggered changes in the definition and alignment of businesses. First, in contexts of stronger business fragmentation, some interesting cases of collaboration and consensus building emerged: i.e. CAMARCO and the CAC's joint document and the creation of the MEBF. Second, the importance of the new trade issues in the negotiation agenda gave prominence to sectoral associations, though not always with a happy ending. Whereas some managed to constitute themselves as leading voices, others were subsumed into leading traditional associations, deepening thus the concentration of representation in already established organizations. The incorporation of the CNE under the SOFOFA is a clear illustration of this process. Third, North-South negotiations promoted the creation of different networks, whose utility in terms of access to technical abilities and expertise varied across associations and also across countries. In this sense, two main traits are worth mentioning. Business networks as in the case of the BNHI and the active involvement in the ABF seemed to be of greater relevance for those who were attempting a significant updating in trade negotiations than for those already having extensive expertise. Contrary to the active role of Argentine associations in these regional forums, Chilean presence in these meetings was not very significant, and businesses more prominently used them as a means for norm diffusion, e.g. the adoption of regulatory standards in Corporate Responsibility (interview with senior ProChile official).

From a cross-negotiation perspective, North-South initiatives triggered the most varied strategies in civil society and hence led to more diverse patterns of trade politics. Moreover, substantial variation became evident across trade unions and NGOs, but also across countries. The launch of North-South negotiations triggered the interest of a wide spectrum of participants—certainly more heterogeneous than in South-South processes—who pursued a broad array of strategies, ranging from collaboration to opposition, contestation and confrontation. Civil society selectively resorted to a completely new repertoire of actions and tactics, including collaborative and competitive strategies as well. Within a limited institutional framework, these strategies led to both subordinated and resistant patterns of trade politics.

This new repertoire was closely associated with the ensemble of social and political networks bridging the North-South divide. Assuming either a more moderate and insider position or an extreme and outsider stance, these networks facilitated access to institutional, material and financial resources together with technical capacities and expertise, which were then in short supply for many trade unions and CSOs in the Southern Cone. Organizations in Chile had already played an important role during the negotiation with Canada and when discussing the possible entry into NAFTA. Consequently, they developed expertise in trade negotiations and in participatory strategies. However, when compared with the private sector, the learning process seems to have been weaker. Actually, the domestic incentive appears to have been absent, since civil society did not enjoy extensive institutionalized access as did leading businesses.

The picture of civil society activism was thus far from simple. On the one hand, organizations like Corporación Participa and Poder Ciudadano deployed an insider, collaborative strategy and made use of the limited opportunities to promote issues of governance, democracy and participation, leaving the trade agenda out of their immediate concerns. On the other hand, several organizations placed higher priority on the free trade agenda and confronted the government because it challenged their material and idealist interests. However, these organizations also used other mechanisms to persuade public officials and negotiators to embed environmental and social clauses more securely into trade agreements, as in the case of the ACJR. Trade unions' opposition to FTAs suggests they were hesitant about following this strategy, as evidenced by the CUT in Chile and the CGT and CTA in Argentina. In time, these divergent positions undermined their effectiveness in making their voices heard in the decision making but also challenged the establishment of broad social coalitions bringing together labour and NGOs across the region.

Finally, the impact of these networks was largely determined by the domestic institutional architecture, as shown by the early activation of trade unions and NGOs in Chile and the rather late configuration of similar opposing voices in Argentina. More importantly still, the particular negotiating counterpart appeared to be a fundamental factor for understanding the responses and strategies of civil society. In this respect, differences between the FTAA and the EU are striking.

The FTAA triggered strong confrontational postures that contrasted with the low resistance and mobilization observed after the launch of trade negotiations with the EU. Even if both negotiation processes did not include the participation of civil society representatives in their initial stages, whereas the launch of the FTAA in Chile in 1998 was met with demonstrations and mobilizations, such manifestations were almost absent in Rio one year later.

### *Multilateral Negotiations under the WTO*

Argentina and Chile followed the conclusion of the UR and the creation of the WTO with increased enthusiasm. Both countries were actively involved in the Doha Round and participated in different formal and informal coalitions intended to promote market access for non-agricultural products and trade liberalization in agriculture.

The creation of the WTO and the later Doha Round faced Southern governments with increased regulatory stakes and the rising legal requirements of the trade agenda. Specific institutions were thus deployed to provide both state and business with useful tools and instruments to deal effectively with these increasing requirements, as in the case of the CACE in Argentina. Additionally, trade policy was to be adapted and modified to comply with the obligations undertaken under the agreements on the new agenda, namely antidumping and IPRs.

Expertise turned out to be a fundamental resource for both public officials and businesses, given the deep and broad character of the WTO agenda. To the already acknowledged complexities attached to the negotiation of the so-called Singapore issues of competition policy, investment, government procurement and trade facilitation, the Doha Round added the questions of market access in industrial products, agriculture and services.[3]

Building on Article 20 of the WTO Agreement on Agriculture, the Doha Round negotiations were to reduce export subsidies and trade-distorting domestic support progressively while at the same time promoting improvements in market access, especially for developing countries. The agenda thus included the establishment of schedules and dates, together with the discussion of complex trade models, requiring sophisticated technical analyses and forecasting techniques, all of which entailed additional challenges for Argentina and Chile.

Governments strengthened their efforts to develop the necessary technical abilities in the agricultural area where the incentives for both countries were strong. In the case of Chile, the creation of the WTO and the commitment to further liberalize agricultural trade resulted in the creation of a trade policy branch in ODEPA. Until then, and after MERCOSUR negotiations, this office had worked as an informal advisory unit to the minister of agriculture. After 2001, ODEPA was reinforced in its role of monitoring agricultural trade discussions and providing assistance in cooperation with the DIRECON. In Argentina, the Secretariat of Agriculture immersed itself in a process of capacity building by training a selected group of economists in state-of-the-art impact assessments.

Governments not only initiated a process of learning-by-doing to develop sound technical abilities but actively sought to engage with the private sector as well. Both in Argentina and Chile, public officials made a concerted effort to reach out to businesses to inform them of the evolution of the Doha Round, but more importantly, to solicit their advice and expertise. A process of extensive inclusion in trade policy making was thus deployed both towards industrial and agricultural associations, whose strategies showed relevant contrasts.

In both countries, the government aimed for close collaboration with leading private sector institutions. In Chile, the SNA, which was then undergoing important institutional reforms that would lead to increasing unity and representativeness, created a special department to provide technical support in the elaboration of the sector's position in trade negotiations, including those at the WTO. In the process, the organization pursued a collaborative strategy with public officials and trade diplomats in the ODEPA and the DIRECON. Multilateral negotiations in agricultural trade liberalization resulted in a similar process of institution building and learning in sectoral associations in Argentina.

Led by the INAI, the agricultural sector sought to strengthen its technical abilities to support the negotiating demands of its associated members but also to provide advice and technical support to public officials and trade diplomats. Thus, leading agricultural associations in both countries more intensely developed a collaborative strategy with the government. Based on their enhanced technical expertise, agricultural interests made widespread use of the extensive institutional architecture, which allowed multiple formal and informal access points to trade policy making. This active collaboration with the government was complemented by the use of investigation and research into acquiring additional knowledge and information. Both elements were part of their strategy to cope with an uncertain environment.

As these practices became routine, they led to a cooperative pattern of trade politics between businesses and the corresponding sectoral public agency—i.e. ODEPA in Chile and the Secretariat of Agriculture in Argentina—but also with the DIRECON and the Ministry of Foreign Affairs. In time, a close working relationship based on the mutual exchange of information and learning, but more importantly on a high level of trust, flourished between public officials and agricultural representatives.

Contrariwise, industrial interests played a negligible role in WTO trade negotiations in both countries. The long-term horizon of this process and the uncertainty of the outcomes led to a rather passive stance, illustrated by the attitude of both the SOFOFA and the UIA, which in the case of the latter was further reinforced by splits across sectors. Though public officials and trade diplomats frequently consulted them about their particular stakes in the multilateral agenda, industrialists failed to produce significant contributions or at least to fulfil the governments' demands. By the time the Doha Round was launched, both institutions had already developed technical abilities through the creation of specialized departments dealing with the WTO, which in the case of the SOFOFA had been even further reinforced by the incorporation of an expert on the WTO. Despite these developments, public officials and trade diplomats in both countries complained of a lack of industrial input to refine the governments' strategy and set out clear negotiation objectives.

Industrialists more strongly resorted to their relations and connections to policymakers and used them for a persistent influencing strategy, while deciding not to specifically cope with uncertainty at all. They assumed a passive stance based on the perception that they could not control developments at the multilateral level, and that to a certain extent neither offensive nor defensive strategies could prevent the regulatory uncertainty emanating from the WTO negotiations.

Complaints among CSOs emerged on both sides of the Andes because of their lack of access to trade policy making. Public officials' exclusive reach to businesses left out a large number of social organizations. In the context of multilateral trade negotiations, technical requirements seemed to exceed the government's need for legitimacy and wide social support. Certainly, the strong development component of the Doha agenda 'is ample testimony of the new proactivist South' (Ostry 2002). Nevertheless, the launch of the Doha Round captured the attention of only a limited number of NGOs in both Argentina and Chile. Whereas governments did not include civil society representatives in the official delegations to the WTO and did not openly invite them to discuss the agenda, CSOs intended to raise social awareness of the impact of multilateral trade liberalization. When dialogue took place, it was the result of the initiative of a few organizations. Thus, the texture of this subordinated dynamic between public officials and trade diplomats, on one hand, and civil society, on the other, remained institutionally limited and thin. The dialogue was intermittent and very ad hoc.

Trade unions and some of the more active NGOs were already involved in regional and international networks, which came as a by-product of their participation in regional trade negotiations or institutions, such as the FTAA or the Organization of American States (OAS), among others. These networks offered advantages for gaining access to available resources, including acquiring additional knowledge to cope with multilateral negotiations and opening channels to decision makers in Geneva. Still, domestic dialogue mechanisms with trade officials and diplomats were scarce, leading in turn to a subordinated pattern of trade politics.

## Comparing Countries

Moving along the national dimension of my cases, I worked on the assumption that national characteristics are relevant. They exert a major impact on domestic trade politics. To this end, I delve into the weight of political legacy and path conditioning to see how well-trodden paths might account for particular strategies and relational dynamics between state, business and civil society in the context of trade negotiations. The idea was that a country's historical, social and political characteristics determine political processes and outcomes in trade politics. As expected, cross-national differences do emerge, and they thus provide controls for the variations observed across South-South, North-South and multilateral trade negotiations.

### *Comparing Trade Policies*

Starting in the 1990s, Latin America underwent both political and economic democratization, all of which entailed a reframing of the relation between state and society. Furthermore, the fall of the Berlin Wall and the increasing integration and globalization provided the region with greater flexibility and more options. Hence, as countries attempted to avoid marginalization and maximize their power, two strategies became key: open rather than closed regionalism as a way to promote political and economic objectives (Bianculli 2016a) and the exploitation of a wide range of external links (Mittelman 2000), including the regional, the interregional and the multilateral arenas.

Argentina's trade policy started to change course in the mid-1970s, at a time when Chile was also opening up to international trade. In 1976, the military dictatorship implemented the first (ill-coordinated) attempt at unilateral trade liberalization, which was then partially reversed. Trade liberalization gained prominence in the mid-1980s as democratic governments undertook important transformations in the country's economic structures and institutions. Nevertheless, trade policies in Argentina remained subject to the instability and vicissitudes of political and policy-making climates.

The first democratic government set the basis for unilateral trade liberalization while at the same time pursuing regional cooperation with Brazil through administered opening and intra-sectoral complementation (Bouzas and Gosis 2014). This gradual and selective approach was left behind in 1994, when the country underwent a deep process of market reform, combining a policy of deregulation, privatization and trade liberalization in a democratic context in an unprecedented way for the Southern Cone. The country's trade strategy reinforced this commitment to reducing and eliminating trade tariffs, starting with MERCOSUR and the adoption of the CET, and the various South-South, North-South and multilateral agreements pursued later in the decade.

As the twentieth century was slowly ending and MERCOSUR underwent a crisis and faced new challenges such as the FTAA, Argentina confronted a chronic trade deficit in a context of unsustainable debt dynamics, an overvalued real exchange rate and weak macroeconomic fundamentals.

Moreover, the international context was marked by financial instability and a slowdown in economic growth. Combined with the recession in the region, these various factors unleashed the 2001–2002 economic collapse. Among other important and fundamental economic decisions and contrary to what had been the experience during previous crises, rather than closing down the economy, the administration of Néstor Kirchner attempted to strengthen trade liberalization through a multipolar trade strategy. Using MERCOSUR as a platform, this strategy combined participation in bilateral, bi-regional, hemispheric and multilateral negotiations as compatible and necessary options to increase and diversify available markets for Argentine products.[4] However, as the new administration pursued policies of stronger state intervention and government control, export duties and taxes increased substantially until 2008 (Brambilla et al. 2010, Galiani and Somaini 2010). Furthermore, this increasingly restrictive trade policy materialized through a variety of non-tariff instruments and undocumented measures (Bouzas and Gosis 2014:64). These measures were even stronger after the Great Recession in the United States and in the EU, which affected Latin America.

In sum, between 1990 and 2005, within a consistent paradigm of trade liberalization, Argentina developed different strategies as the country attempted to adjust trade policies to changes in the domestic and international structural contexts.

In contrast, Chile stands out for its stable and long-standing trade policy. The country started its journey towards free trade in the 1970s, when the dictatorship undertook trade and financial liberalization on a unilateral basis and established a flat rate regime together with extensive export promotion schemes. In the 1990s, after political liberalization and democratic restoration, the Concertación maintained and even increased trade liberalization by promoting a complex and dense web of trade agreements on the regional and extra-regional levels while at the same time pursuing further liberalization through the WTO. Hence, Chile became a pioneer of New Regionalism and of multipolar trade strategy (Robin 2008), and 'has probably gone far beyond any other developing country, be that in Latin America, Asia, or Africa (. . .)' (Mesquita Moriera and Blyde 2006:1).

Over the last 30 years, Chile implemented and sustained a very active and aggressive trade policy, premised on a mixture of three different but complementary strategies: unilateral, bilateral and multilateral liberalization. Despite the continuity of the international trade strategy across regimes, whereas initially trade liberalization relied on unilateral and multilateral mechanisms, with the advent of the left-wing coalition under the Concertación, the trade strategy veered towards negotiations with Latin America and neighbouring countries and extra-regionally in a second phase. Hence, political objectives, namely, the reintegration of Chile in the regional and international arenas and its recognition as a new democracy (Sáez and Valdés 1999), underlay the first South-South agreements.

Purely economic motives explain the move towards the United States and the EU, and with Asian countries in the late 1990s and early 2000s, its largest trading partners. In all, free trade is certainly not only about purely economic factors and gains. Politics and political objectives should also be highlighted when accounting for international trade strategies.

Since the 1990s, trade policy has been an integral part of Chile's foreign policy, and a fundamental tool to promote international links. This resulted in the expansion and diversification of goods and services flows. Exports increased from 8,372 million dollars US in 1990, to 23,316 million in 2005, and new productive areas were consolidated, thus leading to an increasingly sophisticated trade policy (Furche 2011).

Despite the differences, between 1990 and 2005 Argentina and Chile saw an unprecedented surge in the number of international trade negotiations, whose agenda and coverage also expanded from tariffs to an ever wider and more complex range of topics, such as public procurement, trade-related intellectual property issues, services and international investments. How did governments, business and civil society respond to this multi-tier strategy of trade liberalization, involving South-South, North-South and WTO agendas? The next two sections look into the preferences and strategies of state and society, and the last explores the patterns of trade politics that reflect different constellations of actors and relational dynamics.

### *Comparing Governments*

Both in Argentina and Chile, trade negotiations mirrored their strong presidential systems. Executives played a fundamental role in the implementation of this multi-tier trade strategy and the negotiation of international agreements. This applies to the successive governments under the centre-left-wing coalition Concertación in Chile and to the Menemist neoliberal decade, the brief years of the *Alianza*, and the nationalist and statist model under the Kirchnerismo (Godio 2006, Grugel and Riggirozzi 2007) in Argentina. Congresses, on the contrary, played only a marginal role (Spiller and Tommasi 2010, Stallings 2009).

In Argentina, starting with the PICE and the constituting years of MERCOSUR, regional and international negotiations were a state-led initiative where the Executive played the leading role. Yet, differences persisted among the public agencies responsible for trade policy making. Even if with the creation of MERCOSUR by the early 1990s interaction on various policy areas became routine, thus raising the demand for expertise and coordination, the lack of institutionalized mechanisms and channels for information sharing and coordination was still evident in the mid-1990s and early 2000s. Discrepant views among agencies were thus not resolved and sometimes diverged further, to the extent that when differences appeared to be irreconcilable, the president had to mediate.

The design and implementation of trade policy has traditionally remained separated in the hands of various Secretariats and Under-secretariats in the ministries of Economy and Foreign Affairs. Although by the late 1990s and early 2000s, different initiatives were taken to promote a better equilibrium and to enhance coordination between both ministries in all trade policy matters; these failed to reverse the situation completely and waned when the public officials leading these initiatives abandoned office, as illustrated by the CACE under the lead of Félix Peña. Clearly, trade policy making in Argentina was heavily influenced by those in charge—the *persona-grama*—and was marked by a relatively low level of formalization. Within this unstable institutional context, the personnel with professional services contracts—the *contratados*—gained increased importance. Despite the temporary nature of their contracts, provided they remained in their positions for a long time, and in some cases even longer than politically designated officials did, these hired trained personnel worked as the most stable liaison between the government and businesses. With the sole exception of the Ministry of Foreign Affairs, the public agencies responsible for trade policy lacked a stable and highly technical and qualified bureaucracy.

When looking across South-South, North-South and WTO initiatives, it is clear that the FTAA and WTO negotiations elicited several institutional reforms. On the one hand, the CNCE was created within the Ministry of

Economy to face the judicialization of the multilateral agenda. On the other hand, FTAA negotiations triggered the creation of several mechanisms in the Ministry of Foreign Affairs as trade diplomats intended to reach out to business and civil society. At the same time, the then minister of economy and the vice-counsellor and minister of foreign affairs and international trade attempted to promote better coordination and information sharing across these two ministries and with other public agencies. In all, rather high instability in the implementation of institutional transformations,[5] reshuffles in political positions and fluctuations in the rules of the game as political leaders came in and out of office characterized trade policy.

These various factors hindered the development and accumulation of sound institutional and technical abilities, which remained in the hands of a small number of highly professional experts with ready links to the private sector, and slowed the promotion of stable and highly professionalized trade cadres.

In Chile, trade negotiations have also involved a top-down model under the clear leadership of the Executive. However, Chile evidenced a marked institutionalization and formalization of trade policy-making procedures. Since the launch of its active international agenda in the early 1990s, the government promoted several institutional transformations to encourage collaboration, coordination and leadership across ministries and public agencies, and thus develop the government's negotiating abilities.

First, the centralization of foreign trade responsibilities in the DIRECON led to its increasing professionalization. Second, several public officials coming from the previous administration were kept in their positions, and new offices and departments were created to promote specialization in the various negotiating fronts. Finally, the DIRECON coordinated closely with the Ministry of Finance and other Executive branches to provide policy advice to the government and to carry out negotiations (Stallings 2009).

In both countries, the channels opened to allow societal input were a consequence of the regional mandates stemming from North-South negotiations, as in the case of the FTAA, which called for enhanced participation and transparency. Still, domestic factors were also at play.

In Argentina, the opening of the trade policy process to incorporate different civil society voices, apart from businesses, was also linked to the new multipolar strategy implemented in 2003. However, developments were only short-lived, as they did not survive the political reshuffle in these areas. Hence, as FTAA negotiations waned and those in charge left office, these different channels fell into disuse with the exception only of the CCSC. Though still in place, the CCSC has undergone significant modifications. In fact, discussions in this forum now comprise a more heterogeneous agenda, concerning areas of work and related commissions on issues such as food, climate change, sustainable development, natural resources and society, international health, among others (Theiler 2012, Varsky n.d.).[6] In all, the connection with international trade negotiations seems to be practically nil, whereas the emphasis is on MERCOSUR.

North-South negotiations and the launch of the Doha Round revealed the crucial importance of expertise and technical knowledge, and thus became a prerequisite in government solicitation of societal participation. The need to enhance legitimacy in trade policy decisions turned out to be less acute. Thus, whereas governments provided limited and institutionally fragile mechanisms for the inclusion of civil society that did not permit clear input to decision making, businesses relied on extensive access to public officials and trade diplomats. Either on a formal basis but more importantly through informal channels and mechanisms, large businesses and established associations enjoyed multiple access points. Additionally, public officials granted privileged and stable access to those capable of providing technical information and expertise, as in the case of the INAI and the CIQyP.

In Chile, the continuity of the international trade strategy had an impact on the institutional frameworks and the ways in which state and society related to each other. By the early 1990s, the Concertación encouraged the institutionalization of societal participation through several tripartite forums. Early initiatives and mechanisms aimed at allowing the participation of business and trade unions, and to a lesser extent experts and academics. Still, in practice, only the private sector enjoyed extended inclusion into trade policy making through continuous and stable access mechanisms. In the early 2000s, the Lagos administration made a commitment towards the widening of social participation, which required citizen input in policy making. Following this presidential directive, the Ministry of Foreign Affairs and the DIRECON organized joint meetings and seminars to bring together public officials and trade diplomats, on the one hand, and trade unions and civil society, on the other. Nevertheless, these mechanisms remained limited and fragile, especially when compared with those available for business. Public officials and trade diplomats sought cooperation with the private sector more strongly, through both formal and informal mechanisms. As in the case of Argentina, the opening of participatory channels for civil society was also a response to regional mandates, such as those emanating from the FTAA and negotiations with the EU. Bilateral negotiations with Canada also established a precedent for this strategy as they inaugurated areas for dialogue and consultation between public officials and civil society (interview with senior ProChile official), these being later on reinforced in the context of successive North-South initiatives.

In sum, both countries are distinct in terms of the degree of institutionalization and formalization of the various mechanisms devised to promote governments' institutional leadership and technical and legitimacy credentials. Nevertheless, three common patterns emerge when comparatively assessing the institutional architecture devised for dialogue with society. First, governments sought the collaboration and expertise of the private sector more strongly and in a continuous manner, whereas the strategy developed to integrate broader societal interests remained institutionally thin and ad hoc. Second, even if domestic factors contributed to this opening towards civil society, it is clear that this was most actively deployed after the launch of North-South negotiations, following the requirements of Northern partners. Finally, when dealing with trade agendas, especially those involving Northern countries and those under the WTO, obtaining specialized information and technical expertise together with the acquiescence of business was more imperative for governments. Contrariwise, enhancing their legitimacy and base of political support by providing trade unions and civil society access to the policymaking process appeared to be less crucial.

## *Comparing Societal Groups*

Institutional supply is a necessary but not sufficient condition to explain state-society relations in trade politics. Another relevant factor refers to the societal demand, that is to say, the constellations of businesses and civil society representatives that call for spaces to request information and claim a place in trade policy decision making. Whereas the political opportunity structure certainly affects their effective participation, it is equally true that this also depends on their institutional leadership and capabilities, their policy preferences and collective action strategies.

In the absence of stable economy-wide associations, business organizations remained unstable and fragmented in Argentina. Moreover, their conversion to the free trade canon was not homogeneous across all sectors. Apart from the traditional cleavage between import-competing industrialists and export-oriented agriculturalists, whereas the UIA deployed a competitive strategy to demand protection across trade negotiations, the extensive antagonism among economic interests based on their size and sectoral diversity raised barriers to collective action. Hence, major firms, together with concentrated sectors such as food producers under the COPAL and petrochemical and chemical industries under the CIQyP, deployed a more collaborative strategy.

Differences further deepened as the trade agenda gained in complexity and technicality. Based on their collaborative strategy with public officials and trade diplomats and their ready access to decision making, agribusiness associations actively developed their trading abilities and expertise. The enhanced professionalization of the sector, in turn, improved their relationship with public officials and thus increased involvement in policy making. Industrialists, mainly large companies and associations representing competitive and internationalized sectors, undertook a similar learning process. The UIA attempted to develop trade capabilities but with meagre results.

In contrast, by the 1980s, during the military regime, import-competing industrialists under the SOFOFA assumed a free trade stance in Chile. The mediating role of the economy-wide CPC was fundamental then, during the democratic transition and the first years of democracy, just when South-South negotiations ranked high on the Concertación's agenda. When facing highly conflictive situations—i.e. negotiation with MERCOSUR—the CPC played an important role as mediator. However, as trade agendas gained in complexity and government consultations on trade negotiations became more detailed and often sector-specific, a peak number of sectoral associations gained new prominence. In fact, the broad and technical character of negotiations went far beyond the CPC's capabilities. Nevertheless, rather than investing in this multi-sectoral organization, businesses devoted their resources to the development of institutional leadership and technical abilities of sectoral associations, i.e. SOFOFA. Combined with extensive institutionalized access to the policy process, SOFOFA became the main interlocutor and even an ally when negotiating with the EU and under the FTAA, with the government. Unlike their counterparts in Argentina, Chilean agriculturalists were more strongly protectionist. Still, and contrary to their outsider strategies during negotiations with MERCOSUR, they promoted a collaborative strategy with public officials and trade diplomats after the launch of North-South and WTO negotiations. The SNA had undergone a successful learning process and was now interested in establishing a working relationship with public officials in ODEPA and DIRECON. However, these attempts were short-lived because of political changes within the organization.

The private sector resorted to formal and informal mechanisms to raise their demands and proposals in both Argentina and Chile. The SNA's 'outsider' strategy during negotiations with MERCOSUR remains an exception.

The early institutionalization of participatory mechanisms in Chile in the 1990s did not overrule informality. In Argentina, businesses mostly relied on the informal stable channels available but made extensive use of the formal mechanisms set up in the early 2000s as part of the new multipolar trade strategy. Despite considering these new formal mechanisms as mere window dressing, business people felt compelled to attend these meetings while also resorting to traditional informal ones, which in turn proved to be more useful for expressing their own demands and requirements. However, by then, and triggered by North-South negotiations, i.e. the FTAA, businesses including those with a more protectionist attitude within the UIA actively solicited information and called meetings with government, thus showing an unprecedented mobilization. Furthermore, the FTAA spurred their interests in developing institutional capabilities. In the case of rural producers, the launch of the Doha Round also reinforced such interest, as exemplified by the INAI.

In Chile, the SOFOFA had already developed a strong expertise in the negotiation of FTAs when facing North-South agendas. Both the FTAA and the agreement with the EU found the government and businesses forming a strong alliance based on their consensus about the desirability of free trade. This close and collaborative relationship strengthened Chile's position at the negotiating table.

The patterns of preference and collective action definitely came closer in both countries after the launch of the Doha Round. These agendas faced businesses with higher levels of uncertainty given the long-term horizon and the relatively high number of negotiating partners involved. As expected, under conditions of uncertainty, there was a tendency to lean more strongly towards ideas and information and develop a collaborative strategy, this being the case for rural organizations in both Argentina and Chile. These actors saw uncertainty as associated with a lack of information, so that their coping strategies focused on using investigation to collect missing information as well as applying forecasting techniques. In contrast, industrialists as represented by the SOFOFA and the UIA failed to provide public officials and trade diplomats with qualified input. Industrialists under the UIA quite specifically decided not to deal with uncertainty at all on the basis that neither offensive nor defensive strategies could prevent the potential negative effects of multilateral commitments.

In all, the Chilean private sector responded relatively quickly to the continuity in the benefits and selective incentives provided by the state. As the government created different access mechanisms to mitigate vulnerabilities in its policy and enhance its informational and legitimacy credentials, it contributed to the building of long-term institutional and technical abilities in business associations. Yet, in Argentina, the persistence of defensive and offensive business interests led to a complex pattern of collaborative and competitive strategies.

Those developing a collaborative relationship with public officials and trade diplomats undertook a steady learning process to develop their institutional and trading abilities. Stable and constant access to the government offered an important incentive to invest in their own organizations, which in turn reinforced this cooperative pattern of trade politics, leading in time to a close working relationship. Still, this was limited to particular sectors and chambers, namely, highly concentrated and export-oriented sectors. On the contrary, import-competing industrialists followed a historical pattern of reaction and defence despite enjoying extended inclusion to decision making. In turn, as long as their trading abilities were meagre, the chances for the consolidation of a virtuous circle involving a dynamic and two-way flow of information and expertise between public officials and industrialists also remained low. In sum, access to decision making seems to be a necessary condition but not a sufficient one. The quality and stability of available channels and mechanisms are also highly relevant. A strong and coherent demand for broader and clearer mechanisms was still absent. The cost of more transparent and participatory mechanisms could be too high, especially for those maintaining a protectionist stance.

Trade unions and civil society largely remained detached from trade negotiations until the 1990s. Starting with the creation of MERCOSUR and the later launch of external negotiations, trade unions and CSOs—consumers, women and environmental NGOs—started to pay more attention to international trade. Nevertheless, these negotiations, such as those between Chile and the Southern bloc, did not trigger sustained strategies and did not have a relevant impact on these first South-South negotiations (Hochstetler 2003). In fact, there was consensus that South-South negotiations, especially those involving Latin American partners, would promote development, strengthen and consolidate democracies and social and environmental agendas; all of which were also expected to have an impact on the position of the region in the international system.[7]

A relevant change, however, was initiated with the launch of North-South negotiations, as countries discussed the FTAA at the hemispheric level, and negotiations with the EU, at a time when they were involved in other regional initiatives and following the Doha Round of negotiations at the WTO as well. As trade unions and civil society faced these multiple scenarios, they acknowledged how ill-prepared they were to deal with trade, a new issue on their agendas that so far had focused on other, more domestic questions.

The launch of the FTAA in 1998 became especially significant. Starting with this North-South negotiation, trade unions and CSOs initiated an intense learning process, including the development of transnational strategies and the establishment of regional networks.[8] Civil society became very active at various levels—both domestic and regional—and attempted to build a common agenda based on criticism and demands. These ranged from the lack of transparency of negotiations and the absence of dialogue mechanisms with public officials and trade diplomats, to more in-depth arguments related to the 'race to the bottom' that these agreements promoted and the disregard for social, cultural and environmental issues in these negotiations.

However, the picture of trade unions and civil society activism was complex. Fragmentation and divisions ran along various axes, and became more visible only during the negotiation of North-South agreements, as it was these negotiations that mobilized trade unions and civil society more intensely.

First, there were discrepancies between those supporting free trade and those fully rejecting these negotiations. Whereas the first would more strongly focus on procedural agendas, i.e. transparency and participation, the second would bluntly refuse to negotiate on these agreements given their expected negative impacts, i.e. the race to the bottom and the unfair distribution of benefits and costs among Southern and Northern countries. Corporación Participa and Poder Ciudadano, on the one hand, and SERPAJ and ACJR, on the other, are clear examples of such fragmentation. These tensions also permeated the internal logic of organizations as in the case of the Chilean CUT. Second, there were differences between trade unions and NGOs, this being more marked in Chile, where labor oscillated between collaboration and antagonism with NGOs.

Participation also took place at several levels. The launch of the FTAA led to the creation of regional networks, which entailed two important transformations in terms of previous experiences of regional dialogue. First, they more intensively bridged the gap between the North and the South and, second, they widened the debate on free trade by including other issues on which FTAs could have an impact and which were largely disregarded in official negotiations. To the extent that these networks provided 'domestic sites of knowledge production' (von Bülow 2010:137) and for the discussion of a more diverse action repertoire, they reverberated in domestic debates, coordination and mobilization patterns.

Yet, participation at the domestic level remained fragmented and institutionally thin. Once again, even if an early process of institutionalization allowed civil society input in trade policy making in Chile, broader societal interests faced greater obstacles when trying to access public officials and trade diplomats. Moreover, after the creation of formal mechanisms in Argentina, a similar perception pervaded civil society in both countries: existing channels appeared as merely formal exercises as they did not allow real discussion and debates.

From a cross-negotiation perspective, the FTAA elicited the most variegated patterns of preference formation and action repertoire. These strategies oscillated between the outsider-insider dichotomies, while at the same time CSOs resorted to a wide array of collective action strategies.

In Argentina, as in the case of businesses, it was the FTAA that mobilized broader and more heterogeneous interests most fervently. However, even then, consultation mechanisms were limited, and the particular proposals and demands of trade unions and NGOs could hardly find a way to the trade policy process. Moreover, as the FTAA waned, the momentum of participation followed suit, and no other trade negotiation—not even the process between MERCOSUR and the EU that has recently been reactivated (Bianculli 2016b)[9] or the Doha Round—has excited so much social activism and mobilization.

This activism gained prominence in the 2000s in Argentina. In Chile, by the mid-1990s, just as the country faced its first North-South agreement, trade unions and CSOs had initiated a learning process to enhance their institutional and trading abilities. This resulted in the creation of a specialized department on international relations in the CUT as the labour organization attempted to build a more pragmatic approach to FTAs and trade liberalization. In this respect, the negotiation with Canada constituted a fundamental precedent. In Argentina, on the contrary, various domestic and internal factors accounted for the delay in the emergence of solid demand for participation, including the labour reform, changes in the organization of trade unions, and the creation and recreation of new forms of social activism. Based on the regional mandates and domestic pressures on public officials and trade diplomats, the CCSC was set. Yet, given the consultative nature of this body and the dense agenda where trade negotiations were only one topic among many others, their influence remained negligible.

In sum, in both countries the participation of broader civil society actors in the trade decision making was extremely limited, given constant institutional barriers and obstacles. Even if the creation of networks bringing together Northern and Southern organizations granted them access to numerous assets, including financial and technical resources, the absence of selective incentives in the form of institutionalized access at the domestic level seems to have hampered the development of their institutional leadership and trading abilities.

In all, apart from the impressive economic results of Chile's trade policy during the 15 years under study in this book, there is an enormous social and political consensus on the desirability of international trade liberalization and FTAs as a fundamental driver of economic growth and development (interview with senior ProChile). This consensus that makes Chile a unique case in the region, is clearly absent in Argentina, where trade policy has always been subject to intense debate and contestation as different bodies sought to shape the content and outcomes of trade policy. Moreover, in Chile the combined effects of extended inclusion for businesses and the learning process this selective incentive triggered, led in time to a close working relationship based on the mutual interchange of information, expertise and legitimacy but more importantly on personal relationships of loyalty and trust.

### *Comparing Patterns of Trade Politics*

Trade politics remained as the exclusive domain of governments, which more strongly sought the support and input of the private sector, thus leading to the de facto exclusion of wider societal interests. The launch of South-South, North-South and WTO negotiations under the Doha Round led in turn to similar patterns of trade politics across countries.

South-South negotiations elicited a pressured pattern of trade politics as the private sector lobbied for protection against competition from foreign production and even exclusion from the negotiations. The limited character of the trade agenda under negotiation explains the predominance of this pressure. Moreover, if effective participation in trade negotiations is a learning-by-doing process, this process was just beginning when most of these South-South agreements were pursued as Argentina and Chile veered towards negotiated liberalization in the early 1990s. Interestingly though, this business strategy was still persistent more than 10 years later when negotiating with China and India. Even in a country like Chile, with a long and stable trade policy, industrialists sought protection. Judging from the empirical and analytical narrative, businesses are expected to assume a more defensive stance when facing trade agendas that mainly deal with market access and tariffs.

North-South and WTO trade negotiations have more frequently led to a cooperative pattern of trade politics between public officials and businesses, thus revealing the relevance of expertise. Furthermore, trade politics patterns under the Doha Round negotiations at the WTO showed cross-national commonalties but cross-sectoral variations. Though relying on an extensive institutional architecture, agriculturists resorted to a collaborative strategy that contrasted with the difficulties industrial interests faced to define and make specific contributions to these countries' negotiating position. In time, a close working relationship emerged between public officials and trade diplomats, and those business sectors capable of providing technical knowledge. Once again, faced with complex and regulatory agendas, trade politics—as the relation between government and society—is heavily based on learning and the exchange of technical information and expertise. Moreover, in a context of uncertainty, trade politics triggered a learning process whereby businesses' institutional and trading abilities were enhanced, which was reinforced by their role as main interlocutors for governments.

When it comes to civil society, after assuming a cooperative strategy in South-South negotiations, thus promoting a pattern of subordinate trade politics in the early 1990s, the launch of North-South initiatives changed the picture of social activism and trade politics enormously. Following regional mandates and the need to build their legitimacy credentials, governments devised new institutional mechanisms to allow the participation of CSOs and NGOs without dramatically altering the limited character of the institutional architecture in place. However, the broader and deeper scope of North-South agendas elicited the most varied collective strategies and thus of trade politics patterns. These negotiations promoted regional networks for learning and for the deployment of a wider action repertoire to pursue specific issues and policy concerns. However, confrontational strategies were more strongly used after the launch of the FTAA and were practically negligible in the context of EU negotiations. Despite promoting similar economic and regulatory trade agendas, negotiations with the EU were preceded by long years of intensive collaboration and cooperation. The EU financed extensive programs aimed at promoting institution building, as in the case of MERCOSUR, but also at integrating and supporting civil society. Based on the idea of the EU as a civilian or normative power, which has not gone unchallenged especially in recent years, one could expect civil society to feel reluctant to confront one of their most important benefactors. In time, this strong activism, together with the coalitions and networks that framed it, weakened, and when the agenda broadened and became more complex, as in the case of the Doha Round, participation diminished. This is even more striking at the WTO, given the strong developmental component of the Doha agenda. In all, as institutional exclusion persisted at the domestic level, civil society had fewer incentives to invest in its institutional and trading abilities.

## Notes

1 Negotiations with MERCOSUR were the most controversial of all the processes initiated in Chile (interview with senior ProChile official), and the business community still perceives this as the worst agreement (interview with SOFOFA executive). Still, it marked a turning point in Chile's trade strategy as it laid the foundations for the treatment of sensitive sectors in subsequent negotiations (Furche 2011).

2 Acknowledging these demands, the Chile-China regional trade agreement includes a Memorandum of Understanding on Labour Cooperation and Social Security and an agreement on environmental cooperation based on Article 108 of the FTA, signed in 2005 and 2007, respectively.

3 The Singapore issues refer to the regulation of investment, competition policy, access and transparency in public procurement and trade facilitation. These were incorporated in the WTO agenda at the 1996 Singapore Ministerial Conference. Strongly advocated by both the EU and the United States, these issues were to be adopted during the Doha Round. However, due to the strong resistance of developing countries, it was agreed to proceed only with trade facilitation negotiations in parallel with the other negotiations that included, among others, agriculture liberalization and non-agricultural market access. Finally, a WTO Trade Facilitation Agreement (TFA) was passed at the Bali Ministerial Conference in 2013.

4 'La Argentina se va a sentar en todas las mesas posibles', Clarín, 21 September 2003.
5 In 2008, Decree 2025 created the Ministry of Production and distributed trade policy competences between it and the Ministry of Economy. Three years later, the Foreign Trade Secretariat was created under the Ministry of the Economy and Public Finance, which thus regained international trade policy responsibilities (Decree 2082/11).
6 For further details, see http://ccsc.mrecic.gov.ar/, last accessed 15 June 2016.
7 MERCOSUR provided labour unions with a common agenda that included strengthening democratic transitions and dealing with neoliberal reforms (Portella de Castro 2002).
8 The only exception had been the transnational links established in Latin America to denounce the crimes and human rights abuses of the dictatorships that plagued the region throughout the 1970s and 1980s (Bianculli 2003).
9 Even if the negotiation agenda between the EU and MERCOSUR is more reduced in economic terms but more ample in political issues, the liberalization of trade in services and investments is also part of the agreement, though as non-trade issues (Botto and Bianculli 2011).

## References

Bianculli, A. C. (2003). La sociedad civil en la Organización de los Estados Americanos: cambios en la governance de cara al siglo XXI. Master in International Relations Master Thesis, Facultad Latinoamericana de Ciencias Sociales (FLACSO-Argentina).

Bianculli, A. C. (2016a). Latin America, in T. A. Börzel and T. Risse (Ed.) *The Oxford Handbook of Comparative Regionalism*. Oxford, Oxford University Press: 154–177.

Bianculli, A. C. (2016b). Regulatory Governance Regimes and Interregionalism: Exploring the Dynamics of EU–Mercosur negotiations, *Canadian Journal of Latin American and Caribbean Studies / Revue canadienne des études latino-américaines et caraïbes* 41(2): 1–24.

Botto, M. and A. C. Bianculli (2011). Comparative Asymmetric Trade Negotiations in the Southern Cone: FTAA and EU-MERCOSUR, in P. De Lombaerde, D. Tussie and S. (Ed.) *Asymmetric Trade Negotiation*. Aldershot: Ashgate Publishing: 89–116.

Bouzas, R. and P. Gosis (2014). Institucionalidad y actores de la política comercial argentina, in C. H. Acuña (Ed.) *Dilemas del estado argentino: Política exterior, económica y de infraestructura en el siglo XXI*. Buenos Aires, Siglo XXI Editores-Fundación OSDE: 59–103.

Brambilla, I., S. Galiani and G. Porto (2010) "Argentine Trade Policies in the XXth Century: 60 Years of Solitude," Available at http://papers.ssrn.com/sol3/papers.cfm?abstract_id=1680606.

Furche, C. (2011). "Balance de la Política Comercial: Impacto y lineamientos para una nueva agenda." Working Papers ICSO-UDP. Santiago de Chile, Universidad Diego Portales.

Galiani, S. and P. Somaini (2010). "Path Dependent Import-Substitution Policies: The Case of Argentina in the XXth Century," Available at ssrn.com/abstract=1681757.

Godio, J. (2006). *El tiempo de Kirchner: El devenir de una 'revolución desde arriba'*. Buenos Aires, Letra Grifa.

Grugel, J. and M. P. Riggirozzi (2007). The Return of the State in Argentina, *International Affairs* 83(1): 87–107.

Hochstetler, K. (2003). Fading Green? Environmental Politics in the Mercosur Free Trade Agreement, *Latin American Politics and Society* 45(4): 1–32.

Mesquita Moriera, M. and J. Blyde (2006). "Chile's Integration Strategy: Is There Room for Improvement?" IADB-INTAL-ITD Working Paper 21, Washington, DC, IADB.

Mittelman, J. H. (2000). *The Globalization Syndrome: Transformation and Resistance*. Princeton, NJ, Princeton University Press.

Ostry, S. (2002). "The World Trading System in Dire Need of Reform." CEPS Policy Brief. Brussels, Centre for European Policy Studies.

Portella de Castro, M. S. (2002). Contribuição ao Grupo de Reflexão Prospectiva sobre o Mercosul: Propostas para ação e debate, in C. Hugueney Filho and C. H. Cardim (Ed.) *Grupo de Reflexão Prospectiva sobre o Mercosul*. Brasilia, Ministério das Relações Exteriores-BID: 63–76.

Robin, C. (2008). *A Domestic Policy-Making Approach to World Market Integration Strategies in Developing Nations: Chile, Argentina, Peru, and Bolivia in Comparison*. Doctor of Philosophy Dissertation, University of Zurich.

Sáez, S. and J. G. Valdés S. (1999). Chile and Its "Lateral" Trade Policy, *CEPAL Review* 67: 85–99.

Spiller, P. and M. Tommasi (2010). Un país sin rumbo. ¿Cómo se hacen las políticas públicas en Argentina? in C. Scartascini, P. Spiller, E. H. Stein and M. Tommasi (Ed.) *El juego político en América Latina. ¿Cómo se deciden las políticas públicas?* Washington, DC, BID-Mayol Ediciones: 75–115.

Stallings, B. (2009). Chile: A Pioneer in Trade Policy, in M. Solís, B. Stallings and S. N. Katada (Ed.) *Competitive Regionalism: FTA Diffusion in the Pacific Rim*. New York, Palgrave Macmillan: 118–138.

Theiler, E. (2012). *Estado y sociedad civil: la participación ciudadana en los procesos de integración latinoamericanos*. Villa María, Córdoba, Eduvim.

Varsky, H. (n.d.). *La Participación de la Sociedad Civil e Incidencia en las Políticas Públicas, Consejo Consultivo de la Sociedad Civil*. Cancillería Argentina.

von Bülow, M. (2010). *Building Transnational Networks: Civil Society and the Politics of Trade in the Americas*. Cambridge, Cambridge University Press.

# 7 Trade Politics in Latin America

## Past Lessons, Future Challenges

Trade politics is the result of the complex and dynamic interdependencies and interrelations between state and society. Its outcome cannot be predetermined from a set of economic or political structures. Structural and rational accounts of trade policy offer important insights into the behaviour of actors, whose interests are taken as being objectively, materially and exogenously given, when trade agendas involve tariffs and market access and thus have unambiguous distributional costs and benefits. However, they offer few clues as to why state-society relations exhibit different dynamics across trade negotiations. In other words, a question that remains open is why preferences and strategies vary in South-South, North-South and WTO negotiations as domestic actors attempt to respond effectively to the increasing depth of the agendas at stake and the uncertainty of policy outcomes. The framework used in this book spotlights dimensions of trade negotiations that should be considered in order to understand fully how and why domestic actors respond differently to international trade agendas.

In these conclusions, I shall first summarize the main argument of this book that policy creates trade politics, which is taken as a dynamic process of configuration and reconfiguration of state-society interactions. I then highlight the relevance of combining the international and the national levels to comprehend better the various patterns of trade politics. These dimensions became visible because of the focus of the research on the relational and political dynamics underlying trade politics, and the importance attributed to the specific international and domestic political contexts in which governments and societal representatives define their preferences and collective strategies. I conclude by providing a more general review of the legacies of trade politics in Latin America and by discussing the challenges of the current international scene.

### Policy Creates Trade Politics

As is commonly argued, the trade agenda has undergone fundamental transformations since the early 1990s, and these have had important consequences for the ways in which governments and societal representatives define their preferences and collective strategies. From either a regional or a multilateral perspective, studies have portrayed the new trade agenda as creating a far more testing environment for governments as far as their institutional abilities, expertise and legitimacy are concerned. At the same time, the new trade agenda has promoted the direct engagement of new groups, apart from the more traditional distributional coalitions, which are oriented towards the struggle over the allocation of wealth and income. My research has taken this argument a step forward by showing how and to what extent the impact on domestic trade politics varies depending on the nature of the negotiations. The more general conclusion is that the launch of South-South, North-South and WTO negotiations led to different patterns of state-society relations. In other words, policy creates trade politics.

Scholarly literature has distinguished how different policies generate diverse policy dynamics. Different types of issues or regulatory commitments are expected to elicit particular political dynamics: given the relevant variance in terms of the distribution of anticipated costs and benefits, they have a diverse impact on the incentive structure and hence mobilization patterns of different groups (Lowi 1964; Wilson 1980). Consequently, the policymaking process and the underlying political relationships will change depending on the level of conflict over a policy (Lowi 1964).

When analysing the nuances of trade politics in recent years, studies have acknowledged variation across agendas according to the level of political salience and certainty over distributional effects (Poletti 2012). The negotiation of regulatory commitments under traditional trade policy, commercial policy and social trade policy is expected to trigger different policy dynamics (Young 2007). From a Latin American perspective, analysts have contended that market reforms in the region altered policy dynamics depending on how the costs of the particular policy reform were distributed and whether these were certain or uncertain, immediate or longer term, and uniform or uneven (Haggard 2000, Kaufman and Nelson 2004, Murillo 2001, Schneider 2004). Within this scheme, trade liberalization is portrayed as having uncertain outcomes, with multiple and uneven distributional effects depending on how it affected the allocation of a larger number of resources and the interests of many more groups than the more targeted market reforms, as in the case of privatization. This study combines both strands by showing how and to what extent the launch of South-South, North-South and WTO negotiations led to different patterns of state-society relations.

The evidence demonstrates that the institutional architecture provided by the government and societal demand is crucial to understanding the interactions and dialogue between state and society in the context of different trade negotiations.

Governments are in the 'driver's seat'. However, the analytical narrative has shown that governments do not merely respond to societal demands, nor are they pursuing a clear national interest or acting in isolation from social pressures. In fact, government strategies are sometimes undertaken in the context of institutional fragmentation and low-level coordination among public agencies, and are thus the result of power struggles within the state. Nor are the strategies a direct response to private demands. On the contrary, as the trade agenda gains in depth, complexity and uncertainty, new relational and interdependence dynamics are generated between state and society.

The institutional architecture refers to the specific constellation of both formal and informal mechanisms and channels of access to trade policy decision making. Moreover, the institutional architecture or political opportunity structure is neither stable nor unchangeable (Kitschelt 1986, Kriesi et al. 1992, Tarrow 1994). In fact, the analytical narrative reveals that the dynamic character of the institutional architecture relates to the specific, perceived vulnerabilities of governments. Their perceived informational and legitimacy vulnerabilities are crucial to explaining why governments pursue collaboration, with whom, and through which mechanisms. Thus, relevant aspects of the institutional architecture are modified according to the specific needs that governments intend to build on. Governments' informational and legitimacy abilities do not rely on the formal and institutional resources attached to the instruments of command. Rather, they are the result of the governments' ability to define and construct relationships that link different agents and resources to compensate for these perceived deficits, and thus strengthen their own negotiating position.

The empirical work confirms that in a context of continuous and simultaneous trade negotiations, the demand for information and technical expertise is permanent.[1] Nevertheless, this perceived vulnerability increases as trade agendas move from the reciprocal reduction of tariffs to include the negotiation or harmonization of regulatory frameworks. Moreover, as the agenda deepens and gains in complexity, the analytical and technical requirements for governments exceed their need for legitimacy and broad social support.

To compensate or alleviate their informational deficiencies, public officials and trade diplomats consistently involve the business community, the logical reservoir of detailed and technical information, in decision making. Consequently, governments are likely to provide an extensive institutional structure for the private sector. This close collaboration with business certainly fundamentally enhances the informational capacities and expertise of public officials and trade diplomats. However, these interactions may be built at the expense of the equally legitimate participation of broader sections of society. Moreover, to the extent that these mechanisms tend to rely mostly on informal channels and lack clear rules of participation and effective procedural criteria, the resulting governance arrangements do not necessarily promote transparency and accountability in the trade policy process. This is even the case when dealing with trade agendas that include participation, transparency and accountability commitments. As already noted, these external pressures will always be sifted through national traditions and the domestic institutional setting. Hence, an intersection of a limited institutional architecture due to the perception that the governments' legitimacy needs are weak, together with feeble societal demand for change, will not produce results above the threshold level at which the barriers of institutional inertia can be broken through. Arrangements for governance of domestic trade will still favour narrow interests at the expense of wider society, which would find it difficult to hold accountable those who really make trade policy.

As depicted in Chapter 2, looking at societal demands shows that different patterns of preference formation emerge as business, labour and civil society attempt to respond to the challenges posed by particular international trade agendas. At the same time, access to decision making works as a selective incentive for society to act collectively. The definition of preferences and strategies depends on the cost-benefit balance of the possible courses of action, which is mainly given by the political opportunity structure that serves as framework or scenario for strategic action and which defines the modes of interaction with governments and other social groups as well. Moreover, whereas the institutional architecture is a relevant element in explaining trade politics, the extent to which representatives of society are capable of participating and fully exploiting these channels is also fundamental. This certainly depends on their own institutional and informational resources, even if continuous and stable access to policymakers provides incentives for groups in society to invest in their organizations. Thus, over time, their responses and strategies accumulate and enhance their institutional and informational capacities.

The empirical evidence confirms that the institutional architecture is largely determined by the specific vulnerabilities for which states attempt to compensate. Therefore, the resulting structures have a diverse impact on the incentives for collective action and for the promotion of capabilities in societies.

Examining the variety of negotiations through time, the narrative reveals a strong correlation between the perceived informational vulnerabilities of governments and their overtures (both formal and informal) to business. Within this institutional context, business strategies favour more traditional lobbying, either to demand liberalization or protection for domestic-oriented sectors, and this contrasts with the more active response of those already subject to increased economic regionalization resulting from the adoption of varieties of domestic neoliberal policies and the promotion of export growth strategies in the 1990s (Breslin et al. 2002). Information and expertise are not evenly distributed through the business community and tend to be monopolized by concentrated and very competitive sectors, which in time became valuable and irreplaceable interlocutors for state officers. Whereas this fluid relationship enhanced the informational capacities of governments, it also boosted incentives for firms to invest in their respective organizations and cadres.

The analysis also shows that as regional and international agendas deepened and multiplied, trade policy and negotiations occupied an increasingly prominent place on the agenda of labour and CSOs, and also of other social movements and networks that have laxer organizational modes. Whereas stakes were more difficult to evaluate, to the extent that policy outcomes appeared to be diffuse, these deeper agendas were perceived as ambitious and demanding as they impinged on sensitive issues involving governments' ability to pursue a variety of public policy objectives. Still, despite commitments to promote more democratic and transparent procedures, governments' perceived legitimacy vulnerabilities were low. They thus remained liable to be accused of failure in that they offered trade unions, CSOs and NGOs only limited channels of participation. Moreover, these mechanisms did not translate into enduring features of the trade policy sector's institutional setting. This thinly veiled exclusion of wider societal bodies discouraged investment in their own organizations.

Finally, this larger heterogeneity in terms of the societal organizational styles, objectives, and thus in the modes and intensity of collective action will be to some extent discouraged by regulatory agendas demanding enhanced trade capabilities and expertise in the context of long-term negotiations where policy outcomes are more uncertain. Involvement in these processes failed to emerge in the absence of stable and institutionalized access to policy channels and of strong informational capacities.

## Trade Politics at the Intersection of Domestic and International Dynamics

Globalization and regionalization do not entail the demise of the national state and domestic economic, social and political processes. Rather, international developments and challenges add new complexities that require comparative and international political economics as complementary analytical tools. Such an approach is fundamental for capturing the varied configurations of state-society relationships within the context of different trade negotiations. Comparison of trade negotiations between countries enabled the assessment of the relevance of external pressures vis-à-vis national factors. Moreover, it allowed for discussion of the extent to which domestic traditions are decisive elements or alternatively how international pressures exceed the weight of domestic institutionally established arrangements.

### *The International Dimension*

From the perspective of the international political economy, the particular trade agendas at play underlie the constellations of domestic preferences, strategies and political opportunity structures. In this respect, South-South, North-South and WTO trade negotiations can be usefully disaggregated into variations in the scope of the agenda and the uncertainty of the policy outcomes attached to it; all of which impact on the resulting patterns of trade politics.

Trade negotiations range in a continuum from narrow to broad agendas, namely, from tariff reduction and market access to IPRs, investment, services, as well as emerging issues such as competition policy, environmental and labor standards; all of which affect the making of domestic rules. Second, as the agenda gains in breadth and depth, trade negotiations place greater emphasis on the regulatory frameworks that structure trade and thus require greater technical knowledge and expertise. The legalization of trade issues and an increased tendency to resort to litigation further reinforce this trend. Finally, whereas uncertainty is one of the most important characteristics of the political world when it comes to policy outcomes, South-South, North-South and WTO negotiations entail varying degrees of uncertainty. When combining both dimensions, the picture of trade politics becomes more complex and also more varied than originally predicted by the rationalist, and generally, materialistic mainstream of international political economy.

First, South-South negotiations bring in narrow and markedly sectoral agendas. Under these conditions, states more strongly act as umpires between businesses' preferences and demands. Moreover, only those businesses having clear stakes in expanding or limiting trade opportunities are prone to engage after the launch of negotiations. Close-knit interest groups will attempt to prevent policy capture by competitors. Contrariwise, larger societal representatives remain rather detached, since these negotiations do not impinge on the structure of their incentives.

Second, North-South negotiations exhibit the most varied patterns of trade politics as they include elements of the old and the new agendas while also attempting to go beyond WTO-standards. Their potential impact is hence broader: they reach out to domestic regulations in new policy areas and thus impact on the incentive structure of broader societal groupings. Moreover, they impose new challenges on both governments and society. Apart from encouraging further information sharing and coordination among public agencies, governments are pushed to establish a dialogue with a wider array of organizations to increase their store of information and justify their actions as they respond to the Northern partners' requirements of participation, transparency and accountability. Business, as well as trade unions and CSOs, attempt to influence public officials and trade diplomats. In doing so, they resort to new forms of social activism and a more heterogeneous set of strategies, including contestation, opposition and confrontation, and even mixtures of them.

Third, both North-South and multilateral trade negotiations show the pre-eminence of technical information and expertise over legitimacy. As the agendas deepen by including the harmonization and construction of regulatory frameworks that impinge on domestic regulatory and legal systems embedded in the institutional infrastructure of the economy—as in the case of environmental and labour standards—the demand for information, knowledge and expertise expands notably. This leads governments to solicit the collaboration and input of large and internationalized business interests more strongly. The latter will then move away from traditional lobbying strategies and deploy collaborative and strategic relations based on exchanges of information and expertise.

Finally, negotiations under the Doha Round show the extent to which the increasing participation promoted by deeper agendas is curtailed as the uncertainty of policy outcomes increases. In fact, multilateral negotiations involve a large number of parties, deal with multiple economic issues that move simultaneously, often in different directions, and hence have a longer horizon. This complexity adds to the uncertainty of policy outcomes; all of which reduces the likelihood of broader civil society participation despite the strong developmental component of the Doha Round. Businesses, however, show diverging strategies. Those sectors that associate uncertainty with a lack of information (i.e. agriculturists) mainly try to reduce uncertainty by using investigation to collect missing information and applying forecasting techniques while participating in the policy process themselves with the aim of influencing policymakers. On the contrary, those businesses (i. e. industrialists) that perceive WTO negotiations as largely inaccessible and impermeable to their influence deploy passive tolerance: they consider that the potentially negative effects of this regulatory uncertainty cannot be prevented by developing either offensive or defensive strategies. Thus, multilateral trade negotiations under the WTO elicit similar patterns of trade politics across sectors. Certainly, this finding calls for further exploration, all the more so because it seems to contradict the idea that when facing prolonged processes, collective participation is unlikely to emerge, unless strong associations and institutionalized access to policy channels are available (Schneider 2010). Still, this does not seem to hold when comparing the strategies of agricultural and industrial associations in Argentina and Chile after the launch of the Doha Round.

Hence, the variation in the scope of the agenda and the uncertainty of policy outcomes attached to South-South, North-South and WTO negotiations lead to different political and relational dynamics. However, the full pattern of trade politics emerges at the intersection of the specific trade negotiations and requirements at stake, on the one hand, and the domestic institutional setting, on the other.

### *The Domestic Dimension*

Adopting a comparative political economy analysis, state-society relations are path-conditioned and marked by the constraints arising from past policy choices. On this basis, the stability of trade policies explains the emergence and consolidation of a continuous and fluid relationship between the government and the business community. Accordingly, in Chile, a country where a long-term and strategic approach to free trade has been in place for more than 25 years, governments—irrespective of their political colour—have promoted continuous and stable cooperative relations with society. Combined with the public sector's increased specialization and professionalization, governments have offered a crucial incentive for the private sector to invest in their organizational and technical abilities. Premised on the exchange of information and expertise and the consolidation of mutual trust, these dialogues turned into a close working relationship. Transformations in business associations confirmed the importance of this benefit. However, similar incentives appeared to be absent from labour unions and wider civil society bodies. Therefore this close relationship remained biased towards the private sector, mainly large and well-organized associations, at the expense of broader societal interests, namely, SMEs, trade unions and CSOs, which have been largely excluded from the equation.

In contrast, unstable trade policies characterize Argentina's history. Governments' commitment to free trade policies has been fragile and ambivalent there. This policy volatility has hampered the development of a state bureaucracy capable of overcoming policy and political shifts in favour of a sustainable trade policy, whereas trade policymaking procedures remained unstable and informal. Moreover, in a context of high fragmentation across economic sectors and loose organizational and technical capabilities, the lack of sound and constant access to public officials has deprived businesses of a fundamental incentive to invest in their own organizations.

Moreover, from a sociological institutional approach, the coherent and stable trade policy paradigm that has prevailed in Chile is path-dependent. It illustrates the weight of past legacies and policy choices that constrain and limit the ability of all parties to pursue their policy preferences. Whereas the inherited institutional setting imposed strong limitations, the memory of the free-market dictatorship and the three-year period of intense political polarization under the UP that preceded it further deepened the policy path.

Certainly, this policy legacy marked the relationship between the government and the business elite. On the one hand, the new democratic governments did not question the free-market model imposed by the military regime in exchange for greater political democratization. On the other hand, the business community accepted some degree of political change as long as the new government maintained its commitment to the market economy. This constituted the core of an explicit pact between the government and the private sector, which feared a return to authoritarianism and to the political and economic instability of the UP, respectively.[2] Based on their agreement on the desirability of free trade, including establishing closer economic ties with industrialized countries, when facing the more challenging North-South agendas, the Concertación and businesses established a close and collaborative relationship aimed at advancing the country's negotiation position. But in Argentina, in the absence of such consensus, the heterogeneity of the private sectors' preferences, a more complex pattern of relationships including pressure and cooperative strategies emerged.

From an institutional perspective, several elements explain Chile's policy effectiveness and the country's capacity to speak with one voice. They include its strong presidential regime, the reduced number of veto players, a comparatively low degree of institutional fragmentation and a relatively high degree of inter-agency coordination (Bouzas 2006, Meller 2006). Furthermore, international trade is a relevant component of the public administration and sectoral policies and ministries; decentralized institutions and regional governments are also involved in those decisions and commitments that the negotiated FTAs require (Furche 2011). When contrasted with the instability and volatility of trade policies and the difficulties of elaborating a unified position in Argentina, institutional fragmentation, together with the fragility of the public sector organization and the low degree of inter-agency coordination seem to account for the marked differences. Moreover, the relative weakness of effective veto players renders policy change easier and stable bargains more difficult to reach (Leiras and Soltz 2006).

In Chile, this stable and coherent trade policy paradigm relied on public officials and experts with long terms in office, which in turn allowed more autonomy for the state. Rather than totally 'isolating' the state from societal pressures, this autonomy means that the stability and coherence of the trade paradigm offer clear criteria for resisting the demands of those opposing outward looking traders, while accepting those of free traders. Both the stability on the public side and the constant dialogue with the business elite triggered the establishment of a 'policy network', granting further access to the policy process. In time, trade policy generated its own public and private constituencies, making backpedalling and changes too costly and difficult. In Argentina, on the contrary, these factors remained elusive.

However, as the trade agenda gains in depth, complexity and uncertainty, the weight of national traditions seems to dilute in the face of international pressures. Interestingly, patterns of trade politics are quite close in the two countries after the launch of the Doha Round, whereas differences among the trade sectors appear to be more marked. This empirical finding shows that relying on strong institutional abilities and multiple opportunities to partake in decision making is not enough for businesses to cope with uncertainty actively. In this respect, institutionalized arrangements and the incentive provided by the state do not account for the specific ways in which the private sector reacts to conditions of increasing uncertainty. The salience of regulatory issues is certainly a relevant element when analysing trade politics. However, societal groups and more specifically businesses can adopt various strategies, the active search for information and close collaboration with policymakers being just one of the possible responses. They may also resort to other coping strategies: offensive, defensive, passive.[3] It may be useful for further research to analyse how particular uncertainties predispose some sections of society to adopt these different strategies, or a combination of them. This is fundamental given that regulation is growing apace in the international arena, exposing both governments and societies to considerable uncertainty.

## Continuity and Change in Latin American Trade Politics

This book started with observation of the collapse of the negotiations for the creation of a Free Trade Area of the Americas in 2005. It then went back to look at the previous 15 years, during which Argentina and Chile, together with other countries in the Southern Cone and in Latin America, began negotiating multiple trade agreements to reinstate themselves into the region and the world.

Sweeping market reforms, which came as reaction to decades of state intervention and protectionism, included adopting macroeconomic policies, implementing privatization, deregulating, and opening up to foreign investments as prescribed by the Washington Consensus, which was then the orthodox canon of international financial institutions. Trade liberalization was a fundamental pillar of this reform package. However, this failed to promote greater reciprocity in market access, and Southern governments veered towards FTAs and multilateral commitments under the WTO in an attempt to gain it. Moreover, the impact of unilateral reforms was far from homogeneous across countries and also across sectors. Whereas in terms of granting access to their own markets most countries had already made important progress by the early 1990s, in other areas liberalization had not advanced steadily, as had been the case with investment. Hence, in contrast to the experience of industrialized countries, in the case of emerging countries like Argentina and Chile, by the time the trade negotiation processes were launched, economies were not widely and homogeneously liberalized. In addition, while in the developed world market-based economies and democratic governance are usually found together, in developing countries, when these reforms were launched, their grasp upon democracy was still rather fragile. Dealing with market reforms and trade liberalization entailed important challenges regarding fundamental democratic governance principles, namely accountability, representation and transparency. This was especially the case when negotiating South-South, North-South and WTO commitments.

After looking into the patterns of trade politics promoted by these various negotiations, my findings confirm the highly technical and technocratic character of these processes, which thus jeopardized accountability and transparency. These findings are in line with studies highlighting the negative impact of market reform programs on democratic governance (Haggard and Kaufman 1995, Williams 2006).[4] The narrative suggests that international negotiations have made trade politics less democratic by empowering certain groups, such as businesses, and rendering structures and processes more opaque. Therefore, citizens and broader social groups found it increasingly difficult to play an active role in public decisions or to hold accountable those who really make policy. Market-opening policies went hand in hand with democratization, thus leading to technocratic decision making while severely limiting access to the state by wider popular interests in society (Silva 2008). These democratic shortcomings added to the failures and criticisms of neoliberalism and the Washington Consensus, where development turned out to be the missing element.

For over two decades, market reform advanced rapidly in Latin America, bringing new patterns of growth, production, finance, trade and international connections, among others; all underpinned by a different understanding of the relations between the state, the market and society. However, towards the end of the 1990s, and especially at the turn of the century, the challenges and problems associated with free-market fundamentalism became more visible, calling into question the neoliberal model throughout Latin America.

Restructuring proved to be effective at promoting investment and modernization (Stallings and Peres 2011) and technology transfer (Gwynne and Kay 2000), and at the same time integrated Latin American economies more closely with regional and global markets. Nevertheless, all this came at a high cost. From an international perspective, countries became more dependent and hence more exposed to economic fluctuations and shifts. Additionally, the impact on growth was only temporary. Hence, as growth rates slowed down, trade imbalances grew[5] and economic and financial crises became epidemic (Beeson and Islam 2005, Hart-Landsberg 2006, Tabb 2003) since capital openness tended to attract flows into asset speculation and (import-intensive) consumption (Palma 2003).

Social conditions also deteriorated considerably. Unemployment increased, poverty levels in 2005 exceeded those of the 1980s, real wages almost equalled those of the 1980s but income distribution was uneven, and inequality was still persistent and clearly high (Beeson and Islam 2005, Grugel and Riggirozzi 2012).

Similar disenchantment also became evident with neoliberal and market-based regional and international integration strategies. Part of the disappointment may be explained by the biased character of trade policy making that favoured large economic interests and technocrats to the detriment of others and thus undermined the legitimacy and hence the stability of these strategies. Still, whereas one would expect this criticism to be more prominent in countries with unstable and fragile trade policies, as in Argentina, in fact the situation was also present in Chile. Leading representatives of the business community from that country who were interviewed for this study expressed their concerns about a trade strategy that had not led to the diversification of their export production, and called for the deepening of already existing trade agreements rather than the pursuit of new ones. In fact, given the governments' failure to prioritize catch-up, the Chilean economy also had trouble in shifting to higher value-added stages of production (Parrilli 2004, Schurman 2001).

Decades of market reform and trade liberalization gave way to growing disillusionment, rising doubt and new strategies. From the 2000s the region began shifting away from the neoliberal canon, without fully displacing it. There is evidence that supports the hypothesis that 'there has been little backsliding on the reforms' (Stallings and Peres 2011:783). Governments across the region 'hardly advanced neoliberalism, certainly compared to (sic) the 1990s' (Corrales 2012:149). Nonetheless, there was no major reversal in the main reforms undertaken in the heat of neoliberalism, which thus showed its adaptive character as a regime of socioeconomic governance (Peck et al. 2010). Yet the new leftist and left-of-centre governments that, in differing degrees, were elected as a reaction against orthodox neoliberal governments slowly opened a new chapter in Latin America's political economy of development. A variety of names characterized the policies of these new governments: post-neoliberal (Grugel and Riggirozzi 2007, Macdonald and Ruckert 2009, Roberts 2008), new developmental (Bresser-Pereira 2007) or neo-structural (Bielschowsky 2008, Ffrench-Davis and Machinea 2007).

At the policy level, these new administrations incorporated a wide assortment of policies and instruments. In all, because of the particular mix of approaches, policies and instruments, it is widely acknowledged that there is no single Left in Latin America.[6] Hence variations persisted across countries, although important commonalities remained.

The most striking commonalities refer to the search for a new form of social contract between state and society (Tussie 2009, Wylde 2011), which implied restoring the role of the state and reducing or further regulating market power. Re-emphasized citizenship and social rights (Almeida and Johston 2006, Grugel and Riggirozzi 2012) were aligned with greater investment in welfare provision and social policy (Panizza 2005, 2009). All this was in a context marked by a strict vigilance against fiscal deficits, debt and inflation (Bresser-Pereira 2006, Corrales 2012).

From a strictly economic perspective, while retaining important elements of the previous export-led model of growth, these various approaches to post-neoliberalism have affected the formation of new relations with the regional and world economies. As countries attempted to respond to a changing international context, they promoted the construction of new and alternative regional schemes while also diversifying trade relations away from the United States and, to a lesser extent, the EU.

From a regional perspective, countries acknowledged the limitations of free trade and economic liberalization as purveyed by the Washington Consensus. A new regional consensus emerged: it was more focused on development and called for a more active role of the state in various arenas, including that of social policy. This translated into the creation of fresh regional initiatives, as with the Union of South American Nations (UNASUR) and the Bolivarian Alliance of the Americas (ALBA), and into the reframing of already existing blocs, e.g. MERCOSUR. Driven by the need to lessen dependence and promote development, regionalism today encompasses economic, political and social agendas (Bianculli and Ribeiro Hoffmann 2016). Consequently, the focus is no longer exclusively on trade liberalization; rather new arrangements have been instituted to manage investments, infrastructure, security, development and social policy fields as in the cases of education, health and employment, among others. Still, while both old and new regionalism followed a rather common pattern, today the region exhibits at least three different axes of economic cooperation, formed by MERCOSUR, the more liberal and market-oriented Pacific Alliance, and ALBA's model based on twenty-first century socialism (Briceño-Ruiz and Ribeiro Hoffmann 2015). Finally, countries pursued different regional, bilateral and multilateral postures in trade negotiations (Tussie and Heidrich 2008).

In all, the twenty-first century brought in more diversity. Against the background of a rapidly changing international arena, which had transformed the distribution of power, wealth and influence, Latin American countries embarked on different trajectories. Hence, countries in the region are embedded in a network of broader, denser and more diverse international relations in ways not known in the past.

## Broader Contributions and Future Research Agenda

In all, as this book makes clear, understanding trade politics demands that we adopt a encompassing approach. Trade policy strategies, taken as policy choices, are the result of a complex set of factors, both domestic and international. External pressures are sifted through domestic variables before being translated into actual trade policy choices or strategies. Whereas the latter can be partly explained by specific structural factors—namely, economic size, degree of openness and structure of comparative advantage, among others—the domestic institutional configuration offers important insights to account for trade politics. In sum, pressures vary across trade negotiations, and national factors mediate these pressures within countries. Thus, a key theme of the book is the relevance of links between the domestic and international dimensions of public policy, on the one hand, and the patterns of relations and interactions between governments and societal representatives and the arenas in which they operate, on the other.

On an international note, one of the central features of the changing environment of trade politics in Latin America today is the extremely diverse relations and ties within the region but also with Asia, Africa and the Middle East. These add to the more traditional relations with the EU and the United States; all of which further challenge and erode the boundaries demarcating the domestic from the international. In such a context, the study of political economy can no longer be exclusively understood in domestic or national terms. Even if analyses of cross-level connections have arisen during the last 20 years, there is still room for further research regarding the interaction of the domestic and the international in a wider set of arenas, well beyond trade. This becomes even more crucial as Latin American countries show increasing capacity and assertiveness to affect debates and negotiations on prominent global issues as with health, medicine and environment, among others.

In turn, this calls for the investigation of two elements. First, it is clear that the deep transformations of the trade agenda and the regionalization and multilateralization of the political economy of trade policy entail a more complex picture than that originally conceived in the two-level models (Putnam 1988). However, and as shown by the experience of Latin America countries since the 1990s, developing countries have been increasingly immersed in various, simultaneous trade liberalization scenarios. Further research into who are involved in a whole network of simultaneous games may contribute to our understanding of how the international and domestic interact in the context of trade negotiations in Latin America and in the developing world. Second, whereas one could plausibly argue that the leverage of industrialized countries is reasonably stable in these various scenarios, in the case of developing countries their influence is expected to vary, depending on the specific type of negotiation. This calls then for a more nuanced approach to the influence and leverage of developing countries in trade negotiations.

From a domestic perspective, the nature of state-society relations is not static. Rather this book provides evidence that state-society links are constantly modified as the social and political relationships underpinning state capacities change with the need to respond to international pressures. During the last more than 10 years, new modes of statehood and citizenship have been taking shape in Latin America as countries veered towards integration strategies with Southern partners both in the region and beyond. A more careful examination of the interactions between state and societal representatives at the domestic level is fundamental to assessing whether, how and to what extent these transformations have resulted in novel forms of trade politics by including a broader sweep of society, which was marginalized during the previous model of integration. In this respect, whereas policy legacies can certainly determine and delimit the range of legitimate and feasible responses to new international challenges, these can also be reinterpreted and hence provide opportunities for policy and institutional learning.

A final issue, which clearly goes beyond my objective in this book, concerns the relationship between trade and development. In this respect, a crucial question is to what extent neoliberal strategies aimed at (re-)instating Southern countries in regional and international investment and trade flows are intertwined with self-sustained development. Evidence suggests that they failed to deliver on the promise of growth and development, and provoked increasing instability and inequality. In turn, these shortcomings and failures ushered in the construction of alternative regional and international trade regimes in the region, whose impact is still difficult to evaluate.

These changes in the trade strategies of Latin American countries reflect the extent to which political economy cycles in the region are becoming shorter. After more than 50 years of the ISI model, neoliberalism became the predominant paradigm in policy circles in the late 1980s and throughout the 1990s. By the early 2000s, it lost ground, and although not totally displaced, it managed to coexist with neo-developmentalism and post-neoliberalism. At the moment of finishing this book, policy and academic circles are debating the rise of the political right in Latin America and the domestic and international policy implications. Without presuming to minimize the economic, social and political implications of these changes and transformations, it is true that one element continues unaltered: distributive and ideological conflicts remain inextricably linked to trade policy orientations. This might be a moment for Latin America to step back and take stock of what has been achieved, to review the lessons learned and notice how the global economy is currently structured, in order to promote a longer-term vision of trade policy and development, and its complementarity with other policy instruments.

## Notes

1 Studies have shown that the need for expertise is constant in trade policy (Aninat and Botto 2005), contrary to the perceived vulnerability of governments in other

areas of structural reform where the need for technical expertise is restricted to times of crisis.

2 In all, Chile's pre-1973 history of democracy explains its success after the 1990s (Angell 2009), whereas path dependence accounts for its successful trade policy strategies (Meller 2006).

3 Studies have shown that businesses deploy a variety of coping strategies to deal with uncertainty. Apart from the more traditional categorization into offensive, defensive or passive, Engau and Hoffmann (2011) have analysed the impact of the Kyoto regulation and have thus elaborated specific combinations of these three types. In all, they argue that the strategies deployed by firms respond to the perceived level of regulatory uncertainty and their exposure to future regulations. Thus, they conclude that the higher the level of uncertainty, the broader the range of strategies firms deploy. Moreover, those firms that perceive that future regulations are more likely to affect them will seek to cope with uncertainty more actively.

4 Without totally disregarding these negative effects, other analysts have contended that neoliberalism has strengthened democratic survival by enhancing the international protection for democracy and by hindering domestic challenges to democratic stability (Weyland 2004).

5 The average trade deficit of developing countries in the 1990s was higher than in the 1970s by almost 3 percentage points of GDP (UNCTAD 1999).

6 Starting with Castañeda's (2006) distinction between the 'right' and 'bad' left, alternative typologies and labels proliferated as scholars attempted to account for the most relevant differences between governments. Still, these may have run out of steam. Given their focus on the big-picture policy outcomes, they inhibit the most nuanced explanations (Bruhn 2015).

## References

Almeida, P. and H. Johston (2006). Neoliberal Globalization and Popular Movements in Latin America, in H. Johston and P. Almeida (Ed.) *Latin American Social Movements: Globalization, Democratization and Transnational Networks*. London, Rowman & Littlefield: 3–18.

Angell, A. (2009). Democratic Governance in Chile, in S. Mainwaring and T. R. Scully (Ed.) *Democratic Governance in Latin America*. Stanford, Stanford University Press: 269–306.

Aninat, A. S. and M. Botto (2005). *The Influence of Locally Produced Research on Trade Policy Making: The Case of Chile*. Buenos Aires, Facultad Latinoamericana de Ciencias Sociales (FLACSO-Argentina)—Programa de Estudios sobre Instituciones Económicas Internacionales (PIEI), for the Global Development Network "Bridging Research and Policy" Project.

Beeson, M. and I. Islam (2005). Neo-Liberalism and East Asia: Resisting the Washington Consensus, *The Journal of Development Studies* 41(2): 197–219.

Bianculli, A. C. and A. Ribeiro Hoffmann, Eds. (2016). *Regional Organizations and Social Policy in Europe and Latin America: A Space for Social Citizenship?* Basingstoke, Palgrave Macmillan.

Bielschowsky, R. (2008). Sixty Years of ECLAC: Structuralism and Neo-Structuralism, *CEPAL Review* 97: 171–192.

Bouzas, R. (2006). Introduction, in R. Bouzas (Ed.) *Domestic Determinants of National Trade Strategies: A Comparative Analysis of Mercosur Countries, Mexico and Chile*. Paris, MERCOSUR Chair -Science Po: 11–44.

Breslin, S., C. W. Hughes, N. Phillips and B. Rosamond, Eds. (2002). *New Regionalism in the Global Political Economy: Theories and Cases*. London, Routledge.
Bresser-Pereira, L. C. (2006). O novo desenvolvimentismo e a ortodoxia convencional, *São Paulo em Perspectiva* 20(3): 5–24.
Bresser-Pereira, L. C. (2007). Estado y mercado en el nuevo desarrollismo, *Revista Nueva Sociedad* 210: 110–125.
Briceño-Ruiz, J. and A. Ribeiro Hoffmann (2015). Post-Hegemonic Regionalism, UNASUR, and the Reconfiguration of Regional Cooperation in South America, *Canadian Journal of Latin American and Caribbean Studies / Revue canadienne des études latino-américaines et caraïbes* 40(1): 48–62.
Bruhn, K. (2015). Defining the Left in Latin America, *Latin American Research Review* 50(1): 242–249.
Castañeda, J. G. (2006). Latin America's Left Turn, *Foreign Affairs* 85(3): 28–43.
Corrales, J. (2012). Neoliberalism and Its Alternatives, in P. R. Kingstone and D. Yashar (Ed.) *Handbook of Latin American Politics*. New York, Routledge: 133–157.
Engau, C. and V. H. Hoffmann (2011). Strategizing in an Unpredictable Climate: Exploring Corporate Strategies to Cope with Regulatory Uncertainty, *Long Range Planning* 44(1): 42–63.
Ffrench-Davis, R. and J. L. Machinea, Eds. (2007). *Economic Growth with Equity: Challenges for Latin America*. New York, ECLAC-Palgrave Macmillan.
Furche, C. (2011). "Balance de la Política Comercial: Impacto y lineamientos para una nueva agenda." Working Papers ICSO-UDP. Santiago de Chile, Universidad Diego Portales.
Grugel, J. and M. P. Riggirozzi (2007). The Return of the State in Argentina, *International Affairs* 83(1): 87–107.
Grugel, J. and M. P. Riggirozzi (2012). Post-Neoliberalism in Latin America: Rebuilding and Reclaiming the State after Crisis, *Development and Change* 43(1): 1–21.
Gwynne, R. N. and C. Kay (2000). Views from the Periphery: Futures of Neoliberalism in Latin America, *Third World Quarterly* 21(1): 141–156.
Haggard, S. (2000). Interests, Institutions, and Policy Reform, in A. O. Krueger (Ed.) *Economic Policy Reform: The Second Stage*. Chicago, University of Chicago Press: 21–60.
Haggard, S. and R. R. Kaufman (1995). *The Political Economy of Democratic Transitions*. Princeton, NJ, Princeton University Press.
Hart-Landsberg, M. (2006). Neoliberalism: Myths and Reality, *Monthly Review* 57(11), Available at http://monthlyreview.org/2006/04/01/neoliberalism-myths-and-reality/.
Kaufman, R. R. and J. M. Nelson, Eds. (2004). *Crucial Needs, Weak Incentives: Social Sector Reform, Democratization, and Globalization in Latin America*. Baltimore, Johns Hopkins University Press.
Kitschelt, H. P. (1986). Political Opportunity Structures and Political Protest: Anti-Nuclear Movements in Four Democracies, *British Journal of Political Science* 16(1): 57–85.
Kriesi, H., R. Koopmans, J. W. Duyvendak and M. G. Giugni (1992). New Social Movements and Political Opportunities in Western Europe, *European Journal of Political Research* 22(2): 219–244.
Leiras, M. and H. Soltz (2006). The Political Economy of International Trade Policy in Argentina, in R. Bouzas (Ed.) *Domestic Determinants of National Trade Strategies: A Comparative Analysis of MERCOSUR Countries, Mexico and Chile*. Paris, MERCOSUR Chair -Science Po: 45–83.

Lowi, T. J. (1964). American Business, Public Policy, Case Studies and Political Theory, *World Politics* 16(4): 667–715.

Macdonald, L. and A. Ruckert (2009). Post-Neoliberalism in the Americas: An Introduction, in L. Macdonald and A. Ruckert (Ed.) *Post-Neoliberalism in the Americas*. New York, Palgrave Macmillan: 1–18.

Meller, P. (2006). The Political Economy of Chilean Trade Policy: A Review, in R. Bouzas (Ed.) *Domestic Determinants of National Trade Strategies: A Comparative Analysis of Mercosur Countries, Mexico and Chile*. Paris, MERCOSUR Chair -Science Po: 249–278.

Murillo, V. (2001). *Labor Unions, Partisan Coalitions, and Market Reform in Latin America*. Cambridge, Cambridge University Press.

Palma, G. (2003). The 'Three Routes' to Financial Crisis: Chile, Mexico and Argentina [1]; Brazil [2]; Korea, Malaysia and Thailand [3], in H.-J. Chang (Ed.) *Rethinking Development Economics*. London, Anthem Press: 347–376.

Panizza, F. (2005). Unarmed Utopia Revisited: The Resurgence of Left-of-Centre Politics in Latin America, *Political Studies* 53(4): 716–734.

Panizza, F. (2009). *Contemporary Latin America: Development and Democracy beyond the Washington Consensus*. London & New York, Zed Books.

Parrilli, M. D. (2004). Integrating the National Industrial System: The New Challenge for Chile, *Review of International Political Economy* 11(5): 905–925.

Peck, J., N. Theodore and N. Brenner (2010). Postneoliberalism and Its Malcontents, *Antipode* 41: 94–116.

Poletti, A. (2012). *The European Union and Multilateral Trade Governance: The Politics of the Doha Round*. London, Routledge.

Putnam, R. D. (1988). Diplomacy and Domestic Politics: The Logic of Two-Level Games, *International Organization* 42(3): 427–460.

Roberts, K. M. (2008). Is Social Democracy Possible in Latin America? *Nueva Sociedad* 217: 86–98.

Schneider, B. R. (2004). Organizing Interests and Coalitions in the Politics of Market Reform in Latin America, *World Politics* 56(3): 456–479.

Schneider, B. R. (2010). Business Politics and Policymaking in Contemporary Latin America, in C. Scartascini, E. H. Stein and M. Tommasi (Ed.) *How Democracy Works: Political Institutions, Actors, and Arenas in Latin American Policymaking*. Cambridge, Inter-American Development Bank, David Rockefeller Center for Latin American Studies-Harvard University: 217–246.

Schurman, R. A. (2001). Uncertain Gains: Labor in Chile's New Export Sectors, *Latin American Research Review* 36(2): 3–29.

Silva, P. (2008). *In the Name of Reason: Technocrats and Politics in Chile*. University Park, PA, Penn State University Press.

Stallings, B. and W. Peres (2011). Is Economic Reform Dead in Latin America? Rhetoric and Reality since 2000, *Journal of Latin American Studies* 43(4): 755–786.

Tabb, W. K. (2003). After Neoliberalism? *Monthly Review* 55(2): 25–33.

Tarrow, S. (1994). *Power in Movement: Social Movements, Collective Action and Politics*. Cambridge, Cambridge University Press.

Tussie, D. (2009). Economic Governance after Neoliberalism, in J. Grugel and P. Riggirozzi (Ed.) *Governance after Neoliberalism in Latin America*. New York, Palgrave Macmillan: 67–87.

Tussie, D. and P. Heidrich (2008). A Tale of Ecumenism and Diversity: Economic and Trade Policies of the New Left, in J. G. Castañeda and M. A. Morales (Ed.) *Leftovers: A Tale of the Latin American Left*. New York, Routledge: 45–65.

UNCTAD (1999). *UNCTAD Report 1999*. New York, United Nations.
Weyland, K. (2004). Critical Debates: Neoliberalism and Democracy in Latin America: A Mixed Record, *Latin American Politics and Society* 46(1): 135–157.
Williams, M. E. (2006). Escaping the Zero-Sum Scenario: Democracy Versus Technocracy in Latin America, *Political Science Quarterly* 121(1): 119–139.
Wylde, C. (2011). State, Society, and Markets in Argentina: The Political Economy of Neodesarrollismo under Néstor Kirchner, 2003–2007, *Bulletin of Latin American Research* 30(4): 436–452.
Young, A. R. (2007). Trade Politics Ain't What It Used to Be: The European Union in the Doha Round, *Journal of Common Market Studies* 45(4): 789–811.

# Appendix 1: Breakdown of Interviews

*ARGENTINA*

| *Type* | *Number* |
|---|---|
| Public officials | 8 |
| Business representatives | 12 |
| Labour representatives | 2 |
| Civil society organizations | 3 |
| Experts | 3 |
| **Total** | **28** |

*CHILE*

| *Type* | *Number* |
|---|---|
| Public officials | 4 |
| Business representatives | 6 |
| Labour representatives | 1 |
| Civil society organizations | 3 |
| Experts | 7 |
| **Total** | **21** |

# Appendix 2: List of Trade Agreements Signed by Argentina and Chile (1990–2005)

## 1 Trade Agreements Signed by Argentina (1990–2005)

| *Partner* | *Date of signature* |
|---|---|
| Brazil (ECA N° 14) | 1990 |
| MERCOSUR members | 1991 |
| Chile (PS ECA N° 16) | 1991 |
| Paraguay (ECA N° 13) | 1992 |
| Multilateral Agreement: WTO | 1995 |
| MERCOSUR-Chile (ECA N° 35) | 1996 |
| MERCOSUR-Bolivia (ECA N° 36) | 1996 |
| MERCOSUR-Mexico (ECA N° 54; framework agreement) | 2002 |
| MERCOSUR-Mexico (ECA N° 55; auto sector agreement) | 2002 |
| Uruguay (ECA N° 57; auto sector agreement) | 2003 |
| MERCOSUR-India | 2004 |
| MERCOSUR-Colombia, Ecuador and Venezuela (PS ECA N° 59) | 2004 |
| MERCOSUR-Morocco | 2004 |
| MERCOSUR-Peru (ECA N° 58) | 2005 |

Source: *Author-created based on Organization of American States' Foreign Trade Information System, last accessed 4 July 2016*

## 2 Trade Agreements Signed by Chile (1990–2005)

| *Partner* | *Date of signature* |
|---|---|
| Mexico (ECA N° 17) | 1991 |
| Argentina (PS ECA N° 16) | 1991 |
| Venezuela (PS ECA N° 23) | 1993 |
| Bolivia (PS ECA N° 22) | 1993 |
| Colombia | 1993 |
| Ecuador | 1994 |
| Multilateral Agreement: WTO | 1995 |
| MERCOSUR (ECA N° 35) | 1996 |
| Canada | 1996 |
| Peru (ECA N° 38) | 1998 |
| Mexico (FTA) | 1998 |

| *Partner* | *Date of signature* |
|---|---|
| Costa Rica, El Salvador, Guatemala, Honduras, Nicaragua (Chile-Central America) | 1999 |
| European Union | 2002 |
| Republic of Korea | 2003 |
| United States | 2003 |
| European Free Trade Association | 2003 |
| Brunei, New Zealand, Singapore (P-4) | 2005 |
| China | 2005 |

Source: *Author-created based on Organization of American States' Foreign Trade Information System, last accessed 4 July 2016, and DIRECON, last accessed 5 July 2016*

# Index

For Product Safety Concerns and Information please contact our EU representative GPSR@taylorandfrancis.com
Taylor & Francis Verlag GmbH, Kaufingerstraße 24, 80331 München, Germany

www.ingramcontent.com/pod-product-compliance
Ingram Content Group UK Ltd.
Pitfield, Milton Keynes, MK11 3LW, UK
UKHW022119190926
475702UK00013B/1542
*9781138368187*